AFGHAN BUZKASHI:
POWER GAMES AND GAMESMEN

1

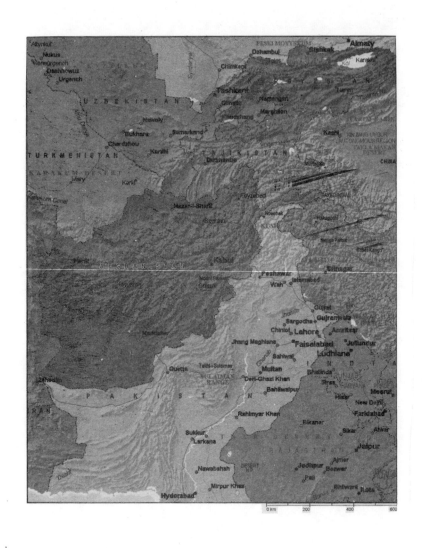

Afghan Buzkashi
Power Games and Gamesmen

1

Sreedhar
Mahendra Ved

WORDSMITHS
Delhi
2000

AFGHAN BUZKASHI: POWER GAMES AND GAMESMEN
by Sreedhar and Mahendra Ved
First published, 2000
Second impression, 2000

ISBN 81 87412 01 1

© Authors
All rights reserved.

Published and Printed by
Arthur Monteiro
for WORDSMITHS
N 11, Xavier Apartments, Saraswati Vihar
Delhi 110034
Tel: (091) (11) 702 6452   Fax: (091) (11) 702 1009

Sales also at
19C, DDA Flats, Masjid Moth I, Greater Kailash III
New Delhi 110048
Tel: (091) (11) 6246180   Fax: (091) (11) 6242860

Cover design: Subir Roy
Pictures courtesy: P. Sarkar

Preface

Why a third book on Afghanistan in as many years? And in two volumes?

We were pleasantly surprised at the warm reception our earlier two attempts received from the discerning public. The first, *Taliban and the Afghan Turmoil* (1997) took note of the capture of Kabul by the Taliban and sought to scrutinize various factors that affected, and in turn got affected by, the turmoil in Afghanistan. It was a collective job with three others that took in the Afghan neighbourhood and the big powers at play.

The second, *Afghan Turmoil: Changing Equations* (1998) focused on the stake of each player in this end-twentieth-century version of the 'great game'. For the second volume, we had the advantage of time and the corollary hindsight. We hoped we had become wiser.

Both volumes attempted to deal with the issue at the macro level from an Indian perspective. The third attempt, needless to say, is meant to tell our readers that we are not running away from this labour of love for the people of Afghanistan who are victims of a seemingly never-ending conflict.

This book is our response to some of the criticism and saying that we stand vindicated by the turn of events. Few believed us in 1997 when we projected the Taliban as a threat to Indian security. Kargil 1999 has proved our point. Today, use of religion as a political and military weapon poses a threat not only to India, but also to others, Chechnya being one example. With narcotics production doubled since 1996, the drug trail gets more menacing. Closer home, the change of guard in Pakistan, whatever the domestic compulsions, has a strong element of what Pakistan is doing to acquire "strategic depth" by nurturing a puppet government on the other side of the now virtually non-existent Durand Line.

We are updating what we said earlier, since the United Nations is constrained to impose sanctions on Taliban-ruled Afghanistan. Osama bin Laden, the bone of contention, is but a symbol, a significant one though, of the larger malaise afflicting the world today. We have tried to put Afghanistan, with or without the presence of bin Laden, in a futuristic perspective.

Among the friends and well-wishers who read the present manuscript, some were of the view that we have indulged in Paki-bashing; that we have made the Taliban synonymous with Pakistan. We may well have, but we have gone entirely by facts on the ground. To delink them would be travesty. We do hope the contents of the book, including the evidence presented, are persuasive enough in making our point.

Our past effort was criticized in some quarters as being soft on the Northern Alliance, in counterpoise to projecting the Taliban in poor light. This book makes an honest attempt to strike a balance: and not because the Taliban control 90 per cent of Afghan territory. We continue to believe that the Taliban's emergence is a major destabilizing factor for the Indian subcontinent and Central Asia—which is a majority of humanity. We have tried to analyse what makes them tick at home, even as they are feared within the country and stand rejected outside.

The sources of our information have been a variety of published sources, with a heavy dependence on the Pakistani media. One of us, Mahendra Ved, also made a field trip to the CARs region and met quite a few valuable sources, who were generous with information and in sharing views. The first person accounts in the book are his exclusively. Both of us also conducted extensive interviews among members of the diplomatic community, military men, policy-makers, Islamic scholars and academics, a majority of whom wanted to remain anonymous, in view of the sensitive nature of the information and views they were willing to share.

A conscious effort has been made not to repeat information presented in the earlier volumes. For this reason, the reader may find our treatment of subjects like pipelines and drugs quite brisk.

If a discerning researcher still finds a gap in our effort, we hope to be excused.

Documents in Volume 2, we assume, will be ready reference to anybody studying Afghanistan. After the international attention it enjoyed in the 1980s, Afghanistan somehow went out of focus in the 1990s. Ours is a modest attempt to fill the gap.

Help came from friends and colleagues at the Institute of Defence Studies and Analyses, Jawaharlal Nehru University and other institutions, who liberally shared information and views with us. We are grateful to them. Our special thanks to Air Commodore (Retd) Jasjit Singh, Director, IDSA and Mr Dileep Padgaonkar and the management of the *Times of India* for their continued encouragement.

Opinions expressed in these volumes are entirely ours and are in no way attributable to the organizations we serve. Also, we alone are responsible for all the views presented and for any lapses.

New Delhi   SREEDHAR
November 1999   MAHENDRA VED

Contents

List of Appendices, Boxes, Maps, Figures, Tables and Charts 10
1. Introduction: Time to Mend a Broken Nation 13
2. The Taliban: Discomfiting the World 25
3. Osama Bin Laden and Other Gadflies:
   For the West, Convenient Hate Objects 59
4. Ahmed Shah Masoud: Hero Awaiting a Script 87
5. Military Structure and Equipment:
   For Suppliers, a Fertile Hunting-ground 101
6. The Drug Trail: For Everyone, a Milch Cow 131
7. Pipelines: Pipe-dreams? 141
8. Pakistan: A Grandiose Agenda 151
9. Iran: Wary Coexistence 174
10. The Taliban "Revolution": A Contrast to
    the Iranian Revolution 187
11. Saudi Arabia: Challenges from Within 195
12. China: Playing for Advantage 207
13. Central Asian Republics: "Back of the Beyond"
    Under Siege 221
14. Peace Initiatives: Till Now, a Mirage 235
15. What Next?: A New Pashtunistan, Perhaps? 252
16. Choices Before India: With Kargil a Nasty Reminder 262
    Epilogue: Taliban and the Hijacking of
    Indian Airlines Flight IC-814 277
    Index 281

Appendices, Boxes, Maps, Figures, Tables and Charts

Appendix 5.1	UN Non-Paper: A Review of the Options on Embargo of Military Supplies to the Warring Factions in Afghanistan	114
Box 2.1	The Dance Macabre	28
Box 2.2	Beyond Good or Evil	54
Box 3.1	The Laden Family	66
Box 8.1	Excerpts from "The Not-So-Hidden Hand"	166
Box 11.1	Excerpts from Junayman bin Mohammad bin Seif al-Oteibi's Writings	198
Map 5.1	Supply routes (Annex B)	129
Map 6.1	The Afghan drug trail	130
Map 12.1	The link between Afghanistan and the Xinjiang Uygur Autonomous Region	206
Map 12.2	China–Afghanistan boundary	214
Map 13.1	The CARs–Afghan border	224
Fig. 1.1	Buzkashi that has torn a country apart	12
Fig. 2.1	Scene from a bygone era: Women pursuing education in public and allowing to be photographed	24
Fig. 3.1	FBI poster sending out the alert on Osama bin Laden	58
Fig. 4.1	Ahmed Shah Masoud	90
Fig. 8.1	Ruined future of a new generation of Afghanistan	150
Fig. 14.1	In its peace initiatives in Afghanistan, the UN at the receiving end	240

Table 2.1	Regional and Sectarian Distribution of Dar ul-ulums (till 1988)	41
Table 2.2	Number of Graduates of Different Levels of Education from Dar ul-ulums, 1982–87	41
Table 4.1	Masoud's Immediate Military Requirements	100
Table 7.1	Oil and Gas Reserves in the CARs	143
Table 8.1	Details of POWs Captured by the Northern Alliance in September 1997	158
Chart 1.1	Current Status of the "Original Seven Sinners" of the Afghanistan Tragedy	19
Chart 2.1	Taliban Ring of Leadership	44
Chart 5.1	Armed Forces Command Structure in Afghanistan	102
Chart 5.2	Armed Forces Command Structure Previously	103
Chart 5.3	Armed Forces Organization	104
Chart 5.4	An Assessment of the Taliban and Northern Alliance Arsenal	107
Chart 5.5	Heavy Equipment in the Afghanistan Fighting Noticed by Various Observers during 1994–99	109
Chart 8.1	Details of Pakistan Army Officers who Allegedly Fought in Afghanistan	159
Chart 8.2	Pakistan's Support to the Taliban in the Summer Offensive of 1998 against the Northern Alliance	171
Chart 8.3	Ethnic Composition of Afghanistan	172

Fig. 1.1. Buzkashi that has torn a country apart
Courtesy: *The News*, 17 March 1999

1

Introduction
Time to Mend a Broken Nation

Buzkashi is a traditional winter game played in northern Afghanistan. Hundreds of horsemen, many of them wrestlers (*pehelwan*) vie to possess a fattened calf. In the free-for-all, the whip meant for the horse is used to lash the rival rider as well. He who manages to carry the calf out of the melée is the winner.

The game has been improvised in recent years to a sport between two teams. That this has not become popular, that Afghans prefer to play their Buzkashi as individual horsemen, typifies the Afghan character.

Heavy betting goes on. The stakes are high.

Buzkashi, it would seem, is synonymous with what is happening in and around Afghanistan today.

For more than a century, the big powers played their so-called Great Game for a share of action in Central Asia. The Europeans strove hard to deny access to the warm waters of the Indian Ocean, first to czarist Russia and later, the Soviet Union. Moscow's effort to gain this access by getting more than a foothold in Afghanistan boomeranged, in part leading to its disintegration.

The number of players in the game has multiplied since. The rules of the game have also changed. More than political domination, economic influence is the prize sought. With the prospecting of oil and gas, and minerals including precious metals and precious stones, the economic stakes have heightened. The waters of the

Black Sea and Caspian Sea are astir with drilling for oil and gas. What was until recently Back of the Beyond has suddenly become the latest discovery of present-day gamesmen.

•

In the Buzkashi being played in the region by external powers, Afghanistan, the nation of rugged mountains and gorgeous vales, is itself the hunted calf. Iqbal Jafar comments:

Soon after the Saur Revolution in 1978, all sorts of persuaders, facilitators, interlopers, mercenaries, pedlars of arms and guardians of ideologies converged on Afghanistan to influence the course of events to their advantage. Since these days, events have repeatedly turned to everyone's disadvantage. One is not sure whether the intruders knew who or what they are dealing with and for what purpose. All that we know for sure is that none of them succeeded in imposing an alien hegemony over Afghanistan. In the process, though, colossal damage has been done to the Afghans and to anyone who intervened. Twenty years have now passed but the last chapter of the saga of the Afghans has yet to be written.

The land known to us as Afghanistan has lain at the crossroads of history for far longer than one can remember. Through it have passed the caravans of traders, missionaries, explorers and adventurers from West Asia, Central Asia, South Asia and East Asia. Through it have also passed the mighty hordes of the Persians, Greeks, Scythians, Huns, Kushans, Turks and Mongols. The last of the intruders to come and go rather bruised and surprised were the Russians of Soviet vintage.

The psyche of the people of Afghanistan has thus, been forged by frequent and hostile contact with some of the most formidable warriors of history and also by its geography that is inspiring in its grandeur, and demanding in its favours. The most significant elements of the Afghan psyche, in the present context can be summarized as follows: unremitting stamina for armed conflict, indomitable spirit of independence, undivided loyalty to the clan, and uncompromising acceptance of its code of conduct, a conviction born out of endless strife and conflict that alliances are temporary and enmity permanent: as a corollary use of deceit more readily and more often than by other nations, in the internal state politics; and a streak of remorseless cruelty of which the Afghans have been both the victims and perpetrators.

All this, however, is not supposed to convey that there is in existence a monolithic culture, ethnic homogeneity or administrative centrality in Afghanistan. The country has three distinct geographical regions, 29 provinces, 105 cities and towns and about 15,000 villages, inhabited by about 18 million people divisible into five major and 15 minor ethno-linguistic groups. It is important to take notice of those 15,000 villages where more than 80 per cent of the population lives for the reason that because of the customary laws, difficult terrain and rudimentary and difficult surface communication, the villages have always been independent of the government. They can be coerced into submission, but only for a while for they are armed, as they always have been, fiercely independent and loyal only to family, clan and the ethnic group. Loyalty to the government in Kabul has never been an obligation in their scheme of things, unless it rules by their consent, obtained in the case of Pushtoons through *Jirga*.

The ethnic grouping in Afghanistan has its peculiar features too. What makes the Afghan ethnic mosaic a political puzzle of international dimensions is the fact that the four largest ethnic groups (Pushtoons, Tajiks, Uzbeks and Turkmen) are not confined within the borders of Afghanistan. Like the rivers of Afghanistan, they are a spill-over from neighbouring countries in the areas of their co-ethnics across the border. This is a situation that offers much temptation for ethno-political intervention into Afghanistan and from Afghanistan. It is thus, a double-edged sword that hangs all along the Afghan border.

Finally, the Afghan economy, in the modern sense, has a history of no more than 76 years, that is from 1904 to 1980. Modernisation of Afghanistan can be said to have begun in 1904 when Habibya School, the first western style preparatory school and the first Military Academy, commanded by a Turkish colonel, were established. This was during Amir Habibullah's rule (1904–1919) which is the period of many firsts—first power station, first pumping station for irrigation, first printing press, first newspaper, first political organization for constitutional monarchy. Amir Habibullah, however, met the same fate of other modernisers of Afghanistan—Amanullah, and in recent years, Sardar Muhammad Daoud and Noor Muhammed Taraki—who were forcibly removed from the scene. Three of them were killed and one—Amir Amanullah—was lucky enough to die of natural cause in 1960 while in exile in Italy.

After 20 years of the yet-on-going process of attrition, not much is left of the human and physical assets created during those 76 years of slow and discontinuous modernisation and development. The intellectual elite of Afghanistan is either living in exile or has been physically liquidated, if not cringing in abject submission before the ever changing and ever more violent rulers of Afghanistan. There is no industrial base left; the roads, bridges and water channels for irrigation are in a shambles; and Kabul, a heap of rubble. About a million Afghans have been killed, an equal number disabled or wounded and millions more are living in refugee camps in Pakistan and Iran.[1]

•

The Soviet Union's invasion of Afghanistan in December 1979 resulted in a host of players—the US and its allies, Pakistan, China and Saudi Arabia—stepping in. Each had its own agenda, and each infused into Afghan society many ingredients calculated to destroy a society. When the Soviets, unable to slug it any longer in the mountains of Afghanistan, withdrew from the scene, the rest too went back to their respective countries, leaving the Afghan people to fend for themselves. Seizing the opportunity offered by the helplessness of a country laid low fighting a mighty empire, smaller players like Pakistan tried to consummate their own extended agenda. The Afghan people's misery continued in a different form for another five years.

Afghanistan would have been forgotten by now by the world community, except that suddenly someone in one of the western think tanks raised the Afghan antenna again, this time as a route to the black gold from the land-locked CARs. The great powers stepped into Afghanistan to convert the black gold of the CARs into hard currency by exporting it through Afghanistan. This drama lasted about three years.

•

In between, Pakistan spawned a genie called Taliban to take control of the situation. Almost everyone in the extended neighbourhood tried to do business with the Taliban. But abruptly, something went wrong in August 1998, and the Taliban became untouchables. The reason given for public consumption is that the Taliban's friends had a hand in the bombing of the US embassies in Nairobi and Dar-es-Salaam. The earlier friends of the Taliban now give the impression that they think they are dealing with fire. The western media hype made Osama bin Laden, a friend turned foe, into a cult figure. Again we witness

[1] "Can Afghanistan Ever be at Peace with Itself?" From *Dawn;* reproduced in *Asian Age* (New Delhi), 21 September 1998.

the romanticization of Osama, like they did with Mullah Umar, the Taliban chief. To an average Afghan, the rationalization being proffered is puzzling: that Osama was a friend if he killed Red Army soldiers in pursuit of his faith; but if he killed a dozen Americans in pursuit of the same faith he becomes a foe. In the 1980s, it was the US–Saudi combine that instigated people like Osama to rush to Afghanistan; and now the same instigators refuse to accept that Osama can be a man with a mind of his own.

•

From King Zahir Shah, deposed in 1973, to the virtual investiture of Mullah Muhammad Umar, the Taliban supremo, Afghanistan has come a full circle. Zahir Shah's ouster marked the end of monarchy. The amirul momineen is now seen as "emperor" or Caliph of the benighted nation, in ruins. Barbarity reigns. An estimated 200,000 people who evacuated to the Panjshir Valley during the last major round of fighting during end-July–early August 1999, are since reported to be fighting disease, especially among children, and braving a severe winter. While flour is scarce, and the prices are rising, the narcotics trade flourishes unhindered. One would have thought that like the Vietnamese, the Afghans would rise from the ashes of conflict and work together in the task of nation-building. They have much catching up to do with the rest of the world. But this gulf has only widened in the last decade.

The Annual Report (1998) of the International Committee of Red Cross (ICRC) gives an inkling of the Afghans' misery:

> Although conditions in rural areas were often harsh and rudimentary, it was urban centres that suffered most from the effects of the seemingly unending conflict. Staple foods were not readily available and spiralling prices put them out of reach of many Afghans. On average, a breadwinner's salary covered only 20% of the family's basic needs and up to 50% of the population was dependent on some form of external aid. The ICRC's relief programme in Kabul focused on 15,000 families headed by widows and 10,000 others with disabled breadwinners. These vulnerable categories received regular two-monthly rations consisting of wheat flour, rice, beans, ghee and soap....

In view of the growing destitution of the capital's inhabitants and the absence of most humanitarian players from the scene, the ICRC carried out limited winter distribution of blankets, clothes, plastic sheetings and fuel to families headed by widows and handicapped breadwinners, street children and orphans....

The collapse of the health system had made it increasingly difficult for paraplegics to obtain adequate care....

For those Kabulis who managed to escape the effects of shelling, poverty and hunger, waterborne diseases remained a deadly threat, particularly for the young and the elderly....

Save the Children Fund (SCF), in its Afghanistan Emergency Bulletin issued on 31 August 1999 notes that the Afghan war (1979–89) created the largest ever flow of refugees from a single country: 6.2 million at the height of the war. An estimated 107,000 refugees returned home in 1998—the largest ever repatriation in the world that year—but 2.6 million live in exile.

The SCF also notes: 90 per cent of Afghans are illiterate. The country is the world's second-most mined, where 700 sq km area needs demining. A third of an estimated 100,000 landmine victims are children. Besides mines, diseases including polio, thanks to delay or denial of proper health care, have caused physical disability to 3 to 4 per cent of the Afghan population.

In this dismal scenario, it may be poor consolation to hark back to the era when the Soviets propped up regimes in Kabul. The governments controlled little outside of Kabul and other major cities. The countryside was relatively free from tensions, and life went on, as it must have been over the centuries. The Moscow-backed regimes, despite the Stalinist repression of their opponents, provided the basics. And they facilitated education, health and housing. Women and children were free to work and learn and were better off.

•

Compounding the Afghan tragedy is the way leaders of Afghanistan, handpicked by external powers to lead the campaign against the Soviets, have ultimately failed their people. Details of these "original seven sinners" are given in Chart 1.1. All the seven came to prominence during 1979–89, and at that time all had close contact with the US at different levels.

After the Red Army's withdrawal, Sibgatullah Mujaddidi

Chart 1.1. Current Status of the "Original Seven Sinners" of the Afghanistan Tragedy

	Organization of Allegiance	Profession	Present status
Gulbuddin Hikmatyar	Hizb-i-Islami	student leader	fled to Pakistan during the Daoud regime; was used by Prime Minister Zulfikar Ali Bhutto against the Afghan government; now 50 years plus; lives in Tehran; has become a *persona non grata* in Pakistan, where he was the most sought after Afghan a few years ago
Yunus Khalis	Hizbul-i-Islami	mullah	in his eighties; lives in the neighbourhood of Jalalabad; physically weak and moves around with a walking-stick; cannot pray standing
Burhanuddin Rabbani	Jamat-i-Islami	teacher of theology	in his sixties; is in Afghanistan, but is always on the move to defend his government
Nabi Muhammadi	Harkat-i-Inqilab Islami	mullah	in his seventies; ill and weak; lives in Cherat, near Pabbi in Peshawar, Pakistan
Syed Ahmed Gilani	Mahaz-i-Milli	pir (spiritual elder)	in his seventies; lives in Peshawar; keeps busy with refugee problems
Sibghatullah Mujaddidi	Jabha-i-Nitaz-i-Milli	mullah	in his seventies; lives in Peshawar; keeps busy with refugee problems
Abdur Rab Rasool Sayyaf	Itchar-i-Islami	mullah	in his fifties; is in Afghanistan as an ally of Ahmed Shah Masoud; his men are fighting alongside Masoud's men in the north against the Taliban

became the President, but Gulbuddin Hikmatyar revolted against his authority. Kabul again became a battlefield. Burhanuddin Rabbani, Hikmatyar, Mujaddidi and Abdur Rab Rasool Sayyaf engaged in armed clashes to grab power. Yunus Khalis, Nabi Muhammadi and Syed Ahmed Gilani were not very much interested in fighting for power. Ahmed Shah Masoud, who was originally in Jamiat-i-Islam, formed his own group, Shoora-i-Nazar, adding another dimension to the power struggle.

A decade after the Red Army's withdrawal almost all these leaders, except Rabbani, Sayyaf and Masoud, have faded away with time. As an Afghan refugee remarked, "No doubt the seven leaders' role against the Russians in Afghanistan will always be in the memory of Afghans. Their post-Afghan war role in turning victory into defeat will be equally unforgettable."

Besides these seven, a number of senior and second-rank former mujahideen live in palatial houses built with money received for the anti-Soviet campaign. Some of them wield influence among the Afghan refugees. "These are people in no hurry to see an end to the Afghan conflict. They behave like gangsters who have used the adversity their countrymen have been facing to their personal advantage", says a European international civil servant who has known many a mujahideen at close quarters. He is not surprised that from the relative safety of Peshawar, they have been cahoots with the Taliban. This is not unmixed with fear, because the Taliban specialize in bumping off any refugee trying to adapt a moderate line or opposing them.

•

To most of the neighbourhood it appears that developments in Afghanistan have been exacerbated by extra-regional players and Pakistan. Probably the neighbourhood except Pakistan would not have bothered whether it was Zahir Shah or Ahmed Shah Masoud or Mullah Umar who wielded power in Kabul. Whosoever was in authority, or at least a semblance of authority, would have been recognized.

But the Taliban and its sponsors introduced two new variables into regional politics. In the name of Islam as perceived by them, they refuse to acknowledge international boundaries between nation-states. They are convinced in the righteousness of their cause in seeking to export their concept of Islam, with the aid of terror and guns if need be. They have brought to the fore the notion that their version of Islam is the ultimate solution to improve the quality of life of Muslims. Some of them have even said that the greatness of Islam diminished with the rulers neglecting Islamic tenets.

This extraordinary perception has resulted in bitter clashes with the State structures in most of the neighbourhood. Whether Pakistan, the UAE and Saudi Arabia who recognized the Taliban subscribe to this thesis is not known. Others certainly disagree with the Taliban on this count.

Also, for building up an Islamic socio-political order in the region, narcotics and terrorism have become basic tools, justified by the so-called doctrine of necessity. The rest of the international community looks upon these two as a menace to mankind. Herein lies the contradiction between accepted nation-sate behaviour in the international order and the Taliban.

Therefore the Taliban are finding it difficult to acquire the needed legitimacy. It is also clear that the Taliban are not a movement or revolution, as some commentators are trying to project, but more of a covert operation by its sponsors—Pakistan, to achieve certain strategic objectives. They are not even an outfit like the PLO of the 1960s or even the Muslim Brotherhood or Hamas. Pakistani armed forces fight battles on behalf of the Taliban (or along with the Taliban); Pakistanis sustain the Afghan economy and a quarter of the Afghan population live in Pakistan.

•

Ironically, the Taliban's consolidation has forced a semblance of unity among their opponents. Conditions on the ground allow only the fittest to survive. This process has eliminated most of the resistance fighters. Dostum and Hikmatyar, who were major players in post-Soviet Afghanistan, are in Turkey and Iran respectively, with little hope of a return to the fight. Their withdrawal from the scene has strengthened Ahmed Shah Masoud, who is today the undisputed leader of the resistance against Kabul. This consolidation has helped the Islamic Front for Deliverance of

Afghanistan (IFDA)[2] led by him not only to hold on to large areas in the north, but also to make frequent and significant military gains.

At the same time, Masoud has severe handicaps. His supply routes are extremely limited, and supplies erratic. While Masoud reigns supreme in the area under his control—Panjshir and Taloqan—his base has narrowed down considerably after the loss of Hazarajat that his Shia ally Karim Khalili held.

It is a military and political stalemate. With Masoud around, the Taliban can never gain full control of Afghanistan. Their pushing for a military solution has prevented a resolution of the conflict. Neither the Taliban nor Masoud is enthusiastic about a role for deposed King Zahir Shah, who has been making tentative efforts from time to time to convene a *jirga* or a *Loya Jirga*, a grand assembly. His efforts in November 1999 ostensibly kept out the two quarrelling contenders for power. While a meeting of the learned and the clergy may be a good idea, its efficacy on the ground in Afghanistan is being seriously doubted.

•

In these circumstances, the turmoil in Afghanistan looks like continuing for quite a while, with its unfortunate fallout on the rest of the region. While the world is becoming increasingly concerned with economic well-being, Afghanistan and Pakistan in this region seem condemned to make do with regularly convulsing polities. On the threshold of the third millennium, they are yet to evolve the basic tools for governance. In the process, 150 million people belonging to these neighbouring polities have to struggle to cope with these convulsions. The conventional wisdom of sanctions against these regimes or hot pursuit of the leadership of these organizations may not produce the desired results. Some new methods may have to be evolved to discipline these nation-states.

Allowing the Taliban to continue in the fashion they are doing

---

[2]The official name is Jabha-yi Muttahid-i-Islami-yi Milli bara-yi Nijat-i-Afghanistan—the National Islamic United Front for the Salvation of Afghanistan.

may give credence to concepts like conflict of civilizations, whereas cooperation among civilizations is seen as the general trend of thinking. The international community, therefore, needs to address three basic questions:

- What is to be done with the Mullah Umar brand of violence and terrorism in the name of Islam? He is averse to conference diplomacy to discuss the problem. In his perception, dialogue is only for endorsing the Taliban point of view, and not for building a consensus.
- How to make countries like Pakistan stop endorsing actions of people like Umar? In fact, allowing organizations like Lashkar-i-Toyyaba to hold congregations with impunity is by itself a subtle endorsement of Taliban policies.
- If we accept the evidence adduced by countries like India and Russia, that the Taliban are nothing but a front organization of the Pakistani armed forces, concepts like terrorism as an instrument of foreign policy may take root. How to tackle this new unwholesome phenomenon—as we enter a new millennium?

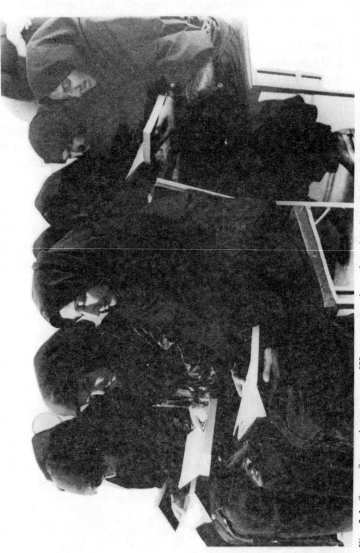

Fig. 2.1. Scene from a bygone era: Women pursuing education in public and allowing to be photographed

2

The Taliban
Discomfiting the World

On 26–27 September 1999, the Taliban completed their third year of rule from Kabul, in itself a remarkable achievement in the twists and turns of Afghan history of the last two decades. This unquestioned success would be ascribed to four factors—(a) their cohesiveness of functioning, (b) their unpurchaseability, (c) their success in maintaining social peace, and (d) the legendary disunity among their opposition.

Cohesiveness. Ever since their movement appeared on the scene way back in 1994, the Taliban have functioned, by and large, as a cohesive and disciplined unit.[1] There was only one documented event of some of their cadres revolting. According to these reports, the Taliban busted a ring of militia activists plotting a coup against the Kabul government. At least 55 senior soldiers, including some Taliban commanders and a number of former Afghan army generals, were rounded up in a midnight swoop in Kabul and Herat on 25 September 1998. It is alleged that these Taliban commanders were negotiating a deal with Ahmed Shah Masoud, offering him a foothold on Tapa Telfizion, a hill overlooking Kabul where the city's television booster is installed.[2] Otherwise, the Taliban have throughout remained a largely Pashtun-

---
[1] Nasim Zehra, "Decisive Factors in Taliban's Victory", *The News*, 20 August 1998.
[2] Rizwan Qureshi, "Conflict of Interest", *The Herald*, October 1998, p. 61.

dominated movement, and maintained a national focus, at least theoretically, with a united backing of their men.

Unpurchaseability. The Taliban leadership has demonstrated that it is not purchaseable, unlike the commanders of the anti-Taliban forces, whose penchant for changing sides has become a byword. No senior Taliban commander has deserted. All Taliban commanders have adhered to the discipline imposed on them by their leader, Mullah Umar.

Success in Maintaining Social Peace. In spite of the widely publicized stories of the social strangling of women, there have been no reports of plunder, loot or rape by the Taliban in the first two years of rule. The Taliban have chosen to administer mostly through local commanders willing to accept Taliban rule from Kabul and adhere to Mullah Umar's decrees from Kandahar, mixing centralized control with local autonomy.

Opposition Disarray. The anti-Taliban forces are disunited. In spite of long years of being in government giving some optimism in their capacity to govern, the later developments have clearly shown that they are a divided and subdivided group.

•

The Taliban had their birth in the mountainous Pak–Afghan border, inside Pakistan territory some time in August 1994. The generally accepted story about the birth of the Taliban is the following: Pakistan's Afghanistan policy-makers were disillusioned with the failure of their agencies like the Inter Services Intelligence (ISI) to bring normalcy back in Kabul. By early 1994 it became obvious to the ISI that the Burhanuddin Rabbani regime, not very friendly to Islamabad, was slowly consolidating itself in Kabul. While they were looking for alternatives, Maj. Gen. (Retd.) Naseerullah Babar, the Interior Minister in the second Benazir Bhutto government, floated the idea of creating a students' militia along with some veterans from the Afghan mujahideen who had fought the Red Army and who had taken shelter in Pakistan. General Babar started his search for suitable leaders from around April–May 1994. In the process, he came across a certain Mohammad Umar Mujahid.[3]

[3]There is some controversy about who actually conceived the idea of the

Very little is known about Umar, a recluse who does not much stir out of Kandahar. He is not known to speak to the media and has not allowed himself to be photographed. Only statements are issued in his name. The mystery about Umar persists.

Some Afghanistan watchers say, however, that Mullah Umar is a Pashtun from the NWFP region of Pakistan. He was doing errand work for the ISI during the Afghan mujahideens' fight with the Red Army. In the process he came closer to the ISI elite, who brought him to Babar's notice. Umar had lost an eye in an accident. Once Umar was selected to lead the movement, to give him legitimacy he began to be called Mullah Umar, in line with the Islamic ideology of the Taliban.

Umar was reported to have had some battle experience. Badly injured in one encounter, he was treated in Pakistan. Since then he has been living in and around Quetta. Apparently, this profile of Mullah Umar fully satisfied the Pakistani authorities in terms of his continued loyalty to Islamabad. The Taliban claim that Mullah Umar was born in the central province of Uruzgan in 1962. They also say that he studied in several Islamic schools outside Afghanistan (Quetta, Pakistan) before joining the jihad against the Russian occupation in the 1980s. Those who claim to have seen him describe him as a determined man with one eye. It is said that he lost his eye fighting the Soviets as a deputy Chief Commander in the Harkat-i-Inqilab-i-Islami party of Mohammad Nabi Mohammadi. The story in Kandahar is that Mullah Umar had a dream in which the Holy Prophet Muhammad (peace be upon him) appeared to him and told him to bring peace to Afghanistan.

His antagonists cry out that he is not a mullah, is illiterate and knows nothing about Islam. He has made many mistakes when it comes to Islamic law, they argue. For example, he stated that the use of opium is wrong, but its sale, especially to non-Muslims, is not wrong under Islamic law—a hairsplitting which would be quite a whale to swallow even for the uninitiated!

On 3 April 1996, about 1,000 so-called Muslim clergymen chose Mullah Umar as "Amirul Momineen" (Supreme Leader of

---

Taliban. The intelligence agencies and Babar all seem to have had a hand in it. Babar being Interior Minister took the credit.

the Muslims) while branding President Burhanuddin Rabbani, a former mujahideen leader, as a criminal. Umar's being a "Caliph" is also touted. Some reports say he styles himself after a namesake, Caliph Umar, the second Caliph.

By the end of May 1994, the basic infrastructure for launching the Taliban was in place. Around this time, the meetings with the Jamiat Ulema Islam headed by Maulana Fazlur Rehman started bearing fruit in terms of deputing students from madrasas run by them for the proposed outfit, which it proposed to call "Taliban", meaning seekers after knowledge. The name, it was felt, would:

Box 2.1
The Dance Macabre
Sunday Times summary from
UN and Human Rights Watch reports (excerpts)

Patrolling the streets in the pick-up trucks, the Taliban members, under the General Department for the Preservation of Virtue and Prevention of Vice (Amr-bil Maroof wa Nahi anil munkar), search houses and destroy any television sets, radios, cassettes, and photographs. The bands of Taliban thugs roam the streets beating those they deem to be violators of the Shariah (Islamic code of Law).

The Taliban's harsh fundamentalist rule has dismantled all civil institutions, and closed all women's institutions. Their leader, Mullah Mohammad Umar, cloaks himself in secrecy, refusing to grant interviews or allow his photo to be taken. He has titled himself "Amir-ul Momineen" or leader of all the faithful in the world, a title that has not been used in 1400 years since the time of the Prophet Mohammad (PBUH).

No Press or international media is allowed in Afghanistan.

Eyewitness testimonies of killings and rape in Mazar-i-Sharif
UN investigator Choong-Hyan Paik, a special rapporteur for the UN Human Rights Commission: "... men, women and male children were shot, while baby girls were kicked or beaten to death."

When relatives attempted to retrieve bodies or bury the dead, they were stopped by the Taliban who told them that the bodies had to lie on the streets "until the dogs ate them".

Human Rights Watch has also received persistent reports that

— indicate the objective of upholding Islamic values;
— provide justification for the creation of a fresh group outside the quarrelling mujahideen groups;
— be acceptable to the tradition-bound Afghan people; and
— attract funds from the international Islamic community.

Accepting the JUI point of view, Babar and the ISI finalized the Taliban's objectives. These, *inter alia*, were:

— Their fighting capabilities being limited, the Taliban were not

---

women and girls, particularly in certain Hazara neighbourhoods of Mazar-i Sharif, including Saidabad, Karte Ariana, and Ali Chopan were raped and abducted during the Taliban takeover of the city.

One witness tells this story: "An acquaintance of ours came to our house seven or eight days after the takeover. She became ill in our house because she had taken over twenty pills to kill herself, I don't know what kind. We called doctors from the neighbourhood who gave her something to wash out her stomach. She lived in Ali Chopan, but her family was staying elsewhere, and she had gone back to check on the house when she was picked up by the Taliban. At first she did not want to tell us anything, but then she said that when she went to their house, the Talibs abducted her and locked her up in a house with twenty to twenty-five other young girls and women. They were raped every night. They were all Hazaras. She was the only one released. One Talib told her now they are halal (sanctified), and she should go to his parents in Qandahar and wait for him to come and marry her. He gave her a pass and his own identity card and told her to go to the Taliban's headquarters and from there to Kandahar, but instead she escaped."

A witness whose testimony is described as "extremely reliable" by aid officials said most of the victims had been shot in the head, the chest and the testicles. Others had been slaughtered in what he called "the halal way"—by having their throats slit.

Another piece of testimony explained why one Taliban was "very worried he might be excluded from heaven". He had personally shot people in nearly 30 houses, opting to kill them as soon as they opened the door. After killing the men in two homes, he learnt they were not Hazara but Pashtun. "That he had killed people in 28 Hazara households seemed not to cause him any concern at all", the witness said.

to engage in pitched battles. Non-military means were to be preferred for conquest.
— Unlike during the Jalalabad offensive in 1989, the Pakistan army was not to be called in for help overtly.
— Pakistani support to the Taliban would be largely in terms of providing logistic support only and was in no way to be open.
— In whichever area the Taliban liberated, Pakistan would provide the necessities of life to demonstrate to the local populace that the Taliban could provide reasonably comfortable conditions of life. Also Pakistan would provide the technical assistance to repair the infrastructure.

In August 1994, the arrival of the Taliban on the Afghan scene was heralded with the reported re-securing by young Taliban of a trade convoy going from Pakistan to Afghanistan. From September 1994, the Taliban went about their job systematically, using mostly non-military means, with hardly any resistance from Afghan warlords controlling various provinces. Some of the drug money and charities received from the Arab world and South-East Asia were liberally used to buy up the adversaries. By about early 1996, people started taking notice of the Taliban's "spectacular" successes on the battlefield and their capacity to enforce some orderliness in war-ravaged Afghanistan. In some quarters, initially, this was even appreciated. In some places the Taliban were welcomed for their effectiveness in bringing peace and security to the population at large. The Taliban's initial successes and popular acceptance may be attributed to the following factors:

— the people's war-weariness and further exhaustion by lack of security;
— the Taliban's stated purpose of reducing the free flow of arms and restoring security;
— the effective neutralization by the Taliban, in the initial phases, of the much-disdained plethora of warlords and commanders, by seizing arms from them and thus providing relative security in which people could pursue their normal lives;
— their Pashtun base and the limitation of their operations mainly to Pashtun-dominated areas;
— their professed adherence to Islam and Islamic values, which

projected them in a better perspective to the people than the warlords;
— the external support they received from Pakistan and through Pakistan from some countries of the Islamic world in the form of resources, manpower and logistic support.

•

In early 1996, the Taliban were faced with a major challenge after the Tajik-dominated regime in Kabul, led by President Burhanuddin Rabbani and his defence minister Ahmed Shah Masoud, decided to acquire greater legitimacy for their regime. They took a major strategic decision of broad-basing their government in the winter of 1995–96 by inviting other leaders to join it. Beginning in January 1996, serious negotiations started between the regime and warlords in various provinces. President Rabbani's emissary, Abdul Rehman, met Gulbuddin Hikmatyar of Hizb-i-Islami near Sarobi on 21 January 1996. Rehman later met General Abdul Rashid Dostum at Mazar-i-Sharif, and Shia opposition groups in Bamiyan in central Afghanistan. By February 1996 all the opposition groups except the Taliban, united and set up a ten-member council to negotiate with President Rabbani in Kabul.

On 27 March 1996 the council of Hizb-i-Islami agreed to empower Hikmatyar to a power-sharing agreement with President Rabbani, which he secretly concluded soon after. By the first week of May 1996 some 1,000 of Hikmatyar troops arrived in Kabul and joined the government troops. On 26 June 1996, Hikmatyar entered Kabul and took up the post of Prime Minister, the Hizb-i-Islami taking up another nine cabinet posts.

The Taliban, however, refused President Rabbani's offer of negotiations, resorting instead to shelling of Kabul. The shelling was quite heavy throughout July–August 1996. Meanwhile, President Rabbani was going from strength to strength with Dostum also expressing his willingness to join the government.

Ahmed Rashid, a leading Pakistani commentator on Afghanistan, reported at the time:

At the same time President Rabbani stepped up his negotiations with

General Dostum while Masoud kept the Taliban at bay outside Kabul. By August [1996] the regime had persuaded General Dostum to agree to a truce and at the end of the month, the Salang Highway which connected Kabul with the north of the country was reopened for civilian traffic for the first time in over a year. However, Dostum still declined to join the government until it was prepared to grant greater autonomy to the provinces under his control.

The Taliban remained the biggest obstacle to peace, refusing to negotiate with anyone and offering no concept of power sharing with its opponents. The Taliban launched a major offensive in April–May [1996] in a bid to capture Kabul but failed to do so. Although they were pushed back some 50 kilometres from Kabul in the southeast of the city, the Taliban held positions just 4 kilometres from Kabul in the southwest and from there they launched repeated rocket attacks on Kabul's civilian population. In April [1996] alone the Taliban fired 866 rockets killing 180 civilians and injuring 550 in the capital.[4]

The Taliban's refusal to join the Rabbani-initiated intra-Afghan dialogue is ascribed by Taliban sympathizers to the Tajik–Pashtun divide. To quote Ahmed Rashid again,

Rabbani's forces are predominantly Tajik who have never before ruled Afghanistan, and have never successfully allied with the Pashtuns even in war against the Soviet Union. The Pashtun Taliban and Pakistan preferred an intra-Afghan dialogue led by the Pashtun.

It could also be that the Taliban and their sponsors were certain of their military success. At one level Pakistan opened negotiations with the Rabbani regime. At the same time, from the first week of September 1996, the Taliban launched attacks on Jalalabad and then on Laghman. After capturing these outposts, the Taliban marched towards Sarobi, which is 70 km from Kabul and is considered to be the gateway to the capital. On 22 September 1996, the Taliban captured Kunar province and three days later occupied Sarobi. On the same day [25 September] the Taliban moved 3,000 troops a distance of 70 km in 12 hours, reaching the outskirts of Kabul the same evening. By the dawn of 27 September 1996, Kabul was captured along with the strategic Bagram airport.

•

The whirlwind nature of these conquests initially drew awe and admiration for the Taliban within Afghanistan, but soon, the secret was out: Pakistani reservists had conducted the whole

[4] Ahmed Rashid, "Politics and State of War", *The Nation*, 23 December 1996.

operation, with some mullahs of the Taliban as a cover. How on earth could a rag-tag bunch with madrasa schooling pull off the transport of 3000 men across 70 kilometres in just twelve hours? Where did they conjure up vehicles and fuel all through September 1996? Where did the "Urdu-speaking" soldiers spring from if not from across the Durand Line? Evidently, banning of photography is a convenient cover. Some commentators have also pointed out that the capture of Kabul was accomplished during the night of 26–27 September, the cover of darkness shrouding the Pakistani troops' presence.

Pakistan directly intervened in the Afghan civil war, perhaps nervous that the intra-Afghan dialogue started by President Rabbani might succeed and get the needed regional support especially from Iran, the CARs and Russia, and in due course these countries might prevail upon the UN representative to join in the intra-Afghan dialogue. This would have totally isolated the Taliban and marginalized their sponsor Pakistan. Perhaps, the oil companies contributed their share by bringing pressure on the Pak–Taliban combine to clinch the job.

Be that as it may. The capture of Kabul only ended up tarnishing the Taliban's image. It was obvious to unbiased observers that the Taliban was but an appendage of the ISI, out to scuttle Afghan nationalism. There was also an upsurge of sympathy and support to anti-Taliban forces. A massive effort was commenced by Iran, Turkey, the CARs and Russia to shore them up both militarily and economically. At the same time, the Taliban's assumption that the capture of Kabul would bring their regime legitimacy proved illusory.

The Taliban's sponsors now accelerated the agenda of military conquest of Afghanistan. They stormed Mazar-i-Sharif, stronghold of the anti-Taliban forces, in May 1997, but ended up with a bloody nose. More than three thousand Taliban attackers became casualties and many ended up prisoners. The Taliban were pushed back to the confines of Kabul. The Taliban rump in Mazar-i-Sharif retreated towards Kunduz. In siege, they were kept breathing with logistical support from Kabul by air.[5]

[5]General Mirza Aslam Beg, "Taliban's Onward March to Mazar-e-Sharif", *The Nation*, 9 August 1998.

The Taliban's 1998 offensive has to be viewed in the backdrop of the all-out effort of their patrons to queer the pitch in their favour. Tim McGirek writing in *Time* (31 August 1998) states that in July 1998, the Saudi intelligence chief, Prince Turki al-Faisal had flown into Kandahar for a meeting with the Taliban leaders. Vast sums of money were then handed over to the Taliban to purchase/bribe the feuding commanders. Logistics had been the Taliban's Achilles heel in the May 1997 fiasco in Mazar-i-Sharif. This time the Saudis had 400 brand new pickup trucks flown into Kandahar.

Over 1700 Pakistani Pashtu- and Urdu-speaking troops in mufti were airlifted to Herat, which was made the mounting base for operations. Some media reports indicate that Pakistani army's 48 Brigade located at Quetta was directly involved, besides ISI's Afghan bureau personnel in mufti. This time airlift of reinforcements was carefully planned.

Early June 1998 saw Dostum's rout. The Taliban regained Murghab in Baghdis province which Dostum had captured from them a few days earlier. Dostum himself was seriously wounded and seven of his senior army commanders were captured and executed. The Taliban entered Maimana in the province of Faryab, forcing Dostum, who had taken refuge there, to flee. During 18–22 June the districts of Shirin Tagag, Faizabad and Pashtun Koh also fell to the Taliban.[6]

The Taliban captured the province of Faryab in early July 1998. In Kunduz, the encircled Taliban forces made advances and captured Haritan and adjoining areas, thus making it impossible for Dostum's and Masoud's forces to receive logistic support from Haritan base. The Hizb-i-Wahdat forces in Mazar-i-Sharif had virtually been encircled and their link with their base in the south severed. Ground contact of Masoud, which extended till Haritan, was also denied.[7]

The Taliban's second northern offensive, which started in July 1998, culminated in the fall of Mazar-i-Sharif on 8 August 1998. Anthony Davies reported in *Asiaweek*:

[6]Ibid.
[7]Ibid.

Wary, weapons at the ready, the first the Taliban moved into Taloqan in the cool of early morning. Advancing in single file into the main bazaar, the troops could hardly believe their good fortune. Instead of the rifle and rocket fire they had faced for more than a year, they were met only by the curious stares of locals. Their enemies, the forces of northern opposition chief Ahmadshah Masoud, had fled in the night. They had abandoned the town of 60,000—and the closest thing they had to a capital—since they ran from Kabul two years ago.

The fall of Masoud's Taloqan headquarters on Aug. 11 climaxed a blitzkrieg campaign in which Afghanistan's the Taliban completed their seizure of well over 90 per cent of the country's territory. Three days earlier they had captured the north's biggest city, Mazar-i-Sharif, scattering the forces of the tripartite alliance that had opposed them since their September 1996 takeover of Kabul. "Mazar and Taloqan were the heart and head of the opposition," says Abdul Maqsud, a Taloqan shopkeeper. "Without a heart or a head, how can a body continue to function?"

The dramatic successes of the Taliban's five-week campaign raise the possibility that for the first time in nearly 20 years, Afghanistan may be reunited under a strong central government, once more dominated by the nation's Pashtun majority. That could mean a long-awaited return of peace and security—along with the imposition of unbending laws and social strictures mandated by the Taliban's ultra-conservative interpretation of Islam. But a more ominous outcome may be continued guerrilla warfare, coupled with dangerously escalating tensions between the Taliban and an angry Iran.

The Taliban's northern offensive opened unexpectedly on July 10. Aided by the paid defection of two opposition commanders, they seized Maimana, capital of Faryab province, two days later. There, the campaign stalled for two weeks as the forces of Uzbek warlord Abdul Rashid Dostam, backed by allies Masoud and the Shia Hizb-i-Wahdat faction, launched frantic counter offensives. By the end of July, they had retaken Maimana's airstrip and were fighting in the city itself.

But the tide turned decisively on Aug 2. After the defection of Pushtun troops of the Hizb-i-Islami,[8] a minor member of the northern alliance but ethnic cousins of the Taliban, the Islamist militia once again surged forward. They fought their way into Dostam's military headquarters in Shiberghan seizing its vital airbase. From Shiberghan, a highway stretches for 90 km to Mazar. "If you break the lines between Maimana and Shiberghan, you are effectively in Mazar," says one diplomat.

Bitter clashes erupted outside Mazar, home to more than half a million

---

[8]Gulbuddin Hikmatyar faction. According to one commentator, this change of sides by Hikmatyar aides proved crucial for the success of the Taliban's offensive.

people. But on Aug. 8, the Taliban entered the dusty, sprawling prize, which they tried in vain to take in May last year [1997]. The defection of a Dostam commander allowed one Taliban column to enter the city from the west, while a second seized the airport 10 km to its east. Mazar's fate was sealed. The civilian population remained under effective house arrest for several days as the Taliban cleared the city, quarter by quarter. "Bodies [were] everywhere," says an independent source. Some were "unburied and being eaten by dogs."

Pakistan-based analysts have focused on two salient elements behind the Taliban's most successful campaign since their emergence four years ago. Once again, Pakistan support seems to have played a key role in terms of logistics, strategic direction and even manpower. According to diplomatic sources, over the two weeks before the fall of Shiberghan, hundreds of Pakistani volunteers were airlifted into the western city of Herat and then trucked to the front to bolster the Taliban push.

Western aid workers in Maimana when it fell estimated that 25 percentage to 50 percentage of some Taliban units were composed of Urdu-speaking Pakistanis. On Aug. 6, Masoud told *Asiaweek* that 1,700 Pakistanis were fighting in a Taliban force of 8.000 with both numbers rising rapidly. Military sources say the reinforcements are part of a multifaceted involvement by Pakistan with the Taliban that began with the movement itself in late 1994 and has since grown dramatically. The northern campaign, the sources add, was marked by impressive logistics support and command-and-control—in sharp contrast with the disastrous Taliban foray into the north last year. "This has been very professionally organized," says one military analyst. As many as 400 new pick-up trucks, imported from Pakistan, were apparently used to spearhead the Taliban advance.

The military analysts say that the Pakistani contingent in Afghanistan has two distinct categories. The overwhelming majority are youths from religious colleges, sympathetic to the Taliban jihad (holy war) and receiving no pay. A far smaller number of Pakistanis are believed to be trained and paid ex-military personal, technically "retired" and now serving in key specialist and liaison roles.

But Pakistani backing for the Taliban could never have had the impact it did without the incompetence and feuding of the northern alliance. Cobbled together after the Taliban seizure of Kabul, the coalition brought together the mainly Tajik forces of Masoud and ousted president Burhanuddin Rabbani, the chronically divided Jombesh-i-Milli Islami (National Islamic Movement) of ex-communist Dostam, and the ethnic Hazara-i-Wahdat faction. Backed by Iran and Russia, this already querulous mix was further divided by the return from exile early this year (1998) of Hizb-i-Islami leader Gulbuddin Hikmatyar, a long-time Masoud rival.

Tensions had mounted steadily following the return from a four-month exile in Turkey of Dostam and his bid to reassert himself as the most powerful partner. Indeed, Dostam spent far more time maneuvering around his rivals than fighting the Taliban. In March, armed clashes erupted between his forces and the Shias. In June, his fighters clashed with Masoud's men. Virtually forgotten was a crucial joint offensive against the Taliban-controlled province of Kunduz Dostam had been "fixated with Mazar," Masoud told *Asiaweek*. "On Kunduz he delayed, delayed, delayed."

In Mazar, meanwhile, where the Hizb-i-Wahdat was entrenched all the old evils of mujahideen misrule in Kabul reasserted themselves—extortion, lawlessness and rape. "Mazar did not just fall because of the Pakistanis," says moderate Pushtun politician Hamid Karzai. "The locals were sick of what was going on."

Beyond the northern allies' squabbling lay a far broader bankruptcy—their failure to present any viable political alternative to the Taliban. Within 24 hours of Taloqan's fall, citizens were commenting favorably on Taliban discipline, ease of movement and trade, and falling prices. "For me, the main change is that I can now travel freely and quickly between here and Kunduz", says merchant Abdul Wahid.

That relatively easy transition is unlikely to be reprised in Mazar and the northwest. There, ethnic tensions between the Hazaras and Uzbeks on the one hand, and the Pushtun Taliban on the other, run far deeper than those between Tajiks and Pushtuns in the northeast. And Mazar and Shiberghan have long seen women at work and girls in school—Taliban proscriptions.

What of the opposition's remnants? Dostam's forces, 30.000-strong before July, have been scattered and many of his top commanders have fled or disappeared. "We estimate 30 per cent to 40 per cent have retreated into the mountains and are still active," says a Taliban commander in Kunduz. Dostam himself has been seen both in northern Samanagan province and talking with Wahdat chief Karim Khalili in central Bamiyan province." He's wandering around in the hills with a couple of helicopters and a satellite phone," says one observer.[9]

To sum up, this success of the Taliban in defeating their adversaries had three components: chequebook diplomacy, Pakistani support, and opposition disarray.

•

[9] "Fateful Victory", *Asiaweek*, 28 August 1998, pp. 30–1. For an interesting analysis of the Taliban's offensive see "Endgame in Afghanistan", *Jane's Defence Weekly*, 26 August 1998, p. 22. See also G.D. Bakshi, "Mono, Ethnic Solutions: Taliban's Cheque Book Campaign Autumn 1998", mimeo, p. 3.

One observer called the Taliban's movement "Islamic Maoism", blending Chairman Mao's "serve the people" doctrine with dogmatic Sunni Muslim beliefs. A more benign description suggested that the Taliban are "in the tradition of the Pashtun reactionary movements recurrent in Afghan history". Another assessment was that the Taliban victory "did more to change the world" than the "Israeli–Palestinian conflict". Because the Taliban have single-minded aim, the redemption of the "entire Islamic world of one billion people", should they succeed in Afghanistan, their impact is expected to be felt not only in Pakistan, Uzbekistan and Kyrgyzstan, but also in Russia, Iran, and India where indeed the vast majority of Muslims are located.[10] In these regions, the Taliban's impact, religious or political, cannot be ignored. In response, as will be discussed in other chapters the governments of these countries have reoriented their foreign policies towards each other and Afghanistan.

Not much can be said at present about the prospects of the Taliban movement's success or failure in its present form. Despite the Taliban's ideological commitment, their economic and military resources are limited and not much political clout can be accomplished by the exuberance of pure zeal. The Taliban's zeal is generally described as Islamic fundamentalism, a kind of transnational street force which has the potential to topple established governments through agitation or spread indiscriminate terror even against the big powers.[11] Increasingly, after Samuel Huntington's thesis of Conflict of Civilizations, it appears that Islamic fundamentalism of the Taliban variety is replacing communism as the bugbear of the West. It may be kept in mind, however, that the exploitation of religion to promote political interests is not absent in other religions like Christianity and Judaism.

The Taliban have recently circulated a substantial amount of information about their view of Islam, and have explained their political and social policies in its light. Their religious, political and social policies can thus be profiled.

[10]Dr Hafeez Malik, "Taliban's Islamic Emirates", *The Nation on Sunday*, 4 April 1999. This four-part article by Malik gives an excellent idea of Taliban moorings from the beginning. We have extensively drawn from it.
[11]Ibid.

To begin with, the term Taliban is derived from the Persian and Pashtu plural of an Arabic word Talib, seeker of knowledge. The Prophet Muhammad (peace be upon him) is known to have urged the believers to seek knowledge even if it meant going to far-off places. Historically, it was practical for the Afghan students to travel to India before 1947, and then to India and Pakistan after partition. In India their favourite madrasa, an institute of higher learning, was dar al-ulum of Deoband in Uttar Pradesh, which had been established in 1862. The Dar al-ulum was known for its anti-colonial orientation and stood for the independence of a united India while it retained a strong anti–Aligarh Muslim University (AMU) policy. The latter was a modernist private university established by Sayyed Ahmad Khan (1817–98) with British cooperation. While AMU offered western education to middle-class students, the Deoband Dar al-ulum trained working and lower-middle-class young Muslims, who received traditional religious education and joined the ranks of "big" and "small" mullahs in masjid (mosques).[12]

Intellectually, the Taliban are heir to the traditional affinity between the Dar al-ulum and the ulema. However since 1947, the leading Deobandi ulema in Pakistan and other sectarian religious leaders as well, established dar al-ulum(s) in all the provinces of Pakistan, including Pakistan-occupied Kashmir (POK) and the northern areas. Their regional and sectarian distribution is given in Table 2.1.

During the years 1982–87, the dar al-ulum(s) of the North West Frontier Province (NWFP) of Pakistan, contiguous to Afghanistan, awarded an "abnormally large number of the highest degrees". This development coincided "with the influx of Afghan refugees and the mujahideen at the height of Afghan jihad" against the Soviet Union (see Table 2.2).[13]

The current Taliban leaders are products of these theological seminaries. The governor of Jalalabad, bordering Pakistan, is a graduate of Dar al-ulum Haqqani of Akara Khattak, Peshawar. The judge of the Jalalabad high court and its qazis are former scholars of another madrasa. The Taliban's Ambassador to the

[12]Ibid.
[13]Ibid.

UN, Maulana Abdul Hakim, though not officially acknowledged by the United Nations, is an alumnus of Dar al-ulum of Binnori town, Karachi; so is the Taliban government's former Ambassador to Pakistan, Mufti Masum. The top echelon of the Taliban leaders are accomplished traditional Islamic scholars, while some of them have yet to complete their education. Their education, however, is frozen in time, an apt description given by a Pakistani scholar. With the exception of the Shi'a dar al-ulum, the curricula of all Sunni theological institutions are based upon Dars Nizamya. The eighteenth-century scholar Mullah Nizam-ud-Din, who established this curriculum, flourished during the period that followed the demise of the Mughal Emperor Aurangzeb (d. 1707). Dars Nizamya teaches young students: Arabic grammar; syntax; rhetoric; philosophy of logic; Lim al-Kalam (dialectical theology); Tafsir (Quranic exegesis); Fiqh (Islamic laws); Usul al-Fiqh (Islamic jurisprudence); Hadith (the Prophet's statements); and Mathematics. None of these disciplines includes nineteenth-century texts, let alone contemporary works of modern scholars whether of the East or the West. One cannot expect a modern outlook on religious and political matters from graduates of these studies. The Taliban's weltanschauung is petrified in this pre-modern mould.[14]

•

There are six elements comprising the Taliban movement:
— the real Taliban, that is young students belonging to both Pakistan and Afghanistan and other nationalities from madrasas in Pakistan;
— former Afghan Mujahideen including Mullah Umar himself and his band of followers;
— veterans of anti-Soviet campaign who do not belong to any group nor committed to any ideology but are individuals who found the opportunity to exercise their vocation of fighting in the fold of Taliban;
— previous members of the Khalq faction of the Communist Party, most of them Soviet-trained professional soldiers;

[14]Ibid.

Table 2.1. Regional and Sectarian Distribution of Dar al-ulums (till 1988)

	Deobandi	Barelvi	Ahl-i-Hadith	Shia	Others
Punjab	590	548	116	21	43
NWFP	631	32	5	2	8
Sindh	208	61	6	10	6
Baluchistan	278	34	3	1	31
POK	51	20	2	-	3
Islamabad	51	20	-	2	3
Northern Areas	60	2	27	11	3

Table 2.2. Number of Graduates of Different Levels of Education from Dar al-ulums, 1982–87

	Nazersh	Hifz	Tajwedd Qirat	Daura-i-Hadith
Punjab	169,688	37,994	21,399	12,252
NWFP	68,529	7,122	9,510	27,906
Sindh	73,623	7,755	18,280	2,552
Baluchistan	32,830	4,645	5,789	2,615
POK	12,460	1,055	1,212	337
Islamabad	3,877	154	357	-
Northern Areas	10,898	243	275	28

Source: Hafeez Mallick, "The Taliban's Islamic Emirates", *The Nation on Sunday*, 4 April 1999.

— former personnel of the Pakistani armed forces; and
— members of the dissident movements in the Islamic world who are supposed to be assisting the Taliban leadership.[15]

According to a Russian diplomat and academic, the Taliban leadership has three broad features, as it happens with any religion-driven militant movement. At the top is the spiritual head—Mullah Umar. He has under him a chain of officials, clergy and military commanders who are controllable. This has been the case in Lebanon, Iran and other places. Under them are commanders, mostly fighting men, who cannot survive without fighting. The third faction is of educated people who form layers of administration, including diplomats and governors. Their number is small and they do not count for much, lacking political or military clout.

[15] Hafiz Sanaullah, "Real Issue Is Economic", *The Nation*, 18 July 1999.

Chart 2.1 presents the Taliban ring of leadership. The Taliban's political structure, which is still evolving, reflects, according to them, the early Caliphate of Khulfa-i Rashdin (AD 632–62), the four "rightly guided" caliphs, who succeeded Prophet Muhammad (PBUH). The Sunni tradition attributed to the Prophet the prediction that the successorship to Prophethood (Khilafa al-Mubuwwa) would last after him for thirty years, to be followed by "biting kingship" (mulk al-'adud), implying oppressive rule of individuals, rather than the rule of law. The Taliban are "committed to establishing an exemplary Islamic rule" for the world and especially for the Muslim states and they are impervious to the possibility that their "exemplary" Islamic paradigm may produce the negative stereotypes of Islam.[16]

Emulating the early Caliphate, the Taliban created a supreme council (Majlis-i-shura) consisting of 20 individuals and in a fairly representative congregation of 1500 Sunni ulema (religious scholars), who supposedly represent various ethnic tribes, elected 33-year-old Mulla Muhammad Umar, the amirul momineen, the Commander of the Faithful or Supreme leader of the Muslims. The majority of the council members are Pashtuns. Fourteen of them lost some part of their body fighting against the Soviet Union. They are determined to implement the Sharia because "the Afghan public has accepted Islam as their religion."[17]

Despite their commitment to the pristine purity of Islam, the Pashtun ethnic composition of the Taliban has turned their jihad into a struggle for power against the Tajiks in the Panjshir Valley and the Uzbeks in the north. The Tajiks are led by the ousted President Burhanuddin Rabbani, and the well-known military commander, Ahmed Shah Masoud, and the Uzbeks were till recently led by the Uzbek General Rashid Dostum, who collaborated with the Soviet expeditionary forces but in January 1982 shifted his allegiance to the Mujahideen seven-party coalition, which was supported by the United States and Pakistan in their war against the Soviet union. The Taliban emphatically reject the ethnic bias of their movement, saying that their true jihad is the

---

[16] Dr Hafeez Malik, "Taliban's Islamic Emirates", *The Nation on Sunday*, 11 April 1999.
[17] Ibid.

war between Right (which they espouse), and Wrong (which is represented by their opposition). In a titanic struggle between "virtue and vice" there is "no place in it for racial prejudice".[18]

•

In consonance with their concept of "Islamic virtue", the Taliban have established a department of moral control—Amar-bil Ma'ruf wa Nahi Anil Munkar—which "enjoins good and forbids evil". This department has enforced hudood punishments ordained by the Quran or the Sunna: (1) Whipping, numbering 100 strikes for having sexual intercourse without being married to the partner or be stoned to death. The moral control department has included homosexuality as a capital offence and punishable by the wall-toppling method, when a 15-foot brick wall is knocked over a guilty person to kill him. (2) Thieves must have their hands and feet amputated. (3) TV stations, "being against the Shariat" have been closed. (4) Photography, singing and music have been eliminated. (5) Those who do not pray five times a day or do not fast for 30 days during the month of Ramadan are imprisoned. (6) Shaving the beard or trimming it less than a fistful is prohibited; so too is keeping western-style hair. (7) Gambling, betting, pigeon-keeping and flying, and dog racing, are forbidden.[19]

The Taliban's repressive policy towards women has evoked the strongest possible indignation from some Muslim countries, and the West. The Taliban assert that Allah has defined and determined women's rights—not the United States or the United Nations or the European states. They reject "the western-bestowed rights of women", and describe their critics' attitude as "entirely absurd and stupid". Islam, according to them, has placed full responsibility of woman's maintenance upon men. If a man cannot pay her dower (mahr) or bear her expenses, his marriage is not valid.

If the husband dies, the woman has the right to remarry, or she can live with her parents, who are responsible for her maintenance. Islam has made woman an heir of her parents' wealth, as well as of her husband's estate. Also, she is an heir to

---
[18] Ibid.
[19] Ibid.

Chart 2.1. Taliban Ring of Leadership

Top Command
Mullah Mohammad Omar

Inner Shura
Mullah Mohammed Rabbani
Mullah Ehsanullah
Mullah Abbas
Mullah Mohammed
Mullah Pasani

Central Shura
Mullah Mohammed Hassan
Mullah Nur al-Din
Mullah Wakil Ahmad
Mullah Shir Mohammed Malang
Mullah Abd al-Rahman
Mullah Abd al-Hakim
Sardar Ahmad
Haji Mohammed Ghaus
Ma'soom Afghani

Liaison Officer in NWFP
Abd al-Rahman (Rashid) Zahid

Liaison Officer in Quetta
Mohammed Ma'soom

Kabul Six-man Supervisory Council
Mullah Mohammed Hassan Akhund (Vice Chair)
Mullah Mohammed Rabbani
Mullah Mohammed Hassan
Mullah Mohammed Ghaus
Mullah Syed Ghayasuddin Agha (Education)
Mullah Gazil Mohammed
Mullah Abdul Razzaq (Customs)

Source: Frontier Post, 24 February 1995.

Note: In October 1999, Radio Shariat, the Taliban's official radio, formally announced the appointment of the following persons as Ministers by Mullah Umar:

Mullah Mohammad Rabbani	Head of the Supreme Council
Mullah Mohammad Akhund	Dy. Head of the Supreme Council
Mullah Abdul Razaq	Interior Minister

her children's property. Contrary to these provisions, the Taliban assert "the West has made woman an object of man's lust and desires". They are also "dragged" into the offices and factories, restaurants and stores. Consequently, the western women lose their "personality and identity". Addressing Europeans, the Taliban have stated that they have no right to force upon others their own failed values. "Your Parliament passes a bill, which makes it legal for a man to marry another man, for a son-in-law to marry his wife's mother, i.e. his mother-in-law. Why do you compel us to do the same?"[20]

The women of Kabul have been divided into two categories: those who were linked to the communist movement, and those who were sent to Moscow. In Moscow, they learned "all the vices" and then returned and were "bent upon destroying the Islamic environment of Afghanistan". They were then appointed to different jobs in the government offices. These women, the Taliban assert, "belonged to the Communists, heretics and atheists" and enjoyed the United Nations' patronage. Their husbands were sent to the warfronts surely to go into the mouth of death. Then, these women became the objects of "leaders' lust".

All these women were removed from their jobs, the Taliban assert, with full salaries, so they are not denied the right to their livelihood. The denial of education is not permanent. Women will receive education in the Islamic madrasas "from which [they] emerge as an epitome of honour and decency, grace and dignity."

Mullah Qaidullah	Defence Minister
Maulvi Wakil Ahmed Muttawakil	Foreign Minister
Mullah Saeedur Rehman Haqqani	Dy Minister of Public Affairs in Kabul
Among the other announced appointments are:	
Mullah Khairullah	Governor of Herat
Mullah Akhundzada	Corps Commander of Kabul
Mullah Abdul Salam Rocketi	Corps Commander of Herat
Mullah Biradar	Vice Chief of the Afghan Army
Mullah Noorullah Noori	In-charge of North Zone Provinces
Sayed Mohammad Haqqani	Ambassador to Pakistan

Source: The News, 28 October 1999.

---

[20]Ibid.

For the establishment of these female madrasas "wait till the end of the civil war!" Consequently, the present generation of girls are being denied the benefits of education at all levels.[21]

•

Despite the Taliban's control of 90 per cent of Afghanistan's territory, President Rabbani's government, which controls 10 per cent of the territory in the north, controls most of the country's embassies abroad, and retains Afghanistan's United Nations' seat after the UN General Assembly deferred a decision on Afghanistan's credentials in September 1997. Indeed, in the Taliban's non-recognition by the world community, the United States has played the decisive role. As on January 1999, only Saudi Arabia, Pakistan and the United Arab Emirates diplomatically recognized the Taliban government, and maintained their embassies in Kabul. The UN again denied recognition to the Taliban in October 1999.

Indifferent to their diplomatic isolation, the Taliban have divided the global state system into four zones:

(a) *dar al-kuffar*, the lands of the infidels, including India and Russia and other non-Muslim states;
(b) *dar al-munafiqin*, the states of the hypocrites, including Iran
(c) irreligious countries, including Turkey; and
(d) *dar al-Islam*, "good Muslim" states, including Pakistan, Saudi Arabia and the United Arab Emirates, and others which have not yet decided on the Taliban's recognition.

If the world governments have not recognized the Taliban government it is because the Taliban are "the true followers of Islam and are extremely sincere in implementing the Islamic system". They call Rabbani "a traitor", and Ahmed Shah Masoud "a communist, who belongs to the Shola-i Javid faction of Afghanistan's communist movement. Their lukewarm adherence to Islam makes them acceptable to the United States and other countries."[22]

Much of the Taliban's invective is reserved for their arch enemy Masoud, who organized the Northern Alliance and at first invited

[21] Ibid.
[22] Ibid., 18 April 1999.

his "Pashtun father" Hikmatyar to join the war against them, then asked his Uzbek "grandfather" General Dostum, to join him, and then "begged his great-grandfathers, India, Iran and Tajikistan" for help. No one could save him. He was driven out of Kabul. Indeed, the Taliban's self-confidence is buttressed by their victories against the Northern Alliance, and by an act of blind faith that "God and Islam are with them".[23]

•

Beneath the façade of solidarity based to a strict Islamic code as they see it, however, a division may be observed in the ranks of Taliban leadership between the arch-conservatives and the less illiberal. After they have unified the country, says Professor Rasool Amin, a former teacher of political science at Kabul University, the more liberal elements within the Taliban are likely to push for women's rights and education for girls. Of course such measures are anathema to the "real Taliban, the madrasa students" whose religion "is embodied primarily in the men's beard and the women's veils", the professor adds.[24] The fault-line is said to cut right through the top Taliban leadership. One group is said to favour monarchy backed up by a system of representative institutions. Given a chance, these Taliban leaders would gladly permit newsmen to shoot pictures, and are willing to sit across the table with other Afghan leaders for the formation of broad-based government of the kind proposed by the United Nations. The head of the interim ruling council, Mulla Mohammad Rabbani, as well as former Foreign Minister Mullah Muhammad Hasan Akhund, now deputy head of the Supreme Council, are said to be sympathetic to this group. On the other side of the divide are hard-core Islamists led by Mullah Muhammad Umar, the amirul momineen. This group includes madrasa students and elements from former mujahideen outfits who together form the military base of the Taliban movement and are the ascendant faction at the moment.

Underlying the apparent political discord is an age-old tribal

[23] Ibid.
[24] See n. 2.

schism between the Ghilzai nomads and the Durrani statesmen. Hard-core Islamists within the Taliban are almost exclusively Ghilzai, including Mullah Muhammad Umar who heads the movement. Although valiant fighters on the battlefield, members of this group mostly hail from the lower echelons of society and lack political training or vision.

On the other side are the Durranis, led by Mullah Rabbani, who have produced landed aristocracies and built empires. Most of them believe that former King Zahir Shah, himself a Durrani, is the only living Afghan leader capable of uniting the country's various ethnic and tribal factions under a central authority.

Differences within the Taliban leadership first surfaced in April 1998 soon after the permanent US envoy to the United Nations, William Richardson, visited Kabul and Mazar-i-Sharif. Richardson later said at a news conference in Islamabad that the Taliban leadership in Kabul (Mullah Rabbani and company) had agreed to put an end to the military offensive, and pave the way for face-to-face talks with the Northern Alliance leaders under the auspices of the UN and the Organization of Islamic Conference. Within hours of this briefing, Mulla Mohammad Umar issued a statement from Kandahar denying that any such agreement had been reached with Richardson, adding that the Ulema Shura proposed earlier by the Taliban was the only forum authorized to resume dialogue.[25]

Political and tribal schisms apart, growing regional rivalries may pose even more serious problems for the movement in the days to come. The Durrani and Ghilzai leaders of the Taliban have at least one thing in common: They all hail from the south and southwest of the country. Mullah Rabbani belongs to Helmand, while Mullah Muhammad Umar is a Kandahari. The domination of the south, in particular Kandahar, is so overwhelming that even the predominantly Pashtun province of Nangarhar feels left out. In Afghanistan, regional rivalries cut across even tribal solidarity, so much so that a Laghmani Ghilzai does not feel at home with a Ghilzai from Kandahar. Contrary to the general impression, the Taliban do have minority Tajiks, Uzbeks and Hazaras in their ranks and in the administration. But their number is small, and they do not hold any key positions.

[25]Ibid. This aspect is discussed in detail in Chapter 14.

The disintegration of Afghan society commenced with the Saur Revolution of 1978 and intensified after December 1979, when Soviet troops entered Kabul. As differences emerged within the ruling People's Democratic Party of Afghanistan (PDPA), the Pashtuns, who were in majority, gravitated towards the Khalq faction while urbanites grouped themselves under the Parcham faction of the PDPA. During this time, the Shola-i-Javed came to represent the minorities while the Sitam-i-Milli party remained confined to the enlightened Tajik leadership.

Pakistan's policy of creating seven mujahideen parties in Peshawar in 1980, mostly led by Ghilzai warlords, took the fragmentation a step further, pitting brother against brother and tribe against tribe. A clear line along the ethnic divide appeared to have been drawn when the ethnic Tajik Jamiat-i-Islami, the Hazara Hizb-i-Wahdat, the Uzbek Jombish-i-Milli and some elements of the Parcham faction of the PDPA captured Kabul in 1992, depriving the Pashtuns of a share in state power.

The mainly Pashtun Taliban movement can be seen as reaction to these events, taking advantage of a state of utter lawlessness to subdue the ruling warlords one by one and bring peace to areas under their control, says Rasool Amin. But the Taliban failed to take into account the egalitarian character of Afghan tribal society and sought to impose their own dictatorship. Such moves have always destabilized Afghanistan."[26]

Rasool Amin believes that the Taliban are making the same mistake as the PDPA by using ideology as a tool to subdue a people who are tribal in character, individualistic in their economic pursuits and almost totally illiterate. Ideologies work only in educated societies, he says. In a society like Afghanistan, they create feuds.

Afrasiab Khatak, a prominent Peshawar-based human rights activist, agrees with this view. The Taliban have followed in the footsteps of their predecessors. These five ways, he explains, are as follows:

[26]See n. 2.

— they have used ideology rather than popular support to legitimize political power;
— they have emphasized a military solution at the cost of a political settlement;
— they have tended to depend on foreign support;
— they have partially shifted power away from the capital. The PDPA moved some key portions of the establishment to Mazar-i-Sharif, while the Taliban have shifted power to Kandahar. This in itself is a destabilizing factor.
— Combining religion with ideology, the Taliban have had an even more divisive effect on Afghan society than the PDPA.[27]

This tactic has not only estranged Afghanistan's Sunni and Shia neighbours and led to Kabul's total isolation, but also prevented the Taliban from adopting a workable political programme. There is no indication that the Taliban are willing or even capable of operating at an all Afghanistan level, says Rasool Amin. They are too tribal and clannish for that.[28]

Initially the Taliban movement succeeded because of its cultural homogeneity at macro-level. As has been mentioned earlier they were Pashtuns; and majority of them operated from Pakistani soil in their fight against the Red Army from 1980 to 1988. In fact this gave them a sense of oneness in the initial stages of the movement. These two factors enabled them to continue to speak in terms of militant Islamic ideology, a phenomenon noticed at the time of "jihad" against the Red Army.

Also, the continued support from Pakistan both physically and diplomatically enabled them to consolidate their position in the areas they annexed. Pakistani support, especially logistic support, facilitated the Taliban's success. The Pakistani recognition in May 1997 provided certain amount of legitimacy; and Pakistani diplomatic support also prompted the custodian of the Holy Places of Muslims, Saudi Arabia, and United Arab Emirates to extend the recognition to the Taliban. At one point of time, 1995–96, even the US was sympathetic towards the Taliban. What put off a possible recognition or a positive relationship

[27]Ibid.
[28]Ibid.

were the reports of barbarity and atrocities on women, which went down badly with the American media.

This diplomatic support from Pakistan also enabled the Taliban to receive liberal doses of financial aid from the Islamic international community to the tune of $100–150 million annually.

•

The important point is that the Taliban control more than two-thirds of Afghan territory. They have been able to maintain a semblance of public order in spite of their internal differences. And if the media reports are correct, they are organizing the apparatus for a state structure. For instance, the Taliban is organizing its militia into a regular army. Initially the ground forces are to be reorganized into two regular divisions while the Islamic militias limited combat and transport air assets are being organized into corps based at Khoja Rawash airbase in Kabul.[29]

In spite of these plus points, the Taliban are not able to get recognition by the international community for three reasons. Foremost is the public perception that the Taliban are a creation of Pakistan, especially Pakistani intelligence agencies, and the Taliban are fighting a proxy war in Afghanistan on behalf of Pakistan. This aspect is acknowledged by even most of the Pakistani commentators. This has resulted in the other neighbours of Afghanistan looking at the Pakistani action as expansionist, and responding sharply to protect their own national interest.

It is clear that without Pakistan's military support, the Taliban all by themselves will not be able to defeat Masoud and unify Afghanistan. Even if, hypothetically, such unification, takes place, factional fights and guerrilla war will continue.

During the 1999 summer offensive of the Taliban, Pakistani armed forces were reported to have been suddenly withdrawn by the Nawaz Sharif government in Islamabad. Whatever may have been Nawaz Sharif's compulsions this resulted in battlefield reverses for the Taliban. Will the Taliban be allowed to be routed by Masoud's forces? That would mean driving them all the way back into Pakistan. That in turn would entail major convulsions

[29] *Jane's Defence Weekly*, 22 January 1998, p. 15.

in the Pakistani polity. The Taliban leadership and their sponsors are well aware of it.

Therefore, one can expect slow but steady efforts for taming of the Taliban by the international community. How far they will succeed is anybody's guess.

Even though the diplomatic isolation of the Taliban government shows no signs of easing, there is little change in the Taliban's hard-line policies. Their determination to enforce their own brand of Islamic law proves their conviction that any compromise in this area may turn the angels against them and deprive them of their victories. To counter growing pressure for change from the international community, the Taliban leadership in Kandahar summoned a grand assembly of ulema (religious scholars) to issue decrees or fatwas on six specific questions. During a four-day gathering in Kabul, 21–24 September 1998 a number of resolutions were also passed.

After the summer–autumn 1999 offensive, Mullah Umar made a cabinet reshuffle. This is being viewed by many as an effort by the Taliban supremo to reassert his authority after the battlefield reverses. Also, it is a subtle indication to the rest of the world that the Taliban administration is going to be Pashtun-dominated and none else.[30]

The Fatwas

1. If Iran or any other country invades Afghanistan, will our resistance constitute jihad in the religious sense or will simply be war?

Fatwa: If Iran or any other country violates the sacred borders of the Islamic Emirate, our resistance will constitute jihad.

2. Is defending our borders the exclusive duty of the military, or is the whole nation obliged to resist invaders?

Fatwa: In the event of an invasion, jihad is obligatory on every Muslim.

3. If enemy soldiers retreat, does the national army have the religious mandate to pursue them into their own territory?

Fatwa: If it is perceived that the retreat is only a tactical one, or the enemy may be capable of influencing the law and order situation in the Islamic Emirate, then it should be pursued.

4. Can the government appeal to Islamic and non-Islamic countries for help to defend the Islamic system of the Emirate?

[30] *The News*, 1 November 1999.

Fatwa: Islamic countries are obliged to offer their help without being asked. In the hour of need, even non-Muslim countries can be approached for assistance.

5. Regarding the Islamic Emirate's laws of qisas, hudood and hijab, some foreign countries say the Taliban have introduced an Islam of their own imagination. Are these laws in conformity with the Hanafi or not? And what does the Sharia say about those who deny these laws?

Fatwa: All injunctions related to qisas, hijab and hudood are [derived] from the Quran, and anyone who denies these laws is an infidel.

6. Has the government of the Islamic Emirate risen from within the people and with their active support, or is it government of a faction that has acquired power forcibly and against the will of the people?

Fatwa: Since the Taliban movement has risen from within the people and has established an Islamic Emirate in the country with the support of the people, the ulema consider it to be a legitimate government and offer their support and cooperation to it. Since this government eliminated those who were committing excesses against the people and brought peace and security to the country, we strongly appeal to the international community to recognize it. As for the limited resistance that still remains, we pray to God to enable the Taliban to eliminate it and to restore the remaining provinces to the divine law.

Resolution

1. We [the Taliban] did not start the [Afghan civil] war, and as such we are not bound to initiate a cease-fire.
2. We have no objection to a broad-based government, provided the participants of such a government are (a) eligible and (b) God-fearing or men of taqwa.
3. We are not involved in training terrorists and have never allowed anyone to carry out terrorist attacks against any country.
4. We are ready to exchange prisoners of war, provided the exercise is undertaken seriously.
5. We have never violated women's rights. Instead we have enhanced the honour of women in the light of the Shariah.
6. We are not involved in drug trafficking and will do everything in our power to prevent it.
7. The issue of mass graves should be investigated by the international community and responsibility fixed for this outrageous act.
8. The NGOs and UN agencies operating in Afghanistan must abide by the laws and instructions of the Islamic Emirate of Afghanistan.[31]

---

[31] Rizwan Qureshi, "Conflict of Interests".

Box 2.2
Beyond Good or Evil
by M. Ilyas Khan

Clad in the ubiquitous shuttlecock *burqa*, she crosses a street in Kabul's Shahri-i-Nau district and enters a cosmetics and toiletry store. She walks up straight to the clerk and stretches out her hand as if to ask for alms. But this gesture is just a ruse. "It'll be two lakh afghanis [equivalent to 250 Pakistani rupees] per head, nothing less", she tells the clerk under the breath, casting a veiled glance at me and the one other man present in the store. "I was expecting some good business, but I dropped it when I received word from you."

"I'm sorry, but this call is just for an interview with our journalist friend here", replies the clerk apologetically, pointing in my direction. "It'll still be two lakhs", she insists. "I told you I dropped some good business to come here."

As radiant as her name, which means an oil lamp in Pushto, Diva is a stunning beauty. In the privacy of the store's attic, she throws off her tattered *burqa* to reveal a beautiful crimson blouse and an ankle-length black Afghani skirt. Diva's shoes are worn, but peeping from underneath the hem of her skirt is a shimmer of gauze stockings. Her neatly trimmed brunette hair falls in straight tresses to her shoulders. Her eyebrows are plucked thin into perfect arches and there is no make-up to mar her glowing complexion. Though she looks barely 20, Diva claims she's 28.

"I graduated from college in geophysics and used to work for the government", she says. But life changed dramatically for Diva in 1995 when she was abducted and raped allegedly by some fighters of the Hizb-i-Islami in the southern Chilsitoon district of Kabul. "I returned to work for a brief period, but in September 1996 the Taliban overran Kabul and ordered women to stay home." Left without a dependable source of income, Diva was forced into prostitution.

Diva lives with her aged mother and three sisters, one of whom is a prostitute and the other a widow with three children. She has a 15-year-old brother who works at a smithy for 100,000 afghanis a month. With their combined incomes, the family appears to be in a position to survive, however modestly, on its own.

Aqazad, a 35-year-old Tajik woman, is not as glamorous as Diva and only half as business-like. But her price is the same: 200,000 afghanis. "The money is only enough to buy 10 *maans*, which is less than what my family needs to feed itself for one day", she points out, defending her rates. Aqazad has four daughters and two sons. The daughters sometimes take in laundry, while the sons, both of them less than 10 years old, beg on the streets. Her husband was an Afghan army officer who died in the battle of Jalalabad in 1989. Between 1992 and 1996, Aqazad ran a grocery stall in the northern Khairkhana district. That lasted till the Taliban ordered all stalls run by women to be closed down.

According to Aqazad, she is extremely good at *tar-shumar*, the cross-stitch embroidery which is used to decorate women's wear and shoulder bags. "I could embroider for large handicraft exporters who pay well, but the Taliban do not allow women to interact with male businessmen. And I have no male relatives through whom I can deal with the exporters."

Both Diva and Aqazad hail from that enormous cross-section of Afghan society whose male bread-winners have either been incapacitated or consumed by the 20-year war, leaving the women and children to fend for themselves. The World Food Program estimates that this segment numbers between 60,000 and 120,000 individuals in Kabul alone. Banned from work by the Taliban, these women have very few options other than begging on the streets or becoming prostitutes in order to feed themselves and their dependants.

"There are hundreds of prostitutes roaming the streets of Kabul and their numbers are rising every day", asserts Zarghuna Hashemi, a Kabul-based spokeswoman of the Revolutionary Association of the Women of Afghanistan (RAWA). "They are not the regular professionals we had in Kabul before or during the war. These women are a product of the economic turmoil of the last three years."

The economic turmoil in Afghanistan has indeed been severe. Over the last three years, the price of wheat flour has risen by around 450 per cent to 80,000 afghanis per maund. While a five-kilogram canister of ghee carries a price tag of 210,000 afghanis, kerosene oil costs 60,000 per gallon. The prices, moreover, continue to escalate while the average government salary remains stuck between 110,000 and 300,000 afghanis per month. The monthly wages of manual labourers are even lower and do not exceed one million afghanis, provided, of course, that work is available throughout the month.

The ban on working women further complicates the scenario

(Continued on page 56)

(Continued from page 55)

for households headed by women. Pushed into a corner, most such women first came out in droves to beg. Now, many of them are turning to prostitution as a more convenient source of income.

"Pretending to be beggars, these women have easy access to clients who are mainly shopkeepers and their trading partners in Pakistan, Iran and Gulf", contends a former member of Taliban's religious police, popularly known as Amr bil Maroof. Most shops in Kabul contain a storeroom or an attic which can be used for the purpose. But more security-conscious clients prefer to fix appointments elsewhere such as their homes. For Diva and others like her, such an invitation can translate into a million afghanis in one night, which, as far as they are concerned, can buy 100 *maans*.

The more wretched of Kabul's prostitutes live in brothels, where they have to share their income with the madam and the resident pimp. RAWA claims that there are some 25 to 30 brothels operating in Kabul. A Taliban source in the Hauz-i-Awwal police cannot confirm this figure, but admits that brothels do indeed exist. "I know of one place in the Ashiqan-o-Arifan neighbourhood, and I have heard that there are others in Qalae Zaman Khan. But they change their location every few months to avoid detection."

When they do get caught, judicial authorities are bribed and the accused gets away with only a few lashes. Aqazad, who worked at a brothel in Qalae Musa, recalls one such incident. "The Taliban once picked up one of the girls on charges of *zina*, but the pimp paid the judicial officer six million afghanis who in turn advised the girl to plead not guilty. The prosecution was reined in, and she was only imprisoned for 60 days and received 20 lashes."

In Kabul, however, court cases based on charges of adultery are few and far between. "It is difficult to keep an eye on all the beggars and monitor shops throughout the day. Even if a suspect is found in a shop, she can conveniently plead that she was just begging. Besides, it is very difficult to prove adultery under the Islamic law, which requires four God-fearing witnesses who have seen the act 'as clearly as a thread going through the eye of a needle' ", explains the source in Hauz-i-Awwal.

As an added protection, the brothels entertain the Taliban free of charge. "One of the reasons I left the house [brothel] was that every two or three days a group of Taliban youngsters would drop in and want to do it for free", says Aqazad. "I already had some steady clients, so I decided to move out."

A former member of the religious police confirms the involvement of the Taliban in such affairs and even provided an explanation. "Communists and lechers have grown beards and infiltrated the Taliban ranks. They will do anything to defame the Taliban." He recalls the time when some of his colleagues took him to a brothel. "There they smoked hashish, performed adultery and cracked jokes about Islam. Some four months later, the entire gang disappeared without a trace. And it was only later that a friend told me that they were ex-communists from the Nangarhar province, out to have fun."

There are indications that poverty-driven prostitution is not confined to Kabul alone. Faced with abject poverty, women in other cities of Afghanistan are also turning to this profession. Mariam is one of them. She lost her husband in a rocket attack on their house in the western border city of Herat two years ago. She lived for six months without the means to buy food for her six starving children. Following a period of acute anxiety, during which she went as far as contemplating suicide, she turned to prostitution. "Among my clients were many Taliban soldiers and *qomandans* [commanders] who were generous as well as gentle", she recalls. But things got really bad when the massing of Iranian troops on Herat's border around mid-1998 brought hordes of unruly Taliban youth to the city. "They were wild and tight-fisted, and when I demanded money, they said they would prefer to pay my daughter who was reaching puberty." Four months ago Mariam sold whatever little she could muster to buy a ticket to Pakistan.

The wisdom of the Taliban's so-called Islamic policies is being debated all over the world. While concerned members of the international community continue to express their outrage at the state of affairs, the predicament of the women living in Taliban-controlled Afghanistan goes from bad to worse. Taliban rhetoric may claim that the ban on working women has been imposed to protect them from the "ignominy" of dealing with men and braving the world on their own. But it is these very repressive policies that are forcing increasing numbers of Afghan women to resort to the basest of professions in the desperate struggle to survive.

Courtesy: The Herald, August 1999.

FBI TEN MOST WANTED FUGITIVE

MURDER OF U.S. NATIONALS OUTSIDE THE UNITED STATES; CONSPIRACY TO MURDER U.S. NATIONALS OUTSIDE THE UNITED STATES; ATTACK ON A FEDERAL FACILITY RESULTING IN DEATH

USAMA BIN LADEN

Date of Photograph Unknown

Aliases: Usama Bin Muhammad Bin Ladin, Shaykh Usama Bin Ladin, the Prince, the Emir, Abu Abdallah, Mujahid Shaykh, Hajj, the Director

DESCRIPTION

Date of Birth:	1957	**Hair:**	Brown
Place of Birth:	Saudi Arabia	**Eyes:**	Brown
Height:	6' 4" to 6' 6"	**Complexion:**	Olive
Weight:	Approximately 160 pounds	**Sex:**	Male
Build:	Thin	**Nationality:**	Saudi Arabian
Occupations:	Unknown		
Remarks:	Leader of a terrorist organization known as Al-Qaeda "The Base". He walks with a cane.		
Scars and Marks:	None		

CAUTION

USAMA BIN LADEN IS WANTED IN CONNECTION WITH THE AUGUST 7, 1998, BOMBINGS OF THE UNITED STATES EMBASSIES IN DAR ES SALAAM, TANZANIA AND NAIROBI, KENYA. THESE ATTACKS KILLED OVER 200 PEOPLE.

Fig. 3.1. FBI poster sending out the alert on Osama bin Laden

3

Osama bin Laden and Other Gadflies
For the West, Convenient Hate Objects

In the two decades-long Afghanistan conflict, one figure that has remained constant, despite periods of absence and preoccupations elsewhere, is Osama bin Muhammad bin Laden. On the day Mazar-i-Sharif was captured by the Taliban, Osama is supposed to have masterminded the US embassy bombings in Nairobi and Dar-es-Salaam; and emerged as a key figure in pulling Afghanistan and his band of men in the Taliban to the centre stage of the globe.

While others who rallied to fight the Soviet occupation of Afghanistan have scattered, died or faded away, or even changed sides, and while the Soviet Union itself has fractured, Osama bin Laden has gone on. In more senses than one he is the child of the Afghan turmoil that refuses to end—he is as meteoric, as isolationist, as ferocious and as inflexible.

The civil war involving Afghan mujahideen disappointed Osama and prompted him to shift to Sudan, where President Omar al-Bashir's government with backing from Hasan Turabi's Islamic movement was pursuing a purist Islamic agenda. But Sudan buckled under American and Saudi pressure to expel him. After five and a half years in Sudan he returned to Afghanistan on 18 May 1996. He had been granting interviews to the western media where he espoused his opposition to the presence of foreigners (especially Americans) in Saudi Arabia and desire to establish a purist Islamic State in his homeland.

Away from Afghanistan after the Soviet withdrawal, he watched from a distance the fratricidal warfare the victorious "mujahideen" were waging. He also watched, although not from any distance and with a measure of participation, the rise of the Taliban. The student militia trained in the madrasas that dot the Pak–Afghan border, in whose creation he played a role, was just the single-minded body of men he needed to establish his brand of an Islamic State and spread the Wahabi sect of Islam among the non-believers. He was encouraged by the advances the militia were making at the cost of the quarrelling mujahideen. He was in Jalalabad when the Taliban captured Kabul in September 1996. According to Jason Burke of *The Observer*, "Many experts believe Osama funded the successful Taliban campaign to capture Kabul."

Today, Osama's singular success lies in identifying the Taliban regime in Kabul with his jihad against the "enemies of Islam". In this mission, he has defied the world community and world opinion. But his role, along with that of Pakistan, has helped the Taliban become an undeniable factor in Afghan politics. This combine has also contributed to the growth of Islamic radicalism in a manner that the western world, which originally created the mujahideen like Osama to fight the Soviets, is now living in fear of them and taking measures to counter them.

Ironically, Osama was on the side of those very "enemies", the western world, in fighting the Soviets. Today, he fights the West that now includes the Russian Federation, but particularly the United States. In a sense, he is consistent. He opposed the Soviet occupation of an Islamic country, Afghanistan and now he opposes the US presence on the soil of the country of his birth, and an Islamic country, Saudi Arabia.

Osama bin Laden comes in a long history of the Islam–versus–Christianity conflict that dates further back than the crusades. He has undoubtedly divided the world on these lines, judging by the hate and adoration he attracts among his Muslim brethren and others. He is the western world's latest hate object, just like Gamal Abdel Nasser of Egypt, Palestine's Yasser Arafat in his younger days as an Al Fatah revolutionary, Libya's Muammar Qaddafi who too has left behind his past and mellowed since 1985, and Iraq's Saddam Hussein. All of them are Arabs, like Osama bin Laden.

Approaching the end of the twentieth century, Osama seems several notches more capable of taking on the American "satan" than all his predecessors. That Osama dons Arab habiliments and sports a flowing beard makes him an instant hit with those portraying him as evil incarnate.

•

Those who have met Osama bin Laden, particularly western media persons, have come away impressed. Media reports have variously described him as "mysterious" and "shadowy." According to some well-informed people, Osama was in Medina University when the seizure of Ka'bah by Junayman bin Mohammad bin Seif al-Oteibi and his men took place in November 1979 (see Chapter 11). Whether Oteibi influenced Osama is not known, but both speak the same fiery language about the Saudi ruling family.

Slightly built, in his mid-40s, he dons white robes and the *qafeya*, the Arab headgear. He has piercing eyes and speaks softly. Used to carrying a gun for years, he now has a back problem and carries a walking-stick.

In Afghanistan, he has changed residence several times. His family of three wives and several children lives in sparsely furnished and heavily guarded homes in rural, remote parts of Taliban-controlled territory. He keeps his operational headquarters away from the family, and keeps changing them.

According to a detailed report by Jason Burke in *The Observer*, Osama's proximity to Mullah Umar is quite close.

He is a good friend of Mullah Umar, the reclusive, one-eyed cleric who is the spiritual leader of the movement. Umar lives in a large new house on the western outskirts of Kandahar that Bin Laden built for him.
The two go fishing together—some say with hand grenades—in lakes in the hills near the city. By February 1999 how close those relations are became very obvious.... Senior American officials hinted that military action was likely if the Taliban continued to give him shelter. So Bin Laden conveniently "disappeared".... Bin Laden moved his three wives from their quarters in a disused air base 20 miles west of Kandahar to a relatively comfortable two-storey house in a former military base called Tora Bora, high in the Springhar Mountains, south of Jalalabad.[1]

---

[1]*The Express Magazine*, New Delhi, 11 July 1999.

His disappearance act was well orchestrated. "In the third week of December, he was interviewed by Pakistani and Arab journalists in a tent set up outside the Kandahar city. In early January, he was seen praying at the city's new mosque during Eid.

His disappearance was conveniently followed by reports that he had boarded an unidentified aircraft that had landed at Kandahar. Various Taliban leaders kept saying they did not know his whereabouts. For Osama, it turned out, it was a period of lying low in Afghanistan itself.

Burke records that around the time he shifted his family near Kandahar, Osama began moving his own organization into Farmihadda, south of Jalalabad, on the Kabul–Peshawar road. According to some reports, his family too shifted to Farmihadda.

For a man worth 125 million pounds—according to the Americans—bin Laden's domestic arrangements are remarkably modest. According to people who have been there recently, Farmihadda is a rotting collection of outhouses, barns, sheds and accommodation blocks with a debris-filled canal on two sides. The living quarters, including those for the wives, are sparsely furnished.

Bin laden has always shunned luxury—preferring to squat on the floor or on a stool rather than use the traditional Afghan cushions and carpets—and his daily life reflects the rigours of his surroundings. Like all devout Muslims, he gets up at dawn to pray, then studies Koran or other Islamic texts before a light breakfast of dates, yogurt, flat Afghan bread and black tea. Until recently, he followed a tough physical regime, with a daily ride and exercises, but now his bad back—possibly a result of the shrapnel wounds sustained while fighting the Russians—has made anything strenuous impossible. He is around 45 years old and uses a cane to help him walk. He is also thought to be suffering from a serious, but unspecified, illness for which he needs powerful medication.

Security concerns, both personal and those of his family members and his close supporters, dominate Osama's life.

He travels constantly between Jalalabad and Kandahar and, according to one source, a remote central mountain district of Oruzgan, where he built a small camp earlier this year [1999].... Bin Laden frequently drives for a time in one convoy and then walks or rides for a distance before switching to a second set of vehicles. His satellite phones are often carried in a third convoy.

Instead of using them personally—he believes the Americans used signals from his phone to pinpoint his location before the missile strikes last year—bin Laden usually dictates his message to an aide, who then sends them on from a separate location.

There have been two reviews of his security arrangements during the last ten months (a period before and after the US embassy bombings)—both prompted by fears of betrayal. Immediately after the American attack, he sacked almost two-thirds of his 200-strong team of bodyguards. Many of those who survived the first purge were Afghans, former comrades from his days with the Mujahideen. But recently, most of these have been fired too and bin Laden now relies on a select group of mainly Arab fighters to protect him.

There are two security cordons around the Farmihadda base—the outer ring is composed of Taliban fighters, the inner of bin Laden's own men.

The massive American reward money was designed to encourage attempts on his life. Three attempts have been made, and all have concluded with the death of the assassins rather than their target.

Burke further records a little-known side of Osama: "He is also increasingly reliant on his eldest son, Mohammed, believed to be around 16."

•

From Morocco to Oman, Osama bin Laden exercises on the Arab populace and among Muslims anywhere in the world, a mesmerizing effect. In Palestine he is described as "beloved of God"; in Pakistan as "Osama the lion"; and in Afghanistan as "soldier of Islam".[2] An interview with him, telecast by a Gulf television channel in May 1999, had millions glued to their TV sets for three hours.

Himself worth millions, he has been able to collect funds for his cause from Muslim sympathizers across the world. With these funds at his command, his critics allege, he has been able to "buy" his stay in Afghanistan. The Taliban and Osama are mutually supportive of each other and together, backed by Pakistan's ISI, they have defied even sympathetic Islamic governments whenever the latter came under US pressure.

Osama has been disowned by his family of a rich businessman

---

[2]Rahimullah Yusufzai, "A Cult Hero Is Born", *The News*, 1 September 1998.

with interests in construction and shipping (see Box 3.1). He left the family initially to take up the gun for the Afghan cause and when he returned, found himself at odds with the family's interests. The change was simultaneous, both for Osama and his country. Interestingly, when Osama first went to Afghanistan in the mid-1980s, he was hailed by the Saudi media as an example of a rich youth taking to jihad.

His style of Islam and, more particularly, his stiff vocal opposition to the US military presence after the 1991 Gulf War brought him in direct conflict with the Saudi royalty. He is supposed to have parted ways with his share of millions from the family business. Today the Saudi authorities, which have stripped him of his citizenship, want him. But it is also believed that his antipathy is a façade. For Osama has the support of Prince Turki al-Faisal, the Saudi intelligence chief.

Notionally, when it comes to governments and authorities, Osama bin Laden stands alone and isolated. Only the Taliban regime hosts him. For the same reason, the Saudi government, which recognized the Taliban regime in 1997, sent back the Taliban envoy after the bombings of US embassies on 8 August 1998, in which Osama's hand is strongly suspected.[3]

In the current phase Osama has been in Afghanistan since May 1996 and has been there, except for reported secret sojourns outside, including two visits to Hyderabad in India, allegedly to be with a female acquaintance. These reports, however, have never been confirmed. There has been no conclusive evidence of when and where he went and on what missions. For the world's most wanted man, these missions must have been important. He is known to be a man who does not waste his time travelling.

•

A US court has issued a warrant and a prize on his head—US$3 million raised to 5 million—for his alleged role in the bombings of US embassies in Tanzania and Kenya, that killed 224 people and injured thousands. Osama has himself variously confirmed

[3]Rahimullah Yusufzai, "Mission 'Get Osama'", *The News*, 8 November 1998.

and denied a role in the bombings. In an interview with a Gulf television in May 1999, he also expressed admiration for the people who bombed American forces in Saudi Arabia in 1995 and 1996 and said that all Americans are his targets.

The *Time* magazine of 11 January 1999 carried an extensive interview with Osama wherein it recorded that, asked about any involvement in embassy bombings, he couched his responses in religious references, as he did with most questions.

"If the instigation for jihad against the Jews and Americans is considered a crime, then let history be a witness that I am a criminal", he said, adding: "Our job is to instigate, and by God's grace, we did that, and certain people responded to this instigation." Asked if he knew the two men in custody in the US in connection with the bombings, he replied: "What I do know is that those who risked their lives to earn the pleasure of God are real men. They managed to rid the Islamic nation of disgrace."

Some of his more notable quotes: "Muslims burn with anger at America. For its own good, America should leave [Saudi Arabia]" (*Time*, 6 May 1996). "If liberating our land is terrorism, this is a great honour" (AFP report).

The Taliban leaders and their Kabul regime have been told several times, mostly through the "good offices" of Pakistan, that they should hand over bin Laden for his involvement in the bombings. He is Afghanistan's "most honoured guest", whom they will not "betray". But a year after keeping Osama in various hideouts, under surveillance, reportedly without his satellite telephones, they are prepared to talk to the US on the issue. While rejecting any attempt at force to evict Osama, they have shown willingness to discuss, which is a significant development.

•

It is rare in world history that a nation risks its own safety for the sake of one individual. There are famous instances of Helen of Troy in ancient Greece and of Prithviraj Chauhan, who invited confrontation with fellow Indian rulers who, in turn invited Mahmood of Ghor after he took away Princess Samyukta in a *swayamwara*. For the Taliban rulers in Kabul, towards the end of the twentieth century, the reason for confrontation is this religious

Box 3.1
The Laden Family

The Laden family is one of the largest and ramified Saudi business empires from the Hadhramaut area in the former South Yemen. The other large business families of that area who have settled in Saudi Arabia are Bin Mahfouz, Bin Zagar, Barouin and Al Amoudi. The government of King Saud used to borrow from Bin Mahfouz's National Commercial Bank in the 1950s.

No other family has progressed as well. The founder, Shaikh Muhammad Ibn Awadh Ibn Laden, an entrepreneur moved in the 1930s from Hadhramaut like many other merchant families, to Jeddah and Makkah to seek their fortune. He started life as a semiskilled bricklayer. Within a few years, he rose to become the largest construction man in Saudi Arabia, particularly in Makkah where most of the rebuilding of the city was taken by his firm. In the expansion of the Holy Mosque he played a big role and a major chunk of these projects were awarded to his construction company. When Ibn Saud (Abdul Aziz Ibn Abdul Rahman Al Saud), the King of Saudi Arabia was confined permanently to his wheelchair because of arthritis in his knees, Shaikh Muhammad's firm was instrumental in building ramps in the Jeddah palace of Ibn Saud in 1950, so that Ibn Saud could be driven by motor-car right up to the roof to hold his majlis in the old style.

Shaikh Muhammad Ibn Laden was a very religious man, worked fifteen to seventeen hours a day and never took a holiday. He with many other Saudi business families such as Juffali, Alireza, Olayan, Bin Mahfouz, Abdullah Saleh Kamel and many more, have done great things for the kingdom of Saudi Arabia. Such was their relation with the government that as and when delegations from America, Europe and Japan came to Saudi Arabia in the 1970s and 1980s to discuss the opportunities offered by the five-year plans, all were shown a list of these business tycoons to choose one of them as their local agent. These families, including the Bin Laden always got preferential consideration from the government.

To the day he died in 1968, aged forty-seven, in a plane crash, Shaikh Muhammad Ibn Laden remained illiterate but left an empire with five thousand employees. After his death King Faisal by a royal decree entrusted the firm to a board of trustees. This board in 1998 consisted of three members: Muhammad Nur Rahimi, Muhammad Saleh Baharis, of Baharis business family, and Khalaf Ahmed Ashour. Any decision concerning their main controlling firm, Muhammad Ibn Laden Co. (Muhammad Ibn Laden Establishment), is to be approved by at least two board members.

Shaikh Muhammad fathered fifty-four children, out of whom fifty, including Osama Ibn Muhammad Ibn Laden, are alive. Two died in childhood and the eldest son Salim and one daughter Ruqayy expired later. Salim was studying medicine in England when suddenly he was recalled home, upon his father' death, to manage the Bin Laden empire.

In August 1997, King Fahd appointed Yahya Ibn Muhammad Ibn Laden (born in 1949), a brother of Osama Ibn Laden, as a member of the newly set-up twenty-member Provincial Council of Makkah Province for a period of four years.

Among the major Bin Laden companies are Muhammad Ibn Laden Co. (Muhammad Ibn Laden Establishment, paid-up capital SR320 million) and Bakar Muhammad Ibn Laden & Brothers (new name, Saudi Bin Laden Group Co., paid-up capital SR220 million). Other companies, owned by one or two or several brothers or where the above two main companies hold equity and controlling stake are: Bin Laden Trading Co. (paid-up capital SR5 million), United Construction & Trading Co. (SR12 million), Saudi American General Electric Co. (collaboration with General Electric Int. Inc.), Saudi Satellite Communication Co., Integrated Computer Systems Co., Marine Accessories & Medicines Co., Universal Brotherhood Marine Services Co., Dana Advertising & Publicity Co., Arabian Soil Contracting Co., Technical Agencies Co., Saudi Tourism And Hotels Co., Space Communication Co., United Medical Group Co., etc. Muhammad Ibn Laden Establishment was also one of the fourteen promoters of Saudi Hollandi Bank. Most of the Bin Laden group companies are based at Makkah and Jeddah. In none of the above companies Osama Ibn Laden has any equity stake. The legal consultant for Saudi Bin Laden Group Co. are the Legal Consultation Office of Shaikh Ahmed Zaki Yamani, the longest serving former oil minister of Saudi Arabia.

Bibliography
Robert Lacey, *The Kingdom*, London, 1981.
Linda Blandford, *Oil Sheikhs*, London, 1977.
Various issues of *Umm Al-Qura* (Arabic), the weekly official gazette of the Saudi government.
Information compiled by
Sharaf Sabri, Research Scholar, Jawaharlal Nehru University, New Delhi.

man from Saudi Arabia, whose Wahabi school of Islam they have embraced and want to make it their State religion. Only one per cent of Afghans are Wahabis, mostly in and around Kunar province. Over 80 per cent of Afghan Muslims are Hanafis.

The US and all those following the Afghan situation suspected all along that Osama was hiding in Afghanistan. But other reports suggested that he might have gone elsewhere. Among the possibilities mentioned were Somalia, Chechnya and Iraq. Six months after the so-called disappearance, Wakil Ahmed Muttawakil, a senior Taliban spokesman, told the Associated Press by telephone on 10 July 1998, "bin Laden is very much here and so is his family, but their whereabouts can't be disclosed."

The AP reported from Kabul:

In a rare admission, a senior official in the Taliban Islamic militia said Saturday that suspected terrorist Osama Bin Laden is in Afghanistan but his exact whereabouts are unknown even to most Taliban leaders.

Muttawakil said that "even high ranking and seniormost Taliban officials" don't know where bin Laden is. Bin Laden is "under the supervision of Taliban's special security committee."

Muttawakil's disclosure came precisely a month after the US imposed financial and commercial sanctions on Afghanistan to punish the country for harboring bin Laden....

"To this day, bin Laden and his network continue to plan new attacks against Americans without regard for the innocence of their intended victims or for those non-Americans who might get in the way of his attack", Clinton said in a statement released on 7 June 1999.

Clinton said his executive order "will deepen the international isolation of the Taliban, limit its ability to support terrorist networks and demonstrate the need to conform to the accepted norms of international behavior".

The US sanctions were imposed under International Emergency Economic Powers Act, the National Emergencies Act and other authorities, which provide wide latitude to the president to impose economic sanctions. At least seven other countries, all on the US list of countries that sponsor international terrorism, are subject to similar penalties. Afghanistan is not on the list.

The order bans US trade with and investment in the Afghan territory under Taliban control. Official figures show the United States exported goods worth $7 million to Taliban Afghanistan in 1998 and imported goods worth $17 million. The sanctions do not affect US humanitarian assistance to the Afghan people. The US provides almost $40 million in such assistance, part of it to Afghan refugees living in Pakistan. Other programmes involve health, education, earthquake relief and elimination of mines.[4]

In Cairo, businessmen from Saudi Arabia and other sources told the Associated Press that Osama bin Laden received a torrent of donations from rich Saudi and Persian Gulf people after the US put the $5 million price on his head. The sources said Osama may have netted more than $50 million before the Saudi government learned of the transfers and ordered them stopped. Saudi officials questioned several leading entrepreneurs in this connection. The Saudi owner of a major advertising firm was severely rebuked, the sources said.

Even though they feared further US missile attacks, "we are not afraid and will not abandon our friend", said Ashabuddin Dilawar, deputy governor of Kabul, the AP reported. Muttawakil said the Taliban would not hand bin Laden over to the Americans "because they don't have an extradition treaty with the United States". In 1998, the Taliban Supreme Court conducted an "inquiry" against Osama and "cleared him of all the charges because the United States did not give proof of his involvement in the African bombings", he said.[5] The Taliban's Chief Justice Maulvi Noor Mohammad Saqib said in an interview in Kabul in August 1999:

> When the Osama issue emerged, the Amir-ul-Momineen asked the world community to produce evidence against him to the Supreme Court. We waited for a long time but no one could produce any evidence. We extended the date by ten days. But still no person and country succeeded in providing any proof against Osama.

Later the Supreme Court decided to clear Osama of charges and closed this chapter.[6]

The US–Taliban contact was direct at the six-plus-two meeting in Tashkent in July 1999. At a meeting on the sidelines of the main conference, US Assistant Secretary of State, Karl Inderfurth,

---

[4] See *The News*, 12 August 1999.
[5] Cited in Izaz Hussain, "Why Extradite Osama", *The News*, 5 December 1998.
[6] *The News*, 30 August 1999.

categorically told the Taliban representative at the talks, Information Minister Amir Khan Muttaqi, that "Arabs and Pakistanis" were among those training terrorists in Afghanistan. "We will fight terrorism", Inderfurth told Muttaqi, according to a Central Asian diplomat who attended the meeting. In response, Muttaqi said through an interpreter: "Osama bin Laden is a good man and a good Muslim. He enjoys our hospitality. He can stay in Afghanistan as long as he wishes." To the charge that his government was spreading terrorism, Muttaqi said that on the contrary, it was fighting the evil "legacy" of the mujahideen government. "We inherited the drugs and Osama bin Laden from the Rabbani government."[7]

•

The US has publicly taken the posture that it is not taking sides in the faction fights in Afghanistan, even though in the weeks after the Taliban captured Kabul in September 1996 and again when they took Mazar-i-Sharif in August 1998, the Clinton administration appeared to veer towards recognition of the Taliban regime.

It changed tack when reports became public about the Taliban indulging in inhuman acts on those they had vanquished and imposing a strict of code of conduct for women, keeping them indoors and out of work and away from educational opportunities. This was in 1996 when the US presidential elections were round the corner and the Clinton administration could not allow human rights in Afghanistan to become a poll-time controversy.

In the second instance, on 7–8 August 1998, the day Mazar-i-Sharif fell, the US embassies in Tanzania and Kenya were bombed. This negated any US intentions to be friendly to the Kabul regime. Through his hosts, Osama thus remains the focus of US attention in Afghanistan.

A US ambassador in one of the CARs said, "He has declared war on us. He has killed our people. I do not think we can let him off. If Osama bin Laden and his supporters are brought to justice, if the US reaches a modus vivendi with the Taliban, then we initiate a dialogue on human rights and rights of Afghan women." He added, "We will continue diplomatic pressures on

[7] Diplomatic sources in Tashkent.

the Taliban so far as Osama bin Laden is concerned. We cannot keep him in that area indefinitely. Once Osama is handed over, then we engage in discussions on human rights and women's rights in Afghanistan. I think the Taliban are amenable to negotiations. We also engage them in a dialogue with other political parties for a political settlement. We need a country, not a faction to deal with", the diplomat observed.

The US stance has drawn flak from various quarters, thanks to its known strategic interest in the region, its amenability to persuasion from its multinational corporations who see business in Afghanistan, its soft corner for Pakistan and its acquiescence with the Sino–Pak alliance in order to counter Russian influence in the region. Even though the US and Russia have joined in a campaign against terrorism, and even though the US has taken a serious view of the Pak–Taliban alliance, these "basics" have not changed.

The Osama bin Laden factor has made the US approach individual-driven. The Indian government, as also the informed public opinion elsewhere, has seen the US role on terrorism as trivializing the issue by centring it on a single person. As Ahmed Rashid, among the better known Pakistani journalists and writers on Afghan affairs notes, "the United States since 1979 had one short-term policy—to get the Soviets out. Ten years later, that has been replaced with another short-term policy—to get Osama bin Laden out of Afghanistan."

Yet, on Osama's "surrender" or "hand-over", the US seems to have reached a stalemate. A CNN report on 7 August 1999, marking the first anniversary of the embassy bombings, took note of this. Among the participants was Robert Oakley, a former Coordinator, Counter-terrorism, and a former US ambassador to Pakistan. He acknowledged that the US cannot confront the Taliban government on Osama's surrender "because he is their guest. They (the Afghans) have their code under which they will not give him up."

The CNN report made another significant point: that the US has not launched any attack anywhere in the world to get Osama. The US has hemmed and hawed about his "plans" to attack more embassies and has issued high alerts time and again. On his part, Osama has adopted a devil-may-care posture about any further US attempt to get him. The Taliban have also showed their determination to face any action and "to save their honour". The fact is that neither side has acted in the year after the US fired its Tomahawks in Afghanistan and on Sudan.

On the other hand, there is also a strong perception in some quarters that the US would not like to press for Osama's surrender, save make the politically right statements from time to time. "Once they get him, a major lever in the region would go", a senior Afghanistan watcher avers. The US can continue to feed its domestic public opinion on the measures it is taking to apprehend Osama as part of its fight against terrorism, he says.[8]

A question being asked through 1998–99 was: if the US can impose sanctions on the Taliban regime, a measure that is hardly effective beyond the diplomatic signals it sends out since there is no State-to-State transaction, why cannot it freeze Osama's assets, which are supposed to be in European and American banks? The US could restrain his activities effectively by freezing these funds the way it has done with Iraq of Saddam Hussein and with Iran. It is further argued that Osama's money power, once neutralized, would make him less capable of funding the Taliban campaign of conquering the whole of Afghanistan and seeking international support. The Taliban would keep their "honoured guest" only so long as he serves their purpose.[9]

The situation has changed only marginally since the US-inspired UN sanctions, imposed on 14 November 1999.

•

Osama's ability to "serve" the Taliban cause is linked to a nod of approval from Prince Turki al-Faisal, a brother of King Fahd and chief of Saudi Intelligence. He has not given such a nod, even though officially, the Saudi government is gunning for Osama bin Laden.

Prince Faisal is said to be working closely in tune with the US interests, especially those of the CIA, in the region. There is strong evidence of a nexus between the CIA, Prince Faisal's

---

[8]The source, who wished to remain anonymous, made this observation in conversation with the authors in New Delhi in August 1999.
[9]Ibid.

intelligence network and Pakistan's ISI, so far as Afghanistan and Osama bin Laden are concerned. This nexus operates effectively in the form of the total ISI involvement in running the Taliban administration and its campaign against the IFDA, besides the production and export of narcotics.

It is significant that when Masoud made out a strong case at Tashkent for the US restraining the Taliban's mentors, the Pakistan government and the ISI, Inderfurth emphasized that the US could not restrain Pakistan on the Taliban beyond a point. In particular, he pointed to Pakistan's "lack of cooperation" so far as the United States' demand for ensuring the surrender of Osama bin Laden is concerned.[10]

This may be contrasted with Pakistan's record in related matters. The US, for instance, had no big difficulty in getting this "cooperation" over Ramzi Yusuf in 1995 and over Mir Aimal Kansi in 1997. The Pakistan government was quick to arrest and hand over a Saudi-born Palestinian suspect in the embassy bombings. Only Osama remains the "honoured guest".[11]

That Osama is not on Pakistani soil seems to be governing the Pakistani approach. Foreign Secretary Shamshad Ahmed Khan told the media on 12 December 1998 in Islamabad that Osama's expulsion was "not a factor in Pak–US relations". "Osama bin Laden is not on our soil, he is in Afghanistan and the matter of his extradition should be taken up with Afghanistan", he said.

It may also be noted that soon after the embassy bombings, the Pakistani foreign office spokesman said: "As a moderate state having links with all sorts of Muslim states and Islamic movements, we will have nothing to do with the anti-Osama crusade."

While the Clinton administration has used a stick-and-carrots policy to get Osama, or at least feed the public opinion at home, the perceptions at the congressional and other levels have varied. For instance, Benjamin Gilman, the New York Democrat who chairs the Foreign Relations Committee, asserted that a new breed of radical Muslim extremists, with possibly the world's largest heroin empire was brewing under the Taliban regime.

[10] Diplomatic sources in Tashkent, in July 1999.
[11] See Abid Ullah Jan, "Osama: The Sovereign Question", *Frontier Post*, 27 July 1999.

A member of the US House of Representatives, he said the Pak–Afghan nexus was "unrelenting in promoting international terrorism". He criticized the Clinton administration "for failing to distinguish between friends and foes".

Gilman said, "The most dangerous example of the lack of this distinction is found in the Clinton administration's attitude towards Taliban, the principal protector of Osama bin Laden and those who continually cross into Kashmir and kill innocent Indians.... Pakistan has also provided crucial diplomatic support for the Taliban regime, hoping it will be dependent upon Pakistan after gaining control throughout Afghanistan and thus provide not only strategic depth in the region, but a corridor to the important energy reserves of Central Asia."

•

Osama's two-pronged attack on the Saudi royal family: (i) disapproving of its policy of stationing American military personnel on the kingdom's soil, thereby disapproving of the Saudi–US security relationship;[12] and (ii) arguing that the Saudi royal family is not following the tenets of Islam in letter and spirit, has brought a whole set of new issues to the fore.[13] In addition, the Taliban–Osama combine has raised a new outfit called Quaida (base) with a mercenary force (known in some circles as 055 Brigade); and is talking in terms of carrying the Islamic Revolution to other parts of the world. A few glimpses of its working are already visible in places like Tajikistan, Chechnya, Xinjiang Autonomous Region in China and India's state of Jammu and Kashmir. Osama is alleged to have transferred US$30 million to Chechen guerrillas. According to the Russian Deputy Interior Minister Igor Zulsov, the transfer was made in favour of Chechen guerrilla leaders Shamil Basayev and his deputy Khattab, "in order to help the duo recruit men and purchase weapons for an invasion of Dagestan and two other neighbouring Russian republics."

When the Taliban–Osama combine tried to undermine the Iranian pre-eminence in August–September 1998, by killing its

---

[12]See "The Paladin of Jehad", *Time*, 6 May 1996.
[13]Rahimullah Yusufzai, "Mission 'Get Osama'", *The News*, 8 November 1998.

diplomats in Mazar-i-Sharif, there was about to be a massive retaliation by Tehran. According to some observers, the Saudis prevailed upon Iran not to precipitate a crisis.

At one point of time, it was alleged that the Saudis did manage to strike a deal with the Taliban about Osama bin Laden. In an interview with the *New York Times,* Prince Turki al Faisal disclosed that he led a small delegation to Kandahar in June 1998. During their three-hour meeting Mullah Umar and his ruling council agreed to end the sanctuary Osama enjoyed in Afghanistan since 1996. But everybody present there felt that the surrender had to be carefully orchestrated so that it "would not reflect badly on the Taliban" and would not appear to be "mistreating a friend".[14]

The *NYT* report says that the key to that initial deal was a Saudi pledge that Osama would be tried only in an Islamic court—a condition of surrender that would have precluded his extradition to face any US prosecution. According to Turki, at the time of his mission to Kandahar, a number of Taliban leaders considered Osama bin Laden an unwelcome burden. His presence was seen by some as an obstacle to foreign investment. Certainly, he was a liability to the Taliban relationship with Riyadh, one of the regime's few friends.

"We made it plain that if they want to have good relations with the Kingdom [of Saudi Arabia] they have to get bin Laden out of Afghanistan", Turki said. "Osama claims the government is illegitimate. He claims we subvert Islam. All these are bases of criminal charges." After his "very friendly" negotiations with Umar, the Taliban made a definite promise to hand over Osama. "It was discussed and repeated many times during the meeting", Turki said. The subject was discussed at subsequent meetings when aides of both sides met to work out the politically sensitive mechanics of how the surrender would be orchestrated, he added. The meetings spanned the next two months.

The Saudis felt frustrated by the delays but did not suspect that their deal was in trouble until after the embassy bombings in Tanzania and Kenya. Suddenly, according to the Saudis, the Taliban officials said they had made no promise to give up Osama. They blamed translation problems for a misunderstanding.[15] While

[14]See *The News*, 9 August 1999, for excerpts of interview.
[15]Ibid.

the Saudis recalled their ambassador from Kabul and asked Taliban's chargé d'affaires to leave Riyadh immediately in September 1998, to keep the lines of communication with the Taliban–Osama axis intact, the Saudi authorities exonerated bin Laden from the truck bombings of Riyadh in November 1995 and in Al-Khobar's case of June 1996. In an interview with *Arab Times*, Saudi Interior Minister Prince Nayef bin Abdul Aziz said that Osama bin Laden was not personally behind the two anti-US bombings that killed 19 American servicemen in Al-Khobar Towers housing complex in Dhahran; that the followers of Osama's ideology could have carried out the attacks.[16]

Dislodging a cult figure like Osama bin Laden is not easy. His continued presence in Afghanistan under the Taliban's protection is giving the latter sufficient leverage. As an Arab diplomat remarked: "Without Osama the Taliban's Afghanistan would not have received the type of attention from the West and Saudi Arabia they are getting now. Why then should Mullah Umar hand him over to the Americans or Saudis and forgo all the bargaining power they have?"[17]

Osama's presence also enables the Taliban to claim that they are not on the payroll of the US or Saudi Arabia or any western power. It also places the Taliban in a stronger bargaining position while dealing with the West and Saudi Arabia. In addition, the Taliban, like many other Afghans believe that Osama with his riches can provide financial support and help in rebuilding the war-ravaged Afghanistan.

The Saudi strategy now seems to be to whip up anti-Osama feelings within Afghanistan in general and the Taliban in particular. The first salvo was fired by Burhanuddin Rabbani's envoy to Iran. He said:

Why should Afghanistan pay for the misdeeds of the few? This is our point. Are the problems today in Afghanistan not enough that we still have to answer Laden's problems?

Laden is a Muslim. Are there not other Islamic countries to shelter

---

[16] See AFP report of *Arab Times* interview in *The Nation*, 5 November 1998.
[17] Rahimullah Yusufzai, "Is Osama a Threat", *The News*, 27 October 1998.

him? He is an Arab; are there not Arab countries for him? Why should our nation take the blows to its head which are intended for Laden?[18]

This line is slowly gaining support. Now they have to coordinate their policies with the other principal players—Pakistan and Iran. The Saudi withdrawal of its Ambassador from Kabul had the desired impact. If they stop the financial aid flowing from the Arab world, the Taliban will have problems.

•

If Osama is to be captured by the US, he would have to come out of Afghanistan. This seems unlikely.

If he stays put in Afghanistan the US would have to wait till there are serious dissensions among the Taliban rulers or the Taliban are ousted from Kabul and are forced to roll back towards Pakistan. As of now, this also seems unlikely.

Osama seems to have kept shifting to Chechnya as an option should Afghanistan become unsafe. If he leaves for Chechnya the US and Russian authorities may combine to get him.

Yet another option for the US is to infiltrate Osama/Taliban ranks and get him through what might be projected as an act of trading. But looking at the four-decade-old effort by the US to get Cuba's Fidel Castro, or Iraq's Saddam Hussein for the last ten years, these prospects seem remote too.

Finally, getting Osama may win President Clinton world accolade and perhaps, votes for the Democratic party in the November 2000 elections. But one Osama may be replaced by a score of them, and not only in Afghanistan. The backlash would be hard to contain. Putting it cynically, the US needs to perpetuate Osama the person as the universal hate object and a symbol of international terrorism—and hope that like a much-travelled Arafat or a subdued Qaddafi, Osama would get disillusioned with the non-fulfilment of his mission and scale down the intensity of his activity.

•

---

[18]Cited by Adan Rehmat, "The Hunter and the Hunted", *The News on Sunday*, 25 July 1999.

Other than Osama, there are a number of well-known persons living in Taliban-controlled Afghanistan. Rahimullah Yusufzai reports:

With all attention focused on Saudi dissident Osama bin Laden, other Islamists from Arab countries who share his ideals and have taken refuge in Afghanistan are somehow ignored. They are important in their own right and are wanted in their native countries or by the US on different counts.

The most wanted man after Osama bin Laden is Sheikh Taseer Abdullah, whose *nom de guerre*, that most Arab militants have, is Abu al-Misri after the name of his firstborn son. He is most probably the same person who the US government describes as Mohammed Atef, the military commander of bin Laden. Washington had charged Mohammad Atef with involvement in the bombings at its embassies in Kenya and Tanzania in August 1998 and has announced a reward. (However, in response to my repeated queries whether he was the same Mohammad Atef, all that I received from Sheikh Taseer Abdullah was silent smiles.)

During this writer's December 22, 1998 interview with bin Laden in his encampment in southwestern Afghanistan, Sheikh Abdullah Taseer figured prominently at every step. He drove this scribe to the encampment from Kandahar city and was responsible for all matters concerning bin Laden's security. It was he who decided when and where would the interview take place. Bin Laden also sought his opinion while answering certain questions and appeared to find happiness in his company. He has been constantly at bin Laden's side, whether it was in Peshawar, Afghanistan during the 1980s, in Sudan and again in Afghanistan after bin Laden's return there in May 1996. No wonder then that Sheikh Taseer Abdullah, who was dressed in the Afghan shalwar-kameez like bin Laden and was bearded and turbaned, was introduced by bin Laden as his right hand man during his last year's famous press conference in Khost, southern Afghanistan.

It was the same news conference where bin Laden announced the launching of the International Islamic Front for Jihad Against the US and Israel and made public the *fatwa* by Islamic religious scholars justifying "jihad" against the "Jews and Crusaders" on account of their occupation of some of the holiest Islamic sites.

Sheikh Taseer Abdullah is a former police officer from Egypt who came to Peshawar in 1983 and started taking part in the Afghan "Jihad". In fact, he was among the first Arabs who responded to the call for "Jihad" in Afghanistan against the Soviet Union and was instrumental in luring and bringing other Arabs to join this cause. He is said to have come to Peshawar before others like bin Laden, the late Sheikh Abdullah Azzan and Sheikh Omar Abdel-Rahman, the blind Egyptian preacher who is now jailed in the US for his role in the World Trade Center bombing in New York.

Sheikh Taseer Abdullah is also credited with convincing Sheikh Abdullah Azzan to give up his job as a lecturer in the Islamic University in Islamabad and devote full time to the Afghan "jihad". In due course of time, Azzan shifted to Peshawar and built a vast network of services to assist the Afghan mujahideen and refugees and help Arab volunteers wanting to receive military training or taking part in the "jihad" in Afghanistan.

Like bin Laden, Sheikh Taseer Abdullah has vehemently denied his own involvement in the bombing of the US embassies in Nairobi and Dar es Salaam or the killing of the American soldiers in Somalia. His argument is the same as bin Laden's; that failure on the part of the US government, especially the CIA, to find those who sponsored these bomb explosions had prompted it to shift the blame to them for the bombings. He also argued that anyone who took part in the Afghan "jihad" is now a suspect in American eyes. Hence the arrest of such people and pinning of all blame on them in connection with the anti-US bombings.

Dr Ayman al-Zawahiri, leader of the Islamic jihad or Al-Jihad group in Egypt, is another important Islamist from an Arab country now living in Taliban-ruled Afghanistan. He is a feared man in Egypt as far as the country's security agencies are concerned because his supporters, whatever their strength, are considered more radical than other Islamists. He hails from a known Egyptian family and his grandfather, Abdul Wahab, had served as Egypt's ambassador in Pakistan. The bespectacled Al-Zawahiri is a learned man and keeps himself abreast of happenings in the world.

In a chat with this writer, he said his wife and children were willingly sharing hardships with him in Afghanistan since the past 15 to 17 years as they considered it a "hijrat" (migration) in Allah's and Islam's cause. He was hoping to forge an alliance with other Islamic groups in Egypt, in particular with Sheikh Omar Abdel-Rahman's Al-Gama at Al-Islamiyyah, in a bid to put up a united front against the dictatorial pro-West government of President Hosni Mubarak and expedite the struggle to make Egypt a true Islamic state. He had no doubt that Egypt's Islamic groups would triumph eventually, though he couldn't tell when and how it would happen.

Sheikh Omar Abdel-Rahman himself is now a prisoner in the US but some of the leading lights of his group are present in Afghanistan. Among them are his two young sons, Mohammed and Abu Asim. Mohammed, 27, is older of the two and it was he who spoke with Pakistani journalists in Khost, southern Afghanistan, in Bin Laden's Badr camp last August and warned of retaliation to avenge his father's unjust arrest and conviction and complained that he was being treated badly in the prison despite being blind and ill. He said the facility provided to his father to talk to family members in Egypt on the phone had also been withdrawn.

Compared to Mohammad, Abu Asim, being a younger man, was more forthright in talking about revenge in case something happened to his father. Abu Yasir Rifa'i Ahmad Taha, also an Egyptian and a leader of Sheikh Omar Abdel-Rahman's party, is also stated to be in Afghanistan. His name was mentioned among those who had authored the *fatwa* that urged "jihad" against the Jews and Crusaders. However his whereabouts aren't known and, again, all that one can get in response are smiles when the Egyptians in Afghanistan are asked about Abu Yasir. However, it is obvious that no other country but Afghanistan would be safe for Abu Yasir or any one else in his Al-Gama at Al-Islamiyyah or other radical Islamic groups.

Some other prominent Islamist Egyptians may also be living in Afghanistan. Among them could be Shawki al-Islambouli who shot dead President Anwar Sadat during a military parade in Cairo. Then there are Arabs from several others countries, some of them wanted on unspecified charges as they constitute a challenge to their respective governments. It is true that Saudi and Egyptian dissidents dominate the Islamists who have sought refuge in Afghanistan but Algerians, Tunisians, Libyans, Yemenis, Syrians, Jordanians, Palestinians and Iraqis are also to be found in their ranks and some of them could be important enough as far as the Islamic movements in their countries are concerned.

All this explains that Afghanistan under the hardline Taliban is now a sanctuary for Islamists who are being hunted by the security services of their own Arab countries as well as that of the US and the West. This reason alone would keep Afghanistan in turmoil for many more years to come.[19]

It is no secret that some of these radical Islamists were in Afghanistan from the early 1980s. They made it a base camp from the early 1990s. The men who matter in the international order know about them. The great powers and their allies hobnobbed with the Taliban knowing full well all these radicals throughout 1996 but ignored their existence in pursuit of their strategic and economic interests. As a Taliban sympathizer said, "supply routes for Turkmenistan's gas through Afghanistan–Pakistan made the great powers ignore the radical ideas of these so-called most wanted men. They even took a Taliban delegation to the US.

[19] "The Last Sanctuary", *The News*, 27 January 1999.

Right now the Taliban have their offices in most of the NATO member countries. All this is being allowed to happen not with some pious intentions of reforming the Taliban but with ulterior motives".

Obviously, the Taliban are not making secret of the hospitality they are extending to these Islamist guests. The reasons could mainly be four: (1) They are seen by the Taliban to belong to their own fraternity. (2) They contribute to the legitimacy of the Taliban movement. (3) They are good for generating sympathy and funds. (4) The Taliban did not foresee the kind of international reaction this would engender.

(1) *A Feeling of Fraternity.* In the Taliban's perception, these mavericks are trying to establish a purist Islamic State like them. Therefore, as forerunners of such a concept they should extend every type of help to them. Some of these people fought alongside the Afghans against the Red Army. When the Red Army was finally defeated, a majority of them moved out of Afghanistan to Sudan and other places. The 1979–89 period was a learning experience of actual combat against the "infidel" (Red Army) for these mujahideen (holy warriors) in launching a jihad (holy war). They were surprised by the support they received from the other faithfuls for their cause. Afghanistan is an obscure country in the Islamic world; and until the mid-1990s not of much consequence to the great powers. It survived on international charity. Now it has a high profile due to the presence of these radical Islamists. This is giving psychological satisfaction to the Taliban that they also matter in the international system.

(2) *Contributing to the Legitimacy of the Taliban.* Since people like Sheikh Taseer Abdullah and Ayman al-Zawahari have become legends in their own way in the Islamic world, their presence with the Taliban provides the latter a measure of authenticity in the Islamic world. From here the concept of Ummah is being expanded to its immediate neighbourhood—Tajikistan, Xinjiang Autonomous Region and Jammu and Kashmir state in the Indian Union. The Taliban and their sponsors say that the concept of national sovereignty is only 300 years old and was superimposed by the West, whereas the "oneness" of Islam is more than a millennium old. Therefore, they have every right to bring together like-minded people, and are not doing anything un-Islamic. They

must be recalling the glory of the Islamic world in the medieval period to rationalize their arguments.

(3) *Sympathy and Money.* The presence of these radical Islamists is generating considerable sympathy among the other faithfuls in the Islamic world. An appeal from Osama or Ayman through their channels has donations pouring in. Their Arab brethren supply fuel oil to Taliban-controlled Afghanistan at a concessional price. Similarly the road repair work or the construction of buildings in Kabul, Kandahar and Jalalabad is being done through donors. In the past five years, it may be noted, no starvation deaths have been reported from anywhere in Taliban-controlled areas.

One diplomat said that compared to the Taliban's income from narcotics and smuggling, the donations from fellow faithfuls are of less significance. He wanted us to examine the imports through Karachi port. The wheat flour (atta) crisis in NWFP 1997 was largely due to the diversion of the commodity from the local market to Taliban-controlled Afghanistan. He says that here the network built by so-called Islamic radicals in and around Peshawar and into Taliban-controlled Afghanistan comes handy. He was certain that food aid being extended by international aid agencies is not the reason for the absence of starvation deaths in Afghanistan but the food going through Peshawar to Kandahar saved the situation. The NGOs and UN humanitarian aid is largely restricted to urban areas.

These radical Arab Islamists were reportedly able to mobilize technocrats from other countries besides Pakistan to keep the Taliban government going. All this shows that besides other reasons, these radical Islamists are helping the Taliban as *they want their experiment in establishing an Islamic State in Afghanistan to succeed*.

(4) *The Strong International Reaction was Unexpected.* The Taliban never anticipated that their providing shelter to their Arab brethren would some day invite suddenly the wrath of the international community. In fact, the way the US dealt with the Taliban till mid-1997 gives an impression that the Great Power just wanted to do business with them. If the Taliban were to question what is so special about women's rights in Afghanistan as compared to say Saudi Arabia, probably no one would have an

answer. A Taliban sympathizer even argued with us saying that in 1979, Ayatollah Khomeini's insistence on wearing *chador* (veil) by women prompted many in the West to accuse him, as now the Taliban are being accused, that he was taking Iran to medieval ages. This media hype about the status of women made Khomeini a hate object all over Europe and North America, and it resulted in a total lack of understanding of the dynamics of the Iranian revolution. However, Ayatollah Khomeini never provided safe haven to any radical Islamists at any point of time.

On the flip side, the Taliban's stock at the popular level in the Islamic world has been considerably enhanced by this particular action of theirs. Pakistan's or Saudi Arabia's inability to exert any serious pressure on the Taliban publicly about these radicals itself indicates the dilemma being faced by the Islamic world. Nawaz Sharif, and now Pervez Musharraf's government in Pakistan would not venture, for instance, to dismantle the Rest House built by Osama bin Laden in Peshawar. Similarly, the great powers cannot prevail upon the Arabs to declare an embargo against the Kabul government for supply of fuel. The Arab governments could not do it without inviting serious domestic problems. In spite of all the noises about the Taliban hosting these wanted men, flights from Dubai to Kandahar continued five times a week, till the 14 November 1999 sanctions.

However, developments in 1998–99 have shown that in the Taliban's dealings with the outside world these radical Islamists have become a liability to some extent. The Taliban are not able to decipher why they are not being extended the needed recognition by the international community. If Afghanistan is having a purist Islamic State, how does it affect the others? argues a Taliban sympathizer. Even the man most wanted by the US, Osama bin Laden, had been acquitted by the Saudi courts. Therefore, why this wrath on the Taliban? he wondered.

For the great powers, the options now seem to narrow down to two: repeat the 20 August 1998 cruise missile attacks and devastate Afghanistan. As an Afghan once told us, "No one can make the Afghans' life worse than it is now. Raining of a thousand missiles is not going to take away the Afghan ego. Only that hardens them more. Therefore, they cannot be defeated so easily."

Alternatively, they can be contained. After another decade, all these people are bound to mellow down. But containing them for a decade requires a lot of sustained political will and understanding from the people who want to do it.

The developments since the Nawaz Sharif–Clinton meeting on 4 July 1999 and the military takeover in Pakistan indicate that such a coordinated policy is being evolved to tame the extreme radical elements in the Taliban. These developments include:

- Visit of two senior Indian officials dealing with Afghanistan and the US to Washington in October 1999.
- A return visit by the US official Michael Sheehan to New Delhi.
- In Dagestan, the use of air power by the Russians against Afghan mercenaries.
- Russian announcement that they are coordinating with the US against cross-border terrorism.
- Nawaz Sharif's younger brother, Shahbaz Sharif's visit to Washington, followed by Lt Gen Ziauddin, the then ISI chief. Both are reported to have discussed cross-border terrorism.
- Developments in Chechnya. Russians march in their troops, declare a martial law and initiate strong military action. Earlier reports indicate that in the Russian Caucasus, Islamic fundamentalists were hoping to install Shariat inspired by Wahabism, close to Islam in Saudi Arabia. Former Prime Minister Primakov says that Russia's enemy is not Islam but extremism.
- Sectarian violence breaks out in Pakistan. The Sunni outfit Sipah-i-Sahaba of Pakistan is alleged to have been involved.
- In retaliation, Tehrik-i-Jafria of Pakistan kills Sunnis. In all 22 Shias and 3 Sunnis are reported to have died in the sectarian violence 1–10 October 1999. Pakistani police killed Khurshid Ahmed, also known as 'Mullah Bomb' on 3 October in a well-coordinated encounter. Khurshid Ahmed was a known radical extremist operating from Afghanistan.
- On 5 October 1999, then Interior Minister Shujaat Hussain blamed Indian security agencies for the current wave of sectarian violence. However on 6 October Shahbaz Sharif stated that Taliban-trained militants were responsible for these

killings. A day later, Prime Minister Nawaz Sharif said that Pakistan had asked Afghanistan to immediately close down the camps on its soil for training of sectarian terrorists. "We have made it clear to the Taliban government that this was not acceptable", he said.[20] When the local Taliban ambassador to Pakistan vehemently denied this, he was summoned and given all the evidence. Immediately, Mullah Umar, the Taliban chief from his Kandahar headquarters issued a statement that he would look into the matter and would not allow Taliban-controlled territory to be used for any activity against a friendly country.

This indicates that all the external powers have started coordinating their approach first to stop cross-border terrorism. Pakistan's ruling elite coming out openly accusing that militants operating in Pakistan are trained by the Taliban indicates that even Islamabad was finally roped in. The success of this operation will largely depend upon to what extent the government in Pakistan has a hold on Taliban sympathizers inside Pakistan. As a Pakistani commentator observed:

It is fair to ask why Pakistan does not stop these students from crossing Pakistani border and entering Afghanistan. Frankly, the answer is very clear. Simply the Pakistani government is logistically and politically unable to stop anyone crossing Pak-Afghan border....

Second, Pak–Afghan border covers about 2000 miles of mountainous territory. It is practically impossible for any government with such limited resources as Pakistan to stop people from crossing the border at different points....

Third, *the residents of Pakistan-Afghanistan border areas are self-governed people where Pakistan has limited control.*

...

Finally even if Pakistan imposes any restrictions, it could become costly to Nawaz Sharif. The Taliban enjoys tremendous support among religious political parties. Although each one of these parties are small, they are well united on issues like Kashmir and India, US vs Osama bin Laden and the Taliban and Islamisation of Pakistan (Emphasis added).[21]

---

[20]*The Nation*, 8 October 1999. Also see Umer Farooq, "Major Shift in Pakistan Policy on Afghanistan", *The Nation*, 9 October 1999.

[21]*Frontier Post*, 8 September 1999.

In other words, containment of the Taliban is not easy without creating serious convulsions in the Pakistani polity.

It is not without significance that many in the world community have pointed to a possible "Taliban angle" to the ouster of Nawaz Sharif. Former Indian Prime Minister I.K. Gujral was among the first to take note of one of the last statements of Sharif cautioning about the role of the Taliban.

It needs to be emphasized that the change in Pakistan came soon after the twin defeat of the Islamists in Kargil and Kapisa. Common elements in both were Pakistan's Northern Light Infantry, the Taliban fighters, and mercenaries of various Arab nationalities. The two debacles, coming in quick succession, were hotly debated at a mid-August 1999 meeting in which Mullah Umar and Osama bin Laden participated. A common theme was that Pakistan's military machine had let them down.

4

Ahmed Shah Masoud
Hero Awaiting a Script

He began as "engineer" Masoud, having been a student of the Engineering Faculty of architecture in the Kabul University. Like his colleague-turned-rival, Gulbuddin Hikmatyar, another "engineer", political activity prevented him from taking his engineering degree. Rather than the drawing-board, he was destined to take to the gun.

Ahmed Shah Masoud has been a homegrown fighter and politician who has stuck to his guns, and his roots. When all other Mujahideen leaders fought the Soviets from Pakistan, Masoud was the lone leader who stayed put in Panjshir Valley. The Soviet aircraft bombed and strafed the Panjshir Valley several times, but the "Lion of Panjshir" could not be dislodged.

Indeed, a key Soviet general got trapped along with troops north of the Salang Pass and requested safe passage. Masoud laid down his conditions, but once the conditions were met, no harm came to a single Soviet soldier and they were allowed to leave Panjshir.

A senior Russian academic and diplomat, who narrated this story, said that although a sworn enemy who never fell for any bait, Masoud was "a worthy enemy, worth having". At a time when others in the fight have changed sides, betrayed, quit after being defeated, quit on receiving money, or have simply disappeared from the scene, Masoud stands tall, all alone.

Panjshir remains his castle, where people revere him and refer to him as "Amir". But Masoud's role pertains to the whole country. He has emerged as the focus of resistance to the present government in Kabul, and thus, to the international power play in and around Afghanistan.

Notionally, he is the Defence Minister of the government of President Burhanuddin Rabbani. It is a government-in-exile, having been made to leave Kabul in September 1996. But it remains the government that the world community, by and large, recognizes.

This is not the only contradiction in the enigma that is Afghanistan. Masoud remains the man to reckon with even as his side has lost nearly 90 per cent of the territory. Military experts surmise that even if the Taliban were to conquer the entire Afghan territory, bypassing the Panjshir, Masoud would be able to offer guerrilla resistance.

•

In a story of unrelenting treachery and bloodletting, Masoud is credited with being humane, considerate and trustworthy. The media in the neighbouring Pakistan pulls its punches while criticizing him. The western media have a few good things to say, even as they pursue the stereotype concepts about Afghanistan and deprecate the Afghan legacy of betrayal and the tendency to take to guns when words could work. Much of the French media have even lionized him.

The reason for this French soft corner is the fact that Masoud, who knows little English, speaks fluent French. He went to a French lycée (Ishtiqlal) in Kabul. He is a Tajik who speaks in French to the French media, something that makes him an instant hit with the European mind-set.

From the "French connections" have also emerged some romantic liaisons, it is being said, with Masoud being close to French-speaking nurses and NGO workers in northern Afghanistan.

A European international civil servant, who worked for a relief agency in Afghanistan for four years during two crucial periods of contemporary Afghan history, 1989–91 and 1995–97, thinks the French have projected Masoud in "trying to be different from others". This is the French approach, be it the Persian Gulf, Bosnia or Afghanistan.

"He is the Che Guevara of present-day France, a special friend. To the post-colonial France, he is a freedom fighter who defies the western attempts to dominate his country in one form or another. *Liberation, Le Monde, Le Figaro and Paris Match*—all speak the same language. But outside of France, the Masoud mystique wears thin. Somehow, he is seen as one of the many warlords responsible for violence and misery in Afghanistan. The British or American media are not particularly kind to him."

Masoud has a reputation of being both anti-American and anti-Soviet, and was generally anti-West during the Afghan War. He was different from Rabbani, Hikmatyar, Gilani and others fighting the same war, "all helping themselves liberally to Pakistani hospitality and western assistance", according to the European official. Much of his military success was thanks to the Chinese arms that he received.

But by and large, Masoud reacted to developments "out of conviction.... He was always the unique one. A cut above the rest, always thinking of higher Afghan interests", the official admitted, while speaking strictly off the record.

He did make a compromise with the Soviets, although none will confirm it. According to recently declassified records of the Soviet 40th Army based in Tirmiz, which directed the Afghan operations, a Soviet operative, Colonel Zakin Kadyrov, struck a deal and reportedly paid him US$350,000. There is no way to cross-check this. Masoud was supposed to have accepted this as his forces were under great pressure. His critics say this allowed the Soviets to be particularly harsh to the people in the Pashtun areas in south, east and west, while sparing the minorities in the north. But he struck back with vengeance two years later at the Salang Pass, causing heavy Soviet casualties.

Indeed, the Soviets made seven major attempts to oust him from Panjshir, carpet-bombing the valley during the decade-long campaign. But Masoud could not be brought to his knees. When the Soviets were withdrawing, however, he did not hesitate to provide them safe passage.

Masoud is also known to have helped himself to the largely

Fig. 4.1. Ahmed Shah Masoud

untapped emerald and lapis lazuli mines in Panjshir. He has also turned Nelson's eye to the rampant opium cultivation and its processing and export through Central Asia. His commanders, whom he tolerates, ostensibly out of necessity, do all this. He cannot afford to discipline them in a situation where bribery has played the key role in his military losses. Those who know Masoud say he is not a person who has amassed personal wealth. The money must go to bolster his military machine and food and other amenities for the thousands who inhabit the area under his control. The "Amir" cannot afford to see his subjects starve.

He can take a principled stand, even where *realpolitik* is sorely needed. Says an official of the International Committee of Red Cross (ICRC), Masoud refused to allow an ICRC team to travel through the north to Herat, as that, to his mind, would have been a conciliatory gesture that was politically unacceptable. Rather than facilitate the work of an international agency, he chose to be politically incorrect.

For his opposition to the US (CIA)–Pak combine and to its protégé, Hikmatyar, during the fight against the Soviets, Masoud was "sentenced" to death by Pakistani authorities during one of his brief stays just inside Pakistani territory. Masoud escaped, and never went to Pakistan as long as the war was on.

Indeed, Masoud and Hikmatyar have been traditional rivals. Nobody seriously believed that the two would coexist in a government. Masoud agreed to be defence minister under Hikmatyar as *de facto* prime minister only because Rabbani was the president. But by a strange mix of circumstances, it was Hikmatyar who cried off and went into the mountains, to rain rockets on Kabul ruled by a government of which he was supposed to be the prime minister.

A compromise bid by Rabbani and others brought Hikmatyar back to Kabul in June 1996. But it also fuelled a conspiracy, according to a European official then based in Kabul. A plan was hatched to kill Masoud, allegedly with Rabbani's consent, and with Hikmatyar playing a role. Masoud smelt the conspiracy and retired to Jabul Siraj, seething with anger. It required numerous messages and conduits from Rabbani to bring him back to Kabul.

But by then, mutual distrust among the main players was complete and the Rabbani government was weakened beyond repair.

Dostum, who was the third party of the ruling alliance, betrayed it and allowed the Taliban into Kabul in September 1996.

Hikmatyar has never been able to live down this act. No tears were shed when the Taliban ousted him from his base. His efforts to return to action and even his teaming up with Masoud for a brief period in 1997 has not helped salvage the reputation of a one-time hero, who could have been the natural leader, being a majority Pashtun, but for his repeated chicanery. His proximity to the US–Pak axis during the resistance against the Soviets and the hospitality currently extended to him by Iran have not helped him to get back home.

•

Masoud married late. His wife and five children live in Panjshir but move to Dushanbe, Tajikistan, when the going gets tough. A photograph of him with his son in his lap made it to the world media at the height of the war after the Taliban ousted him and his forces from Kabul. The Robin Hood cult has persisted, even as the world tires of the stories of Afghan betrayal and brutality, and the never-ending civil war.

Masoud was born in 1956, according to some accounts, which makes him the youngest Afghan leader of reckoning. He is about five feet ten inches, tall, and not very large. Has a wheatish complexion, perhaps partly the result of years of living in the open, is bony and sturdy in build, with an aquiline nose. His eyes are typically "Panjshiri", like large black almonds.

He has a steady gaze, but does not always meet the eyes of his interlocutor. While making a point about his fighting, he often uses his Afghan cap dramatically. He drops it on the ground and snaps: "I need this much space to fight." His arms almost reach his knees as he stands, arms that in Indian legend describe their possessor as *ajanbahu*. He dons military fatigues, when not in the traditional Afghan attire with headgear.

Masoud can sleep at will, and sleep deep. Catnaps permit him to work or travel long hours.

Constantly under threat, he is known to sleep at different places each day. At any given time, ten armed men, mostly those hailing from Panjshir, guard him.

He is fond of poetry and music. The Afghan envoy to New Delhi, Masood Khalili, says Masoud listened 57 times to a cassette of poetry presented by him, each time travelling from Kabul to Jabul Siraj. He loves to share jokes and has a hearty laugh. When he laughs, he covers his mouth with his palm.

"In the twenty years-plus that I have known him, he has not changed much," says Khalili.

Masoud relaxes by playing judo, karate and volleyball, all of which he has cut down after he developed a problem with his lower back. He loves to play chess—"as long as he is winning. He quits before he is checkmated", says an aide who has watched him at play.

Perhaps, this was what he did in striking an understanding with the Soviets in 1983 to save his Panjshir from being ravaged; and in quitting Kabul in September 1996.

Son of a military officer in King Zahir Shah's court, Masoud comes from a well-known family from Panjshir. His grandfather was an influential man in the valley. Both his parents are dead. In private conversation, he is known to praise his mother. He prays five times a day and is known not to miss his prayers under any circumstances.

He is fond of friends and is exceptionally warm. But he is an extremely private person. He does not take people home, where his world is his wife, from a relatively commoner family who can read and write, and five children.

Those who have conversed with him say he speaks extremely softly, and to the point. He is a careful listener, but pressed for time, pushes the other to come to the point quickly. He gets to the bottom of the subject quickly and once he absorbs what the other has to say, responds briefly and makes his points clearly, before moving on to the next topic or person.

His demeanour is of one supremely sure of himself. He is also extremely conscious of the responsibilities on his shoulders. An aide says he is very keen and meticulous for military details, but tends to be less concerned on political ones. "Masoud's strength is that he can resist, he can fight. But he cannot build. He is a good military man, a good strategist. But he is not good as a politician. He has not been able to build a political movement, despite political convictions", the aide concedes.

This imbalance in approach has made Masoud rush to conclusions and change course later. Privately, he has not been averse to accepting an error of judgement, but generally, he is very confident that his decision is what is required and is bound to work.

He has not travelled much outside the country, save brief visits to neighbouring Iran, Uzbekistan and Tajikistan. According to Khalili, he went to Pakistan only once in 1992 to attend the Mujahideen commanders' meeting in Peshawar and travelled to Islamabad because the local and international media were clamouring to talk to him. Among his recent trips has been one to Tashkent, at the end of the six-plus-two conference in July 1999.

He is media-savvy and relates himself well with media persons, but is visibly shy with women journalists.

Masoud is a member of Jamiat-i-Islami Afghanistan, a non-Pashtun organization, headed by Burhanuddin Rabbani. Although a member of the radical Islamic movement, Masoud is not known to be a religious bigot. Not much is known of his younger days except that he has worked under this flag throughout his life as a student-activist and then as a mujahid.

•

Masoud has miscalculated quite often. One was when he failed to grab the opportunity to lead the mujahideen government when Najibullah was willing to abdicate in his favour. There was in fact a direct contact with the Najib government when the then Foreign Minister, Abdul Wali, made him a specific offer. Najib was willing to trust him, but there were hitches in the person of Hikmatyar, the favourite of CIA–ISI, well-placed Afghan sources say.

Also, Masoud considered himself too young for the job and felt that he could work under Rabbani's tutelage. Being a Tajik, an ethnic minority, he feared that he would have a problem being accepted by the majority Pushtuns. One of his preoccupations has been ethnic balance in the Afghan society.

Amidst many marquée names that emerged from the Afghan resistance to the Soviets, Masoud remains the most successful mujahideen commander. In September 1996, he was forced to flee Kabul by the Taliban militia. Some supporters claim that he voluntarily left Kabul. Although Masoud is considered a master of the guerrilla technique of tactical withdrawal followed by a surprise turnabout and counter-attack, this withdrawal seemed to have been undertaken without that tactical element. The counter-attack did not come for months and he has not so far reached Kabul.

Possibly, Masoud calculated that he would be able to take Kabul once the Taliban weakened. At that time he obviously did not calculate the role Pakistan has been playing in the Taliban's military successes and in keeping the Taliban regime going by propping up the administration right up to the district level.

The Rabbani–Masoud debacle was just like any other military development in Afghanistan, today or some centuries ago. It was driven by betrayal. Uzbek warlord Abdul Rashid Dostum, who had earlier betrayed Najib, betrayed him.

Masoud was outnumbered and outflanked. Till the last minute, he found himself arguing with other commanders who should defend which part of the city. The Taliban were just 15 kilometres away from Kabul's city centre. Rabbani, Masoud and others quit the city by vehicles and rushed to the safety of Panjshir.

The most charitable thing that can be said, which is factually fairly credible, is that the Rabbani–Masoud combine quit because, had they stayed on in Kabul and fought, there would have been more bloodshed.

Masoud's force has lost ground since and is confined to about 10 per cent of the territory in the north. Masoud was unable to reconcile his differences with Dostum, who adopted an off-again-on-again policy towards the alliance of which he was a part. Masoud has had numerous setbacks because of Dostum and other generals who have chosen to fight each other, or betray each other, even to the extent of inviting the Taliban. That was how Mazar was lost and regained in May 1997, and eventually lost again in August 1998.

Asked about the Mujahideen's failure to work together, a top military aide of Masoud, who did not wish to speak on record, had this to say:

Our basic mistake, both military and diplomatic, was that we invited war on different fronts. We had bad relations with neighbours. Among us, we never reconciled. We were four major forces: Hikmatyar's Hizb-i-Islami, Mazari's Hizb-i-Wahdat, Jombesh of Dostum and our own

Jamaat-i-Islami. At any stage, each was fighting the three others. At that time, each of us was supported by Pakistan, which benefited from our internecine quarrels.

We fought the Russians, and then had our factional fights with other mujahideen. In the Taliban, we found a younger enemy with support and supplies from foreign countries. Some of these had supported our cause earlier. But we failed to see the danger and unite when the Taliban emerged. The worst thing is, each of us fought the Taliban separately. You can see the results.[1]

This perceptive military man put it more succinctly:

When Hikmatyar fought the Taliban, we were watching from the sidelines. When the Taliban attacked Dostum, others watched on. We united only when seriously threatened by the Taliban. Only military pressure united us. The way we performed, we had to lose. In a sense, the loss of Mazar united us.

Today Dostum, who had Uzbek support, is not around. Iran has changed its view about Wahdat. Everyone has realized that Afghan resistance needs a single leader. Now we have to make the best of this situation.

It is no secret that the anti-Taliban alliance remained plagued by frequent internecine quarrels even after Kabul was lost. This is clear from the way Mazar was lost, regained, and lost again. With Dostum's departure, as also that of Shia leader Karim Khalili of Hizb-i-Wahdat, and a number of smaller warlords, the command has "unified" under Masoud since early 1999. This has given him unhindered powers to run his campaign. The base of the Northern Alliance, renamed Islamic Front for Deliverance of Afghanistan (IFDA) to signify the departure of Dostum, has considerably narrowed, but in military terms, it has become more coherent and effective, as was evident from the July–August 1999 round of fighting.

With the Rabbani government in exile, there is little by way of administration of areas under Masoud's control. As it happens in Afghanistan, towns are provided for, while the villages are remote and fend for themselves with the help of their tribal set-ups.

Masoud's task is mainly military. He commands all the forces. There is a Military Council for advice. It has fighters, some from civilian-political background, while there are others who have

[1] Interview in Dushanbe in July 1999.

had a military background. The civilians are referred to as "Ustads" or "Commanders", while the military ones retain their ranks.

The Military Council comprises Bismillah, a Tajik from Jamaat-i-Islami; Anwari from Harkat-ul-Ansar; Commander Kazmi, a Hazara from Hizb-i-Wahdat; and Commander Sher Alam, a Pashtun from Kabul, from Ittehad-ul-Islam. Anwari, Bismillah and Sher Alam are former colonels who got their ranks while fighting as mujahideen. Among other council members is Gul Mohammed, an Uzbek. He hails from Faryab and is a brother-in-law of Abdul Malik Pehalwan. Malik, who fought Dostum and invited the Taliban to Mazar, and then threw the Taliban back in May 1999, is now a spent force. He reportedly lives in Turkey and is not directly involved in Afghan affairs, though he keeps tab on developments.

Being a mix of civil and military (not in the formal sense of a conventional army, though), Masoud's military machine is representative in ethnic terms and feels close to the people.

•

The Masoud-led alliance has inherited Russian-made armament from what the Soviets left. Much of the armoury is obsolete, but is kept in use. Supplies come in fits and starts, depending upon the funds and the "black" market in Eastern Europe, which is offloading old Soviet armoury.

There is no clear estimate of who has how many troops in the Afghan conflict. This is understandable from the fact that both the militias are loose forces commanded at different levels by local chieftains.

There is constant change of loyalties and changing of sides. Unless in groups, fighters scatter away for fear of being identified and punished by the "other side".

The changing loyalties have often turned the tables of war. Masoud's side has suffered more since many of its commanders change sides for money. They are derisively called "chequebook victories". That the Taliban control over 90 per cent of the territory and have all the advantages also works on the minds of the Masoud commanders. Many of them changed sides earlier when they found their top commanders quarrelling.

The round of fighting at the end of July 1999 also saw money changing hands when two commanders, one of them at Najrab, both Pashtuns, changed sides. Money, plus the fact that the attack was combined with artillery fire and strafing by the air force, weighed heavily in favour of the switch of sides. They had defected earlier also, but had returned to the Masoud fold. The ground realities are such that both sides, particularly Masoud's side, are compelled to trust these local chieftains.

The switch-over is largely one-sided, from Masoud to the Taliban, although Masoud's side has not been averse to purchasing and has actually made occasional gains. A Masoud aide said his side did not purchase rival chieftains because it simply does not have the money for it. "Such gains are always for the short term."

Although they are dubbed "chequebook victories", there is no cheque transaction. Senior military hands change sides when paid in US dollars. Accounts are opened in banks in Pakistan where transactions take place. At the lower level, the deals are struck in afghanis. In the prevailing volatile situation money is simply buried and hidden in the compounds in the homes of many a fighter, to be dug out, spent and enjoyed, if they live to fight another day!

•

Masoud won appreciation from the Americans, Russians and others whom he met at Tashkent in July 1999 by appearing to be flexible and conciliatory. He won Uzbek support when during a three-hour meeting with President Islam Karimov, he was assured that Uzbekistan would stand by him and that it would not encourage parallel resistance forces.

Many observers of the Afghan scene, particularly the Russians, says a Russian diplomat in a Central Asian capital, feel that the Uzbeks have a track record of putting all their eggs in Dostum's basket and then feeling let down. Indeed, Tashkent played a crucial role when Najibullah was ready to give up power. But its actions prevented a smooth transfer of power and in the process, triggered instability.

In those twilight days of the Soviet Union, Mikhail Gorbachev had virtually stopped functioning and Karimov, then close to

Boris Yeltsin, played a crucial role in Afghan affairs. Fearing that Najibullah's successor from among the mujahideen might once again be a Pashtun, Karimov signalled to Dostum to change sides and move over to the mujahideen's side.

Dostum's unreliability became public when it transpired that he had purchased property in the US and UK and now lives in style in Ankara. The Turks hosted Dostum with the hope that they would have a role in Afghanistan.

Before quitting Afghanistan the last time, Dostum allegedly sold the 180 Scud missiles under his control to the Taliban. Sources say Dostum could have had them towed to safety or made them unworkable, but he did not. The "deal" with the Taliban, it is being said, was brokered by the CIA, which did not want the Scuds to leave the Afghan territory. A possible use of Scuds on the Afghan soil could be to use them against Iran, should Iran get restive along the border or try to have a larger say in Afghan affairs.

Uzbek sources admit to being let down by Dostum. All that has happened, so far, is that they have accepted Masoud, albeit grudgingly, since both Dostum and his aide-turned-foe, Abdul Malik, another Uzbek warlord, have proved unreliable.

More than once in the past, the Uzbeks sought to persuade Masoud to accommodate and rehabilitate Dostum. Masoud, in his turn, has been pointing to Dostum's track record of being unreliable. For the present at least, the Uzbeks have given up asking him to accommodate Dostum, who has completely lost his base in Shebergen. His Uzbek fighters have either joined the Taliban, or Masoud, or have scattered. Given the record, it is not unlikely that Dostum would like to stage a comeback in future. A reliable assessment about Dostum, however, is that he has enough property to retire comfortably. But he has age on his side and he lacks liquid cash. An antithesis of Masoud, he has enjoyed the patronage of the Russians in the past, then moved on to Najibullah and from him, to the Mujahideen. A "Soviet" general, he won grudging acceptance of the Mujahideen, mainly because of the patronage of Uzbekistan and his loyal militia. But Dostum has proved to be chameleon-like, keeping in touch with the ISI. The Russians consider him closer to the ISI and through it, the Americans, than the Uzbeks.

Masoud is also aware of the threat from Hikmatyar, on whose behalf Pakistan could play the Pashtun card at some stage in the future.

For the moment, in their absence, Masoud has full run of the resistance movement. His recent successes in fighting the combined force of the Taliban, Pakistani regulars and "volunteers" and Arab mercenaries have established his prowess and his hold. That, and his track record, make him Afghanistan's man of the hour.

What does the future hold for Masoud? This question arises because Masoud has territory, enough firepower to hold out and, most of all, the will to fight on. He is also not short of trained, trusted men for a concentrated, all-out attack on Kabul.

For Afghanistan's neighbours, he seems to be the rallying-point. Iran, CARs and Russia—all want him to stay on and fight. For he is the only buffer between the Taliban ideology and the CARs, the only one who can fight the Taliban.

Table 4.1. Masoud's Immediate Military Requirements

No.	Item	Cost (US$ mn)	Total (US$ mn)
20	helicopter gunships	0.3	6
2	Mi-26 transport helicopters (to transport men and material to theatres of operation)	2.8	5.6
8	Mi-25 and Mi-26 attack helicopters	4	32
	Along with small-arms and ammunition, the cost would not exceed		US$100 million

The moot point is: Just what will ensure a Masoud victory? According to defence analysts, such a victory could change the entire political scenario in the region. A top Masoud aide listed his military requirements as given in Table 4.1. With that assured, a short, limited, but intensive operation would get them Kabul. The logic is: once Kabul falls, the Taliban would have no choice but to surrender without fight or switch sides.

Masoud is waiting for this golden moment, while he fights on.

5

Military Structure and Equipment
For Suppliers, a Fertile Hunting-ground

A major factor in the Afghan polity, both the cause and consequence of the conflict, is that along with the political leadership, the traditional armed forces have disintegrated. Nurtured on modern lines in monarchal times, they had a clear-cut command structure. In addition, the Maliks leading various tribes, and later warlords like Abdul Rashid Dostum, worked along with the armed forces through their militia.

This continued even under the communist-backed regimes, although the armed forces were no longer apolitical and represented various political factions. The top brass had strong political connections, but the basic command structure did not change.

The Afghan army disintegrated after the Najibullah government was toppled by the coup in 1992. Under the provisions of the interim government accord signed between the various groups, a major portion of the army was divided basically between these groups. They were, among others:

— *Jamiat's main commanders*:
  Ahmed Shah Masoud; Toran Ismayel Khan; Mullah Najibullah
— *Kabul regime's militia groups*:
  Abdul Rashid Dostum; Sayed Jafar Naderi
— *Parchami generals*:
  General Momen, General Baba Jan
— In the Paktia, Ghazni and Nangarhar provinces, the army

divisions were divided between Gulbuddin Hikmatyar, Mohammad Yunus Khalis and Sayed Ahmad Gailani's Tanzeems.

In some places, particularly in the Bagram and the Shindand airbases, Gulbuddin's forces confronted the members of Itelaf-i-Shamal and each side captured as much of the Afghan army military equipment, including transport and fighter planes, helicopters, tanks, APCs, artillery pieces, etc., as they could. Charts 5.1 and 5.2 show the armed forces command structure as of now and previously. Chart 5.3 gives the armed forces organization.

The capture of Kabul by the Taliban changed much of the military scenario in Afghanistan. The Taliban do not have a regular command structure. Indeed, they are not organized on conventional army lines. They count on the individual commanders, as expected in a tribe-dominated social and political structure.

The Taliban maintain a fighting force of 25,000 to 30,000, going by the arithmetic of commitments made by the Taliban administration in different parts of territory under their control.

That a force of this size is able to maintain control of a vast territory, while serving as a fighting force against resistance from the north is a subject of keen debate and speculation among military and political observes alike. This is explained variously, but reliably, by the role of the ISI. The Pakistan Army personnel (both serving and ex-servicemen) command the garrison that defends Kabul, as also the air defence, not only of Kabul, but all

Chart 5.1. Armed Forces Command Structure in Afghanistan

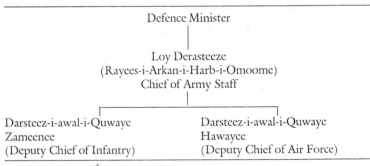

Source: Afghan Home Page.

major and minor cities under Taliban control. Pakistani personnel also man the intelligence, communication and other key posts.

In the assessment of the resistance leaders, Pakistani personnel also man the civil administration right up to the district level.

Chart 5.2. Armed Forces Command Structure Previously

Ster General (Nayeb Saalar) 4 star	Senior General
Dagar General (Nayeb Saalar) 3 star	Lieutenant General
Toran General (Ferqameshar-i-Awal) 2-star	Major General
Brid General (Ferqameshar-i-Sani) 1-star	Brigadier General
Dagar-wall (Lewa Meshar)	Colonel
Dagar-man (Ghond Meshar)	Lieutenant Colonel
Jagran (Kandak Meshar)	Major
Jig-Toran (Tolai Meshar)	Captain
Toran (Tolai Meshar-i-Sani)	Lieutenant
Lomray Brid-man (Zabet-i-Awal)	Second Lieutenant
Brid-man (Zabet-i-Sani)	Third Lieutenant
Brid-gai (Khurdzabet)	Sergeant

Source: Afghan Home Page.

Chart 5.3. Armed Forces Organization

```
Urdu Structure
Qool-hae-i-Urdu      Corps, (usually four)
                     Quway-i-Markaz,
                     Kabul
                     (Central Corps)   Corps 1
                     Kandahar          Corps 2
                     Paktia            Corps 3
                     Mazar             Corps 4
                     Shamal (Herat)    Corps 5

     Ferqa           Division, 2–3

     Lewa            Brigade, 3

     Kandak          Battalion, 3

     Tolaly          Company, 3

     Delgai          Squad Sect, 3
     ┌────┴────┐
   Type 1    Type 2
(11–33 soldiers) (33–99 soldiers)
```

Air Force
(Information not available)

```
                Ground Forces
   ┌──────┬──────────┬──────┬──────┬──────────┐
Peyada-Nezam  Quwa-      Toopchi   Lawazem   Istekhbarat
              i-Zerahdar                     wa Kashf
(Infantry)   (Mechanized) (Artillery) (Logistic) (Intelligence
                                                & Recce)
```

Source: Afghan Home Page.

"Afghans have a tendency for constant infighting and only the ISI presence bonds the Taliban together. But then the ISI is also able to manipulate the Taliban in political, military and diplomatic matters", said a top military aide of Ahmed Shah Masoud.

The Taliban maintain an expeditionary force of 5,000-plus, which is totally ISI-trained. It is lightly equipped, moves rapidly and goes in groups owing allegiance to their respective leaders for attacks.

Although the Taliban military headquarters are in Kabul, as are the government's, the real control rests in Kandahar, with Mullah Umar. The Taliban supremo controls the military personnel, particularly the expeditionary force, through trusted commanders. One of the trusted commanders is Amir Khan Muttaqi, who is also the spokesman and the Information Minister.

Muttaqi, along with the Taliban Defence Minister, Mullah Obaidullah was taken prisoner in Andarab during the 1997 abortive attempt to capture Mazar-i-Sharif. The latter remains in Masoud's custody, while Muttaqi was among those commanders who were "sold" by local chieftains and managed to get back to safety in Kabul. Obaidullah was involved in terrorist activities before the Taliban captured Kabul. He was caught and detained in 1995, but was later "exchanged" for a key commander, Masoud's aides recall.

Among the seniormost leaders concerned with military decisions are Mullah Dadullah and Mullah Biradar and Mullah Obaidullah. All are from Kandahar, which explains their proximity to Umar. But their precise position in the military hierarchy, if any, is not clear. There is little doubt, however, that along with the ISI deputationists, these three mullahs form the top military command of the Taliban.

A significant part of the military high command, and thus of the Taliban military planning and execution, are officers who belonged to the Khalq faction of the Communist Party that ruled the post-monarchy Afghanistan. They are General Issa Khan and General Bahlol. All Afghan War veterans, they dominate the Taliban military and have trained Taliban personnel in air defence, armour, communication and other key operations. This is done in close coordination with the ISI deputationists.

All the key figures in Taliban politico-military brass are Pashtuns. While the clergy is from Kandahar, the former Khalqis are from different parts of the country. But Kandaharis dominate the decision-making process. Tribe-wise, a majority of them are Ghilzais, the most prominent being Umar himself. But Durranis dominate. Mullah Rabbani, who is the *de facto* head of the government, is a Durrani. Their differences can grow in future.

Guiding and manipulating them all is the ISI's brass. Although the Punjabis dominate it at the top in Islamabad, the Pashtuns, almost entirely Ghilzais, are in total charge of the Afghan operations. This is obviously a lollipop given to the Pashtuns, who are left fairly free to work as they find it essential in guarding the Pakistani interests.

This has been the case since Lt Gen. Hamid Gul was the ISI chief. Maj. Gen. Nasirullah Babar, the alleged brain behind the Taliban, is also a Pashtun. So was the Chief of Defence Staff of Pakistan Army, Lt Gen. Aziz, who had a long tenure with the ISI earlier.

Indications are that the Taliban military is not a homogeneous force and the political differences get reflected in the military hierarchy as well. There are no basic differences, however, and disagreements are only on approaches. Messages intercepted by the opposition indicate strongly that the differences surface on issues pertaining to clan, tribe and regional loyalties. They assume political dimensions from time to time. But the ISI manages to paper over them and keep them functioning together.

The cash-strapped Taliban commanders have also been known to indulge in corruption, selling off truckloads of weapons to Masoud's men. Masoud's forces have continued their fight in Darai Suf throughout 1999 basically with weapons got from the Taliban.

•

Equipment used by the warring groups is mainly of the erstwhile Afghan armed forces and left behind by the Soviets. In addition, the small-arms and Stinger missiles are of the cold war era supplied by the CIA through Pakistan. Large quantities of arms were also procured covertly from the allied countries and from arms factories at Darra Bazar in NWFP of Pakistan. The procurement of arms and ammunition has been mainly through the proceeds of narcotic trade and donations from the fellow faithfuls.

Due to the ongoing fighting the equipment has been extensively used, poorly maintained and damaged, and is therefore less reliable. Maintenance and repair of heavy equipment and ordnance of the Taliban are reportedly undertaken by technicians of Pakistan Army. The weapons are at times employed by the warring groups in roles different from their primary task. For instance air defence guns are deployed in ground role. Similarly artillery guns are used in direct role; and artillery shells are catapulted by innovative means, and so on.

The Northern Alliance's main source of military hardware had

Chart 5.4. An Assessment of the Taliban and Northern Alliance Arsenal

Taliban

Infantry: Pistol; 7.62 mm SMG; 7.62 mm LMG; 7.62 mm GPMG (Kalashnikovs); Assault Rifles (AK Series); 12.7 HMG; Greade Launcher; RG-42 A/Personal Hand Grenades; RPG 6; RL; 82 mm A/Tk RL; 82 mm RR (Recoilless Rif); 107 mm RR; SPG

Mortars: 81 mm, 82 mm, 107 mm, 120 mm and 160 mm.

Artillery: 100 mm Gun (Towed); 122 mm HOW (Towed); 122 mm Gun D-30; 130 mm Gun; 152 mm Gun (Towed); BM 21, 13, 16 and 27

Tanks: T-54/55; T-59; T-62; T-72 (Reported to be procured by Pak from Ukraine for Taliban. Money paid by Saudi Arabia).

APCs: BTR-40, 50 (tracked); BTR-60 (wheeled); BRDM - 2; BMP-1

Air Defence Systems
  Missiles: SA-2, SA-3, SA-7, SA-9, Stinger; Lunar (?)
  Guns: 23 mm ZSU; 37 mm Gun AA

SS Missiles
  Scud-A, Scud-B and FROG - 7

Air Force: MiG-19/21; SU 7B, AN-12

Helicopters: MI-17, MI-25, MI-35

Northern Alliance

By and large the same as that of the Taliban. No worthwhile Air Force. A few helicopters are held for transportation and logistic duties. The Northern Alliance also has about a 1,000-horse-strong cavalry, which played a decisive role in mountain warfare.

Source: Collated from various published sources and from information given by NGOs and diplomats.

been neighbours in addition to the weaponries of erstwhile Afghan armed forces. The extent of neighbours' assistance may be gauged from the fact that when 16 wagons were intercepted at Osh railway station Kyrghyzstan, they contained the following: Grad rockets; Machine-guns; F-1 grenades; mines; 700 tons of ammunition; FOL. This is only one example. An assessment of the Taliban and Northern Alliance arsenal is given in Chart 5.4.

•

An unexplained phenomenon noticed in almost all post–World War II civil wars and ethnic conflicts is that the warring factions have not experienced any serious shortage of money and arms to flight. At least that was so in the first ten years after the war. This part of the world witnessed this phenomenon at the time of, say, the Cambodian crisis; and is again witnessing it for the last fifteen years in Sri Lanka. Interestingly, neither country has an indigenous arms industry to mobilize the arms. The arms were acquired from outside sources through clandestine means. In Cambodia the narcotics trade from the Golden Triangle did play an active role in mobilizing resources. In the case of the LTTE, in the initial years, the smuggling of consumer goods raised funds; and later on there have been stray reports about Sri Lankan Tamils smuggling narcotics. Of far greater importance is the vast expatriate Sri Lankan Tamil population—Sri Lankan Tamil diaspora, as some would call it—who provide the needed infrastructure. However, one commonality in both Cambodia and Sri Lanka is that neither country had effective armed forces, trained to meet the threat posed to the State structure.

In the ethnic conflicts witnessed in India, in the northeast in the 1950s and 1960s and in Punjab and J & K, the State managed to contain them through a political process and State power. Though India has a an arms industry to reckon with, in terms of developing-world standards, the arms outside the governmental apparatus are insignificant. The Indian republic did not allow the grey arms market to grow to unwieldy proportions. Clandestine arms production is restricted to manufacturing a double-barrel gun of World War I vintage. However, with the resolution of most of these conflicts it became evident that the nexus between narcotics and arms did operate in intensifying the conflict. Once the Indian republic confronted this nexus with a political solution, it petered out.

In Afghanistan, evidence suggests a mixture of Kampuchea and Sri Lanka.

Officially, no government supplies arms and ammunition to any faction in Afghanistan. At the same time, a million AK-47s were in circulation in Pakistan–Afghanistan as in December 1998. There was also no disruption in supply of ammunition. Chart 5.5 presents a list of some of the heavy equipment noticed by various observers over the five years 1994–99, besides a variety of small-arms.

From where do the Taliban and the Northern Alliance mobilize aircraft, tanks and rocket launchers to attack each other? There is no arms industry in Afghanistan. Even the extent of cannibalization of the equipment during the 1980s would not meet the requirements of the decade-long civil war. Media reports indicate that the Taliban are mobilizing their cadres in brand new Nissan pick-up vans. Two hundred of these were captured along with thousand men by Ahmed Shah Masoud's forces in July–August 1999. There was a report that the Taliban are getting ready to have an air force with 20–21 aircraft.

Even if the contestants were getting clandestine arms supplies from some countries, the watchful eye of the international media would have exposed it after a couple of transactions. No country would like to be exposed in this manner. Alternatively, the contestants must be buying equipment from the open market, which also looks like the only possibility. But where does the

Chart 5.5. Heavy Equipment in the Afghanistan Fighting Noticed by Various Observers during 1994–99

- main battle tanks (mostly T-54/55)
- light tanks—PT-76
- armoured infantry fighting vehicles
- towed artillery
- multiple rocket launchers
- air defence guns

- surface-to-air missiles
- surface-to-surface missiles
- anti-tank guided weapons
- fighter aircraft (MiG-19/21)
- armoured helicopters (Mi-8)
- transport aircraft (An-12)

Source: Same as Chart 5.4.

hard currency for the purchases come from? Apparently, they manage to generate money from two sources, namely, through drug trafficking and from the network of Islamic solidarity organizations that have sprung up all over the world during the past few years. According to rough estimates, the Golden Crescent at the Afghan end generates around US$5–6 billion, if not more annually. As regards the Islamic solidarity organizations, they support some faction or the other in the name of Islam. There are Islamic solidarity groups for Afghanistan even in South-East Asia, the Far East and Europe. Some of these outfits also facilitate arms acquisition from the open market, through their networking.

Chief among the open market sources for weapon acquisition are Eastern Europe and the CARs, which are keen to offload their Soviet-origin armouries for hard currency payment. Even obsolete weapons are bought up for cannibalizing by Afghan factions.

Media reports in early 1998 indicate that Iran and Russia have been pouring in arms and ammunition to the Northern Alliance. Relief workers who visited northern Afghanistan also say that they have seen hundreds of new rifles and other military equipment in the hands of the Northern Alliance militia. Similarly, Pakistan and Saudi Arabia are reported to have helped with funds and organized the purchase of new weapons and their supplies for the Taliban. Quoting intelligence agencies, a *Washington Times* report[1] said that 55 cargo aircraft carrying arms from Ukraine had landed in Peshawar. More Ukraine arms had arrived in Karachi by ship and had been delivered to the Taliban. The report added that Ukraine was a major arms-for-cash supplier to the rebel movements in the developing world and had sharp differences with Russia, which was backing the anti-Taliban alliance. Ukraine also had developed differences with Iran, another country that supported the anti-Taliban alliance.

Since Pakistan is a party to the Taliban movement, the old supply routes perfected during the fight against the Red Army seem still to operate quite effectively: the arms coming via sea land at Karachi and by air at Peshawar. Of late there have also been reports that arms consignments by air land directly at

---

[1] Reproduced in *Times of India* (New Delhi), 22 February 1999.

Kandahar. All these consignments are first assembled at Dubai, where their mode of transport is decided.

The anti-Taliban forces in the north are getting weapons by road and air from the countries across the border. On the face of it, the whole thing seems to have emerged as a multi-million dollar business with many vested interests developing. An Asian diplomat said that even if there is peace in Afghanistan, the arms-loving Afghans are unlikely to allow the supply network to be disturbed. Also, arms buying and selling has become a big business for laundering money earned from narcotics. This linkage is difficult to dismantle.

Published sources 1994-98 indicate that the Afghan factions receive arms and ammunition from seven countries. Except Uzbekistan others in the list are also confirmed by Pakistani commentators like Ahmed Rashid. They are: Pakistan; Russia; Iran; Turkey; Saudi Arabia; Uzbekistan; Ukraine; France; Singapore; UAE. Since officially none of these governments acknowledges that it is supplying arms and ammunition to Afghanistan, one has to assume that this arms in flow into Afghanistan is largely through non-official/clandestine channels.

An arms merchant explained to us how the deals are struck for the supply of spares to Russian arms in the Taliban's inventory. First, the representatives of both parties meet in country 'A' to assess demand and supply. If there is common ground, the parties again meet in country 'B' and finalize the details like price, quantity and delivery. All transactions are cash down, with some advance paid. The remainder is paid from country 'C' by some outfit. Arms and ammunition are actually assembled in country 'D' and charters of country 'E' are used to ferry them.

Whether these arms are supplied directly to each Afghan faction from the supplier or the arms are purchased and delivered to Afghan factions by a third party is difficult to say. UN officials in the know say both are happening, and it is difficult to pinpoint these sources of supply. "With so much quantity of arms easily available in the open markets, it is difficult to identify the source and route, especially when the drug money is involved", one UN official said. "Afghanistan is surrounded by countries who are looking for hard currency earnings by any method. Most of them have arms industries. Since arms exports is a big business every one is an it", he added.

Some of the major countries mobilizing finances or helping to procure arms or providing transit routes are: all Asean countries except Vietnam; most of the CARs with an arms industry; most of the former Warsaw Pact countries; People's Republic of China; Qatar; Sudan; Lebanon; Egypt; Libya; Brazil; Argentina; some West European countries (Britain, France, Italy); UAE; USA. In all 32 countries could be identified. The governments are not involved. One Asean official said, "If an organization like Islamic Solidarity with the People of Afghanistan [in his country] decided to send some money, officially we cannot stop them."

Therefore, one can draw the following conclusions about the arms supplies to Afghanistan:

- To fight the Red Army, the US and its allies dumped a variety of arms in Afghanistan. The arsenal was disproportionately large.
- The Soviet Union had a massive arms industry spread over all the Soviet republics. The disintegration of the Soviet Union led to most of the new republics, to mobilize resources, selling arms to any customer for hard currency.
- The South-West Asian region being a heavily armed region and the birthplace of a number of militant movements, there are well-established channels for mobilization of arms.
- The Golden Crescent being a pre-eminent narcotics production and export centre on the global narcotics map, the disturbed conditions in Afghanistan provided an enviable market to enhance the trade.
- To the Afghan war, which from the outset was being fought in the name of Islamic ideology, the faithfuls all over the world contributed generously.

How can this inflow of assistance and arms to Afghan factions be stopped? The only feasible solution is to ask the international community to ensure that no arms from their respective countries are allowed to go to Afghanistan. A UN appeal might be tried, but the effectiveness of such an appeal is limited because government control on the small-arms market is extremely limited. Also, four of the five permanent members of the UN Security

Council are involved in the supply of arms to Afghanistan. A country like China having entered into a non-official defence cooperation agreement with one faction in the Afghan civil war, it is difficult to impose any type of arms embargo. Also, there cannot be any check on arms trade through countries like Sudan.

Therefore, along with a UN appeal for a voluntary arms embargo, there should be effective policing of the Afghan borders by the UN. In other words, the UN should appoint inspection teams and place them in all the bordering countries to monitor the flow of traffic into Afghanistan. These teams, it they perceive any cargo to be lethal, should have the right to stop the consignment. Since all of Afghanistan's neighbours except Pakistan would agree on the need for an arms embargo, such a UN initiative has a reasonable chance of being accepted. Since the policing of the entire Afghanistan border with all the countries is physically impossible because of the rugged terrain, one method could be the identification of routes and placing UN inspectors. Such an exercise would reduce the inflow of arms and ammunition by as much as 90 per cent. This may incidentally also help to monitor the drug trade from the region.

According to a study by the UN, such an exercise would involve about 50,000 UN personnel (see Appendix 5.1). But a Pakistani study estimated for total blockade of 362 supply routes to Afghanistan would require only 100 international observers and would cost about $30 million over a two-year period.[2] These conflicting assessments have made the arms embargo initiative against Afghanistan dormant. There is an urgent need to revive it.

---

[2] See Nasim Zehra, "Pinning Hopes on US Engagement", *The News*, 2 April 1998.

Appendix 5.1

UN Non-Paper: A Review of the Options on Embargo of Military Supplies to the Warring Factions in Afghanistan

Introduction

This document has been prepared by the Secretariat, taking into account informal papers provided to it by the Russian Federation and the United States of America. In response to requests made during the drafting period, a US team of experts visited New York and provided additional information and ideas. Further discussions were also held with Russian experts.

The Government of Ireland kindly accepted to release Colonel Kevin M. Hogan, former chief military observer of the UN Special Mission to Afghanistan (UNSMA), who provided valuable assistance with the preparation of this study.

The following preliminary observations should be borne in mind:

a. Based on the experience in other theatres, the effectiveness of an arms embargo that is not mandatory is questionable. Furthermore, it might be desirable to establish a supervisory machinery in order to monitor the flow of goods into Afghanistan and to help the governments of the transit countries to discharge effectively their responsibilities arising from the embargo.

b. The warring parties in Afghanistan have relatively few large weapon systems, and the war consumes only a limited amount of material, most of which can be carried by small trucks or pack animals. Given the length of the border of Afghanistan and the nature of the terrain, it would be quite impossible to prevent such shipments entirely. The best that one could hope for would be to made the supply of arms, to slow it down and make it more expensive. Over time, this might affect the behaviour and expectations of the Afghan parties and of their suppliers.

Background

The Taliban (controlling two-thirds of Afghanistan), and the Northern Alliance, (the forces of General Dostum, Commander Massoud and Mr. Khalili) have been locked in conflict for several years. The parties, lacking locally produced military supplies, are known to be supported from outside Afghanistan. Military supplies are regularly brought inside the country by roads and by smaller less accessible passes through mountains. They are also flown into airfields. Smuggling of goods is a traditional

Military Structure and Equipment 115

and now, highly "sophisticated" operation. Afghanistan is now the world's largest supplier of opium and it is common knowledge that the illegal drug industry and trade contribute substantially to the war.

Situation

A near stalemate exists on the military front with little hope of the parties resolving the situation militarily.

One way to end what is seemingly an endless conflict in Afghanistan would be to curb the flow of arms and other war materials. To this end, studies have been undertaken on the feasibility of an embargo on supplies that continue to fuel the conflict.

Assumptions

This paper makes the following assumptions:
i. Any embargo should be effective and verifiable at least to some degree;
ii. An embargo ought not to confer any advantage to any faction in the conflict;
iii. For any embargo to be effective, it, should be verifiable and supported by all Member States, especially the neighbouring countries;
iv. Costs wilt be a limiting factor that must be taken into consideration.

Embargo General

An embargo entails:
a. Selection of items to be embargoed;
b. Establishment of level of detection;
c. Selection of monitoring method;
d. Selection of supply routes to be monitored;
e. Selection of monitoring posts and areas of mobile patrolling;
f. Selection and assembly of monitoring teams;
g. Provision of infrastructure (logistic support, communications, etc.);
h. Monitoring of the selected routes;
i. Detection of the embargoed supplies;
j. Assembly of evidence;
k. Establishment of a supervisory organ and reporting mechanism for oversight and to deal with complaints or allegations of violations;
l. Enforcement of sanctions.

Geographical Considerations

On first inspection, because Afghanistan is land-locked and has little or no indigenous capacity to manufacture war materials, it would appear to be very vulnerable to an embargo. However, when geographical considerations and historical orientation of the Population is taken into account an embargo becomes extremely problematical. Annex A-1 describes airfields in Afghanistan, while A-2 depicts the type and size of roads in the area.

Afghanistan is land-locked mountainous area of 647,500 square kilometres with 5,529 kms of border with six neighbouring states, as follows:

a. Pakistan   2,430 km
b. Iran   936 km
c. Turkmenistan   744 km
d. Uzbekistan   137 km
e. Tajikistan   1,206 km
f. China   76 km

a. The Pakistani Border

This border has the following characteristics, which need to be considered.
1. Principal roads
2. Secondary roads   itemized in Annex A-2
3. Minor trails
4. Tribal areas
5. Air route
6. The terrain varies from mountainous to level desert like plains.

There are two principal roads—one between Quetta and Kandahar and the other connecting Peshawar and Jalalabad. See Annex A-2 for carrying capacity of these routes.

The border is crossed in many places by secondary, minor routes or trails. The characteristics of some of these areas allow these routes to vary at short notice.

The tribal areas in southern and eastern Afghanistan possibly pose the greatest difficulties. In these areas, traditional migratory populations show little or no recognition of the state boundaries.

Afghan factions are also supplied by air. Generally, longer range air supply requires major airfields, but this is NOT a guarantee as supplies could be air-dropped, or minor airfields or roadways could be converted to receive longer range aircraft.

b. The Iranian Border

Though this is considered to be a well controlled border, it could be used for illegal supply for private gain by a third party.

With the Taliban controlling the Afghan side of the border with Iran, no special considerations need to apply for land supply. However, air routes over this border have allegedly been used for supply purposes.

c. The Turkmen Border

This border is well controlled with few major crossing points. However, illegal crossing at minor junctions is difficult to control.

d. The Uzbek border

This has a short, well controlled border with only two major supply routes, one land bridge and one barge ferry. These channels could also hypothetically be used for arms supply.

e. The Tajik Border

This border is patrolled by CIS forces. However, because Tajiks live on both sides of the border, movement is known to occur in connection with annual migrations, and both legal and illegal trade take place. This area also suffers from ongoing civil strife. Supplies to Afghanistan could hypothetically be arranged from southern Tajikistan.

f. The Chinese Border

Because of the location and small size of this border no special considerations are necessary.

Supply Routes

Approximate number of crossings are as follows: (Ref. Map Annex B)

a.	Major routes	x	6
b.	Major airfields	x	6
c.	Minor roads	x	40
d.	Minor airfields	x	7
e.	Tracks and trails	x	300
f.	Ports	x	3
	Total		362

Experts advise that some 40 minor routes and approximately 300 tracks and trails should be considered for planning purposes to cover the land borders of Afghanistan.

Logistic Considerations

Estimates of logistic capacities needed to supply conflicts vary from many thousands of tons per day for the bigger conflicts down to a few thousand tons per month for low intensity operations. The Afghan conflict would be on the lower side of the scale. It is estimated that between 2,000 to 4,000 tons per month is all that is needed to support the present level of fighting. For planning purposes, a rate of 3,000 tons per month is used.

Annex C indicates the requirements to transport this supply rate. Larger rates require ships, large vehicles and large transport aircraft. As Afghanistan is land-locked, has relatively few large airports and a poor road network, it would be comparatively easy to detect large quantities of supply.

Scale of Detection

An unknown quantity of arms, ammunition and petroleum, oil and lubricant (POL) is at present being supplied to the warring factions by:

a. friendly governments
b. commercial suppliers and
c. "grey market" arms dealers.

Supplies are entering Afghanistan by:

a. air and possibly by
b. major and minor land routes and by
c. barge.

It would also be possible to deliver smaller quantities by many minor overland and air routes. It is unlikely that these more difficult routes are being used to any great extent at present because other routes are open, but they could be used if the easier routes were denied by an effective embargo. For an embargo to be effective it would be necessary to monitor all routes because of the low level of supply (estimated at 2 to 4,000 tons per month as already stated) that is required to go undetected to sustain the present and average level of hostilities. This level of supply could easily be reached by using minor routes and trails, some of which could have lain dormant for years and be brought back into operation rapidly as an embargo becomes more effective on the larger supply routes.

Conflict Characteristics

Annex D lists the military equipment commonly in use in Afghanistan by all sides.

a. Factors such as geography, lack of maintenance, high fuel usage and the fat highly maneuverable type of fighting in which they are experts, reduces Afghan reliance on heavier weaponry.
b. Tanks in use are rarely used conventionally, but more as a mobile gun or for morale or propaganda purposes.
c. Similarly the use of air power is rarely used to effect. Likewise maintenance and high fuel usage are very problematic.
d. Weapons mainly used for the fighting are artillery, such as rockets and shells, mortars, RPGs, anti-aircraft (in ground mode), and small arms.

e. For mobility the preference is for 4" pickup trucks for troop movement rather than armoured personnel carriers, and small to medium size trucks/lorries for logistics.

Monitoring Overview

The international inventory for a monitoring operation could include any of the following:

Aerial   satellite imagery
manned aircraft
remote pilotless vehicles (RPV) (drones)

Ground   electronic
manned posts and checkpoints
mobile patrolling

Intelligence agents
signals intelligence (sigint)
money trail—controls on financial transfers, freezing of assets, etc.

Having considered each resource under the headings

a. available to Afghanistan theatre,
b. costs,
c. usefulness on stand alone basis,

and relating same to the Afghanistan scene, it follows that manned posts and checkpoints supported by mobile patrols must be employed.

Recommended Levels

The UN norm staffing level is 24 to 32 persons per post. For planning purposes this paper uses 30 persons.

Where neighbouring countries supply the staff, an international staff of supervisors is recommended. For 24 hours monitoring to be effective, a HQ staff of five to six in each country and a post staff of eight persons at any one time would be required. The degree of support given by host countries would (as in the experience of the embargo on Yugoslavia) affect the numbers of international staff.

Stationing UN Monitors in Afghanistan

Effective control of the flow of arms into Afghanistan would be best achieved by observers being placed on the ground inside Afghanistan itself. Not having observers on the ground in Afghanistan, especially at all ports, would make monitoring, detection and assembly of evidence virtually impossible.

However, the stationing of UN monitors in Afghanistan would

require the consent of all Afghan parties as well as credible assurances by the parties for the security of observers.

As an alliterative, detection and prevention might occur at the suspected points of departure. However, this would not guarantee that aircraft flights planned for one (seemingly innocent) destination would not be rerouted, stopped and unloaded elsewhere or en route.

Local Enforcement Agencies

Each neighbouring country, the Northern Alliance and the Taliban all have border enforcement agencies in situ. They vary from high levels of efficiency down to token only. However, they are in place and could be utilized to obvious advantages.

The Options

When considering the monitoring options for an embargo of military supplies and the assumptions and conclusions made earlier, there are two main variables.

a. *Level of Detection Required*
The level of detection and the' capability of land, sea and air routes will determine the number of posts to be manned and the positions of mobile patrols. This paper considers four such levels, i.e.

Level 1   to detect heavy weapons only
Level 2   to detect supply rates of 50,000 tons per month
Level 3   to detect supply rates of 10,000 tons per month
Level 4   to detect supply rates of 3,000 tons per month

b. *Composition of Monitoring Teams*
1. Self-monitoring with UN supervision (in accordance with agreed international standards)
2. International UN monitors
3. Teams drawn from neighbouring states and supervised by UN
4. UN team of experts "shadowing" local enforcement agencies

Self-monitoring

Option 1—Self-monitoring with spot inspections by UN specialists. This option envisages the neighbouring states supporting an embargo and assisting UN specialists by allowing spot inspections, i.e., lowest level of international involvement.

Advantages: 1. Puts onus on neighbouring and second tier countries;
                 2. Least expensive in manpower and infrastructure;
                 3. Wide ranging—not limited to pre-selected posts.

Disadvantages:
1. No guarantee states will respond in an even and fair manner;
2. Difficult to verify;
3. Even if supported at Governmental level, difficult to enforce everywhere;
4. Security of UN personnel may be problematic and costly to ensure.

UN International Monitors

Option 2—UN/international monitors at level 1 sites. This option envisages independent UN monitors at the major all-whether routes which are allegedly used to supply

Advantages:
1. Only nine sites to be staffed;
2. Legitimacy and credibility of independent monitors not influenced by local allegiances;
3. Staffing level of 30 per site = 270;
4. Small infrastructure needed.

Disadvantages:
1. Detection of heavy weapons which are die least desired materials;
2. Supplies could be transferred to minor routes;
3. Security would be required to protect teams;
4. Little effect on factions' ability to fight.

Option 3—As 2 but to supply rate of 50,000 tons per month. i.e., major and secondary routes

Advantages:
1. Sixty-two sites to be manned;
2. Staffing level of 62 x 30 = 1,860 (still modest in relation to the task);
3. Forces suppliers to more difficult and costly routes;

Disadvantages:
1. Supplies detected not the most desired;
2. Could be switched to other routes;
3. Little effect on factions' ability to fight,

Option 4–As 2 but to rate of 10.000 tons per month, i.e., auxiliary routes

Advantage:
1. Detection rate could affect the supply;
2. Forces suppliers to more difficult routes and consequently more costly.

Disadvantages:
1. Some 362 sites would need to be monitored;
2. Staffing level of 362 x 30 = 10,860;
3. Need for sophisticated command and control;
4. Large infrastructure.

Options 5—as 2 but to detection rate of 3.01 month, i.e., supplementary routes.
Advantages: 1. Best possibility that embargo would "bite".
Disadvantages: 1. Much higher vigilance and more diligent searching needed;
2. Consequently more human resources or more specialists than Option 4;
3. Large infrastructure to including holding areas, search areas, loading and unloading bays, parking and detention capability;
4. Disruption to local legitimate trade.

Monitoring from Neighbouring Countries Supported by UN

Option 6—This option envisages neighbouring states supplying members of the monitoring teams under the supervision of the UN to major routes

Advantages: 1. Involves neighbouring states;
2. Could build confidence;
3. Better chance of success of even-handed enforcement;
4. Capable of development;
5. Small UN international staff required.

Disadvantages: 1. Compatibility of members-Some members may notBe acceptable to others;
2. Security;
3. Traffic could switch to other minor routes;
4. Only the heavier weapons detected, which are not the most needed;

Option 7—as 6 but to rate of 50,000 tons per month

Option 8—as of 10.000 tons per month

Option 9—as rate of 3,000 tons per month

Advantages: 1. As Option 6;
2. Detection rate could affect conflict.

Disadvantages: 1. As Option 6;
2. Staffing level of 3,000 international staff.

UN Team "Shadowing" Local Enforcement Agencies

Option 10—This option envisages international team 66 "shadowing" local enforcement agencies with extended brief to enforce arms embargo

Advantages: 1. Access to local knowledge;
2. Knowledgeable local staff in place;
3. Availability of State resources, i.e., aircraft, transport, infrastructure;

4. Economical in human resources;
   5. Security supplied by local agencies;
   6. Confidence building;
   7. Verifiable;
   8. Local arms manufacturers and suppliers known to local authorities-end user certification.;
   9. Small number (100) international staff.

Disadvantages: 1. Local enforcement agencies not developed to equal standards in all neighbouring countries;
   2. Depends on willingness of local authorities to assist.

Calculation of Staff in Levels

Factors affecting level of staffing:
i. Support from host countries
ii. Level of detection required
iii. Budget
iv. Other considerations such as involvement of local population to "win them over".

Staffing Level Calculation—International Staff

	Level 1	Level 2	Level 3	Level 4
Total routes to be Monitored	9	62	362	362
HQ staff x 5 persons				
6. China + N/S Afg = 7 x 5	35	35	35	35
Post staff x 30	270	1,860	10,860	10,860
Total Staffing	305	1,895	10,895	10,895

Staffing Level Calculation—International Staff Supported by Member States

	Level 1	Level 2	Level 3	Level 4
Total routes to be Monitored	9	62	362	362
HQ staff x 5 persons				
6. China + N/S Afg = 7 x 5	35	35	35	35
Post staff x 8	72	496	2,896	2,896
Total Staffing	107	531	2,931	2,931

Summary of Options

The monitoring options are summarized as follows:

Option/Remarks
Self-Monitoring
1   Unlikely to be fair and verifiable
UN International Monitors
2
3   Little effect on conflict as sufficient arms could be delivered delivered through alternative routes
4
5   Needs over 10,000 international staff
Monitors from Neighbouring Countries Supervised by UN
6
7   Little effect on conflict as sufficient arms could be delivered through alternative routes
8
9   Needs 3,000 international staff
UN Teams "Shadowing" Local Enforcement Agencies
10   Needs 100 international staff and support of local authorities

Security

Operating in Afghanistan or the surrounding areas will necessitate large numbers of security personnel. Consideration should be given to locally hired security personnel. This, of course, means "buying into" local faction corni-nanders.

Observations

The effort and cost involved in policing the arms embargo effectively would be considerable if the task were to be undertaken by international personnel. A less costly arrangement would be to rely primarily on the national authorities already responsible for border control. They could be linked in the form of an international body chaired in the field by a United Nations coordinator, who might report to the Security Council and its sanctions committee through the Secretary-General.

Such an international body might comprise Afghanistan's six neighbours plus Russia mid the United States and any other States whose contributions may be considered useful. Together they might provide the personnel to staff offices to be set up in the six neighbouring countries to assist the national authorities in their task. Such an arrangement might help build confidence between the participating states concerning each one's observance of the embargo.

However, even in this case, the participating states would be required to dedicate significant additional resources for the purposes of the embargo.

The embargo would be more effective if it were also monitored inside Afghanistan. However, this would raise additional political and practical problems (e.g. security) which would need to be addressed at a later stage.

Conclusions

The paper reaches the following conclusions:
i. Arms are being supplied to the warring factions in Afghanistan by land, air and ferry port.
ii. There an estimated 362 such points of entry.
iii. Any such point of entry could accommodate the required supply rate of 3,000 tons of arms and ammunition per month to the conflict.
iv. To be effective all these points of entry would have to be staffed 24 hours per day and a very high standard of search required to detect these small quantities.
v. There are no technological "miracle" systems available to replace "on-the-spot" manual monitoring.
vi. An international staff of monitors of over 10,000 would be needed to monitor these routes, *or* An international staff of approximately 3,000 supported by neighbouring states.
vii. Each of the neighbouring states, second tier countries and the Taliban and the Northern Alliance have their own On-Site Border Control Posts and Enforcement Agencies.
viii. A relatively small staff (Central Coordination Headquarters d a cell in each sector totaling approximately 100) given the access to national agencies, border control, emigration, customs, drug enforcement authorities, etc. activities could give acceptable and verifiable monitoring results.
ix. The UN has a satisfactory experience of one such embargo in Yugoslavia.

Annex A-1. Routes to be Monitored

Any attempt to impose an embargo on Afghanistan will be complicated by the number and variety of transportation nodes that are likely to require constant international monitoring to prevent large-scale, organized smuggling from undermining the embargo. These nodes include:

(a) Airfields
(b) Ground Transport 1. Major highways
2. Minor roads
3. Trails

Airfields

Afghanistan has a number of major and secondary airfields that would require constant monitoring during embargo enforcement. Absent such enforcement efforts, routine cargo flights to these airfields could deliver some tens of thousand of metric tons of goods annually.

Six Afghan airfields probably can handle long-range, heavy transports such as the Il-76, capable of carrying up to 40 metric tons of cargo:

Airport	Runway length (metres)
Bagram Airbase	3,000
Herat	2,600
Kabul International	3,500
Qandahar	3,200
Shindand Airbase	2,700
Mazar-e Sharif	3,100
Total six major airfields	

Another seven smaller airfields can handle at least short-range, light-to-medium transport aircraft-such as the An-26, An-32, and C-130-which can carry up to 20 metric tons of cargo:

Airport	Runway length (metres)
Bamian	1,500
Feyzabad	1,800
Jalalabad	1,800
Konduz	2,000
Meymanch	2,000
Sheberghan	2,600
Taloqan	2,000
Total seven minor airfields	

Annex A-2. Ground Transportation with Neighbouring States

Afghanistan relies upon ground transportation from its neighbouring states to receive most of its imports, and monitoring this traffic would be critical to enforcing an embargo. Ground transportation links include:

Major Routes. Afghanistan's major highway links to the front-line states are sufficiently developed to handle up to 85,000 metric tons (mt) of cargo per day, although actual usage typically is considerably less. These major routes include:

Route	Capacity (mt/day)	No. of Lanes
Maza-r-i-Sharif–Termiz, Uzbekistan (port)	11,000	2
Jalalabad–Peshawar, Pakistan	21,000	2
Qandahar–Quetta, Pakistan	11,000	2
Herat–Kushka, Turkmenistan	17,000	2
Herat–Tayyebat, Iran	21,000	2
Delaran–Zabol, Iran	5,000	1
Total six major land routes		

Minor Routes. Any attempt to circumvent an embargo would be likely to place special emphasis on supply routes that avoid major highways in favour of more remote trails and mountain passes.

During the 1980s anti-Soviet jihad, Afghan insurgents were primarily resupplied by such routes, and factions would likely seek to re-stablish them to counteract any embargo.

Total forty minor routes. Tracks and Trails. Mountain passes—many part of old caravan trade routes that are located along the Afghan–Pakistan border from the Wakhan corridor in the north to Qandaliar Province in the south can be used to move goods into Afghanistan. At least six of these passes can accommodate motor vehicle traffic, while another 56 can handle pack animals during at least summer and early fall. Most of the northern and central passes are open only during summer and early fall, although the more southerly passes are typically open year round.

An undetermined number of trails—most of which likely can accommodate cargo trucks—also cross into Afghanistan through the and flatland along the country's southern and western borders. These remote regions are likely to require constant mortitoring to enforce ail embargo.

Cargo Caravans. Caravans following ancient trails through remote regions have been one of the primary means for moving cargo into and within Afghanistan, and would be likely to be used during attempts to circumvent an embargo. These caravans typically consist of:

Pack animals—including camels, horses, donkeys, and mules—have been the traditional means of transportation in Afghanistan for centuries, especially to cross rugged mountain terrain. Although each pack animal typically carries only several hundred kilograms of goods, organized caravans likely could deliver some 10-15,000 metric tons of cargo yearly.

Cargo trucks frequently are used when conditions allow, such as crossing flat-to-rolling desert terrain. Depending on the specific vehicles involved, each cargo truck would be likely to be capable of delivering some 2.5 to 5 metric tons of goods per trip, and organized truck convoys through remote regions would be likely to be used to deliver 20,000–30,000 metric tons of cargo annually.

Total 300 trails

Annex A-3. Amu Darya (River) Ports

Cargo destined for Afghanistan, especially commodities transiting through Central Asia, is also handled at three river ports located along the Amu Darya (river) on the northern Afghan border. Together, these ports would be likely to be able to receive up to 4,1 00 metric tons of cargo daily, although their actual usage is typically less. The ports are located at:

Jeyretan. Located across the river from Termiz, Uzbekistan, this port can handle up to 500-ton capacity barges and includes some 550 metres of quay frontage and 500 metres of improved riverbank for vessel berthing. The port receives bulk, containerized, and POL cargo. Maximum cargo transferred through the port is estimated at 2,800 mt/day, although the port typically handles only 500-600 mt/day.

Sher Khan. Located about 60 kms north of Konduz, opposite Tajikistan, the port, handles commercial goods and fuel shipments. Facilities include a 180 metre quay for vessel berthing and about 200 metres of riverbank. Maximum cargo transferable through the port is estimated at 1,000 mt/day.

Keleft. The smallest of the three port facilities, Keleft is located some 100 kms west of Jeyretan, opposite Turkmenistan. The port has a total of only some 175 metres of riverbank being space, and maximum cargo transferable through the port is estimated at only some 320 mt/day.

Total three ports

Annex A-4. Tabulation—Routes To Be Monitored

		Heavy Weapons		Heavy Weapons, Small Arms and Ammunition (tons/month)		
				50,000	10,000	3,000
Major routes	6	✓		✓	✓	✓
Major airfields	6			✓	✓	✓
Minor roads	40			✓	✓	✓
Minor airfields	7*			✓	✓	✓
Tracks and trails	300*				✓	✓
Ports	3	✓		✓	✓	✓
Total routes to be monitored		9		62	362	362

* As minor airfields can include prepared portions of roadways and tracks and trails can be opened or altered at short notice–these numbers are used for planning purposes only. Under estimates could be rectified by use of mobile patrols.

Military Structure and Equipment 129

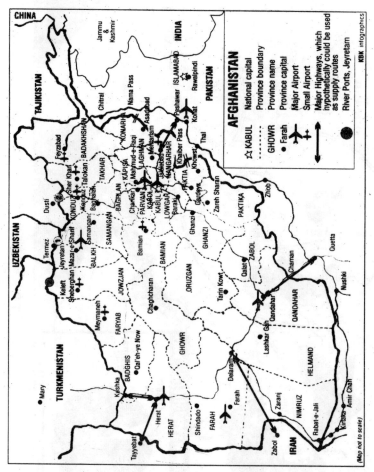

Map 5.1. (Annex B) Supply Routes

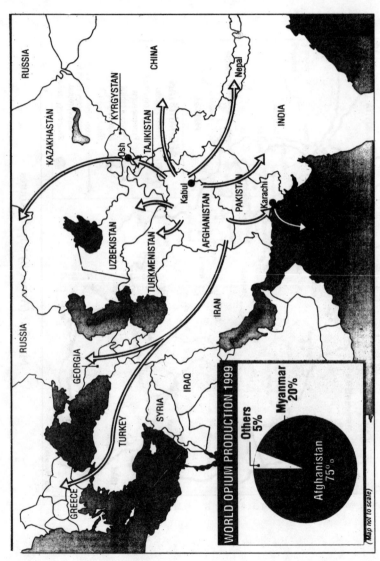

Map 6.1. The Afghan drug trail

6

The Drug Trail
For Everyone, a Milch Cow

How prolific is the drug trade in the Afghan–CARs region? A Russian diplomat stationed in one of the CARs, when posed this question, preferred to dramatize his answer: he pointedly filled up his cup of tea to the brim till it spilled on to the saucer. The drug trade was feeding a trade in illegal arms and in turn terrorism, he emphasized. Eighty per cent of drugs of the opium group flow out of Afghanistan. The destinations are Europe, the Americas and other parts of the world, "and unfortunately, also Russia. The number of drug addicts is increasing everywhere, but in Russia, the change is noticeable", he said. Other sources confirmed that large-scale trafficking in narcotics has been going on among all the three CARs bordering Afghanistan.

Although Russia's 201st Motorized Division is guarding Tajikistan's border with Afghanistan, this border, as he described it, is "most active". Quoting figures of the UN Drug Control Authority (UNDCA), he said that during 1998, 140 drug carriers were seized on this border, while 70 attempts were foiled.

The 201st Motorized Division comprises 80 per cent-plus of local personnel. It operates under a defence agreement to which other CARs are also parties. The civil war in Tajikistan that has brigands, drug-traffickers and armed mercenaries active, has necessitated the continuation of this arrangement, which other CARs see as an unwelcome, but necessary presence of a former colonizing power.

Tajikistan is widely believed to be a major transit route for narcotics from Afghanistan. Well-placed diplomatic sources say this is because the Russian force is under-armed and underpaid. They do not rule out local-level corruption and inefficiency.

Compounding the difficulty of border management is the mountainous terrain along the porous borders, especially during winters. Similarly, the Amu Darya, which forms the 157 kilometre riverine Uzbek border with Afghanistan, is difficult to manage for the nascent Uzbek force.

Well-placed sources say that the problem has lessened in 1999. Surveillance has been tightened and there have been more catches. These add up to US$30–35 million of drugs, both raw and processed, as compared to US$69 million in 1998. "New York's daily drug trade would be more than Tajikistan's annual turnover", an intelligence source said. However, these figures and trends stand thoroughly discredited by the latest UNDCA report that 4600 tonnes of drugs emanated from Afghanistan.

The flip side of the story, closer to reality, comes from none else than President Imomali Rakhmanov of Tajikistan himself, who shocked the world community in 1998 with his disclosure at a CARs conference on drugs. He said that right at that moment, 2000 tonnes of narcotics were ready to be transported across Central Asia for European and other markets.

Evidence suggests that the Afghan area that abuts Tajikistan, which is under control of the Northern Alliance, now renamed Islamic Front for Deliverance of Afghanistan (IFDA), may also be engaged in cultivating opium, totally contrary to its stated public position. Well-informed circles, both official and non-official, in Central Asia give credence to this phenomenon being the result of the Front's dwindling political and territorial support and also the paramount need for funds to feed people under its control, without collecting any tax or revenue. Pushed out of Kabul, the Front is in dire needs for arming its military operations against a more powerful Taliban force, which specializes in buying over the Front's garrison commanders.

The Front's leadership, particularly the military commander Ahmed Shah Masoud, is firmly opposed to the cultivation of opium, but he is perceived as unable to dictate terms to his local commanders at this stage and may leave enforcement of his anti-narcotics agenda to a later date. Responsible Central Asian and Afghan quarters maintain that this is only in Badakhshan and Kunduz. The area around Mazar-i-Sharif, which the alliance held till August 1998, also has poppy fields. But they argue that the quantity is nothing compared to what the Taliban are doing. International agencies confirm that the Taliban, who control 90 per cent of the territory, also have that much, and more, share in drug production and its illegal export.

A high level of corruption among the political leadership and the bureaucracy, both civil and military, in all the three CARs bordering Afghanistan, is suspected of turning a blind eye towards the drug trafficking. Even so, a strong political will to eliminate the drug menace exists among the CARs, stated publicly and repeatedly. Diplomats from missions of major powers and officials of international organizations confirm that some of it does get translated into coherent, concerted action. Presidents Islam Karimov of Uzbekistan, Imomali Rakhmanov of Tajikistan and Supermurat Niyazov of Turkmenistan are all committed to ending this menace. Officially, all the governments in Central Asia say that they are not allowing drugs to come into their countries. Neither do they agree that the narcotics pass through their territories to lucrative markets in Europe, the Americas and elsewhere in the world.

Officials of these countries admit in private that all the five CARs, especially the ones bordering Afghanistan—Turkmenistan, Uzbekistan and Tajikistan—are the recipients and transit points for the narcotics produced in Afghanistan. But they also declare their firm intention to stamp out drug traffic.

Borders among the CARs were basically administrative divisions and have become political only after the break-up of the Soviet Union. Border management was simply not required earlier. The drug menace is largely a post-Soviet phenomenon fed by the loosening of controls on the borders and the advent of disparate mujahideen groups who came to power in Afghanistan after the fall of Najibullah. The drug trail was established during the Afghan War as a source of income needed to run the resistance movement against the Soviets. The new rulers, competing for political supremacy, either continued with this lucrative phenomenon, or had no time to curb it.

Even so, the problem multiplied with the advent of the Taliban. The last three years have witnessed a phenomenal growth in the production and export of opium. While hardly any processing was done earlier and opium was sent out in raw, resin form, now a hundred laboratories, small in size but effective in output, have sprung up in areas under Taliban control.

The biggest outlet is Pakistan, which has an "open" border with Taliban-ruled areas. Significantly, all druglords of Afghanistan are based in Peshawar, living well, and operate through conduits in Afghan territory. Neither the authorities in Kabul nor in Islamabad are interested in really curbing this activity. Drugs flow out of this border with ready sea outlets among Pakistan's seaports. The hand of Pakistan's ISI in the lucrative narcotics trade is an accepted fact. In an otherwise mutually compatible relationship between the ISI and the Taliban, however, fissures have surfaced about sharing of earnings from narcotics. The ISI has generally allowed only 10 per cent of the total to the Taliban, retaining the rest to finance its activities, including training of a large number of Pakistanis, Afghans and Arab mercenaries of various nationalities. In the name of jihad it deploys these trained, armed and highly motivated mercenaries in various places from Kashmir to Chechnya and Kosovo. From an estimated US$432 million earned during 1998–99, it allowed the Taliban about US$45 million, according to intelligence sources, leading to serious protests by the Taliban leadership, which is having to run a cash-strapped Kabul administration.

The Afghan–Pak drug axis has also made India a transit point; and also drug money is being used to give a violent turn to the ethnocentric ambitions of some groups. According to officials of Indian intelligence agencies with whom we talked, Karachi–Kathmandu/Dhaka to eastern India seems to be one route. While Kathmandu is used for onward transmission to the Far East, of late the focus seems to be on eastern India. Drugs are converted into currency in Kathmandu by the Afghan–Pak drug barons. From there it is decided who gets how much.

The other route is reported to be the less guarded Pakistan–India border in Rajasthan, and different points on India's west coast. From Afghanistan, the focal point seems to be Peshawar in NWFP; and from there the consignments are dispatched by various modes of transport to either Karachi or Lahore. From then on it operates on demand–supply basis. Since a large number of politicians and personnel from the security agencies are involved, the movement is not difficult within Pakistan.

•

Traditionally, Taliban-controlled Afghanistan is known as one of the largest poppy-growing areas of the world. According to various estimates, this region produces a few thousand tons of poppy annually; and the area under this crop is increasing in recent years. Pakistani media reports say that the Taliban have imposed a strict ban on making of hashish, but have declined to ban poppy production from which opium and its derivative heroin are made.

The return of refugees to southern Afghanistan, the peace and security established by the Taliban and the relative rehabilitation of agriculture through project aid is in fact fuelling greater opium production. The Taliban leaders say that hashish is consumed by Afghans and is therefore anti-Islamic, but as opium is only exported to the West and there is no cash crop alternative for farmers to grow at present; there is no urgent need to ban poppy growing.[1]

In 1996, Afghanistan produced an estimated 2300 metric tons of opium, rivalling Myanmar as the world's largest producer of opium. Afghan dealers as well as those from neighbouring Pakistan, Iran and Turkmenistan buy the raw opium and then refine it into heroin in their own countries for onward export to the West. UN officials said that in 1996, Kandahar province (the headquarters of the Taliban) alone produced 120 metric tons of opium harvested from 3160 hectares of poppy field, a staggering increase compared to 1995 when only 79 metric tons was produced from 2400 hectares. The drug issue has

inadvertently become a means for the Taliban to blackmail the West. The Taliban makes no bones about the fact that the western demands to curb opium production would be implemented if the West and the UN recognize the Taliban government. Although all the Afghan warlords

---

[1] Ahmed Rashid, "The Year in Afghanistan 1997", *The Nation*, 7 January 1998.

use drug money to fund their military campaigns, none have been so brazen in declaring their intention on drug control as the Taliban.[2]

According to Mohammad Hashem, Afghan Chargé d'Affaires in Tashkent, who represents the Rabbani government, the Taliban regime is "forcing" opium cultivation in place of wheat and other crops. Most of the money earned from opium trade, he said, goes to "high levels" in Pakistan. Through business firms, "contacts" are also funded in Tajikistan, Uzbekistan and Turkmenistan.[3]

Nevertheless, from time to time, the Taliban indulge in public awareness campaigns to send politically correct signals to the people, donor countries and international agencies. An AP report from Kabul by Amir Shah reads:

Afghanistan's ruling Taliban Army used three military helicopters to drop thousands of pamphlets on the capital of Kabul warning against drugs.

Poppy cultivation and narcotics manufacturing is banned all over Afghanistan, the pamphlets warned. Those people who violate the ban will be punished according to Shariat (Islamic law).

The Taliban who rule 90 per cent of Afghanistan, including Kabul, launched a massive anti-narcotic campaign to mark international anti-narcotics day.

According to UN statistics, Afghanistan is the world's largest opium producer, the raw material used to make heroin.

Drugs destroy health, the pamphlet said. If you want good health and life, do not use drugs.

People, including children and old men, ran to gather the pamphlet. Some people, who could not read, looked around for someone to read it.

Religious leaders, parents and doctors all should play a role in fighting narcotics, the handout said.

The Taliban promised an all-out effort to fight drugs along with international agencies. However, earlier, the Taliban warned that they need greater assistance to help poor farmers find alternative crops to replace the lucrative opium crops.

Most of the opium grown in Afghanistan is grown in the 90 per cent of the country ruled by the Taliban. However, there is a large quantity grown in Northern Badakhshan province controlled by opposition leader Ahmed Shah Masoud.

Earlier this year, the Taliban destroyed dozens of laboratories where

---

[2]Ibid.
[3]Interview in Tashkent in August 1999.

opium was being converted into heroin for sale in Europe and North America.[4]

Orozbek Moldaliyev, Director, Bureau of International Trade and Security, a non-government organization based in Bishkek, Kyrgyzstan, charted on a map the 600 kilometre-plus drug trail that starts from Badakhshan in Afghanistan's north to Osh in Kyrgyzstan. According to *Nasha Gazeta* (1997), 85 per cent of Kyrgyzstan's illicit narcotics makes its way through Osh, whose image as a "second Mecca" is now being replaced by its reputation as a drug distribution centre. Osh also serves as the point for distribution of the consignments to other parts of the CIS and beyond. It is hilly terrain, but has a fairly good road to Kharokh, capital of Gornyi-Badakhshan in Kyrgyzstan, 417 kilometres from the Tajik–Afghan border. From Kharokh, it is another 200-odd kilometres to Margab. On this segment is the Kyzylhart mountain pass, 4280 metres high.[5]

At Saratosh on the Kyrgyz border, a border check-post deals basically with customs. Drug and population movements go virtually unhampered. The other check-post is at Kharamukh. That the annual catch was 200 kilograms in 1998 is strongly indicative of poor surveillance. "It shows that much is needed to be done", a senior official in Bishkek confessed, on monitoring of the movements and compiling data.

The people of Margab, roughing it out in the mountains, make a living by transporting drugs. Moldaliyev said pregnant women, old women and children are employed for drug trafficking, since the law is benign towards them.

There is a strong element of coercion on the population that is Ismaili by faith. Prince Karim Aga Khan, the religious head, has helped the community, sending humanitarian help and medical help. But there is no way they can keep off the drug trade.

This population, especially the young, is taking to drugs. The outcome of the schemes initiated by the Kyrgyz government to contain the drug menace is yet to be assessed. A UNDP-supported project, called Osh Deadlock Convention and Border Management Scheme, are also under way.

[4]AP wire service, 26 June 1999.
[5]Interview at Bishkek in July 1999.

Moldaliyev noted that before 1997, about 700 tonnes of opium came into Kyrgyzstan from Afghanistan. But during 1997–98, it went up to 3000 tonnes, ostensibly under changed political conditions in Afghanistan. There have been further "improvements" in that it now comes in processed form.

In Osh, one kilogram of heroin sells for US$8000. But in Moscow, transported through a network of routes, with bribes paid to "contacts" along the way, it can go up to US$170,000 per kilogram, said Moldaliyev.

Moldaliyev is among those who are convinced that the drug and arms trail is the same. But the governments in CARs reject the general perception. Emphasizing that "we are part of the international effort to curb narcotics movement", Turkmen Foreign Minister Boris Sikhmuradov insisted that "not a single bullet" had passed through the Turkmen territory for either side involved in the Afghan conflict. "What you hear is rumours and concoctions," he said in the course of an interview.[6]

In Tashkent, Kadirjon Yousopov, Head of the Asia and Africa Department at the Ministry of Foreign Affairs, said that the Uzbek–Afghan border is short. It runs along the Amu Darya and is easier to manage. But the quantity of drugs passing through this border "is not inconsiderable" mainly because borders of other neighbouring countries also converge, making monitoring of drug movement a major challenge.

There is "big punishment" for traffickers. None the less, some consignments do pass. But the official firmly said: "I do not agree that Uzbekistan is a major transit point."[7]

Afghanistan's border with Tajikistan has been "live" due to opposition groups fighting the Rakhmanov government, crossing the border at will. Save this exception, the CARs present a contrasting situation: their borders are "peaceful", officially speaking, even as contraband goods move, as it happens along international borders anywhere in the world. For instance, Yousopov emphasized that there was "no border problem" in that there are no open hostilities. In Ashkabad, Sikhmuradov also emphasized the point about the border with Afghanistan being "peaceful".

[6] Interview in Ashkabad on 28 July 1999.
[7] Interview in Tashkent in August 1999.

Even so, the present state of all the CARs borders is precarious, allowing transit for contraband drugs and other items to other parts of Asia and Europe. A US diplomat said he believed that the destination of much of the contraband drugs flowing out of Afghanistan through Central Asia was Europe.

Border management in Uzbekistan, Yousopov said, was not a question confined to Afghanistan. There is a 2000 kilometre border with Kazakhstan to guard and customs offices were established only recently.

Most affected by drug trafficking from Afghanistan is the Ferghana Valley, an area formed by intersecting territories of Kyrgyzstan, Tajikistan and Uzbekistan. *Interfax* comments that "Unfortunately, the Ferghana Valley's importance as a centre of religious thought and transit has been overshadowed by its prime importance for drug trafficking from Afghanistan to Russia and Western Europe via Tajikistan."[8] The proceedings of a Central Asian Conference on Regional Cooperation, UNDP, Bishkek, 1995, placed on record:

> In opening up new surface transportation routes, Central Asian officials often compete with the region's narcotics traffickers, who have revived the Great Silk Route as a new drug route, becoming one of the new examples of coordinated inter-ethnic cooperation. The war in Tajikistan is a tragic example of problems created by the region's organized criminal elements, as many observers believe that competition between criminal clans in establishing control over the supply and trafficking of illicit drugs and arms is a serious obstacle to the peaceful resolution of the conflict. Although Central Asia has traditionally been a drug producing region, increasing corruption and drug trafficking have reached unprecedented dimensions, particularly in the Ferghana Valley.

In her paper "The Challenge of Regional Cooperation in Central Asia", written for the United States Institute of Peace, Anara Tabyshalieva, Director, Institute of Regional Studies, Bishkek, comments:

> At present, large numbers of people all across Central Asia are involved in the trafficking and production of illicit narcotics, and state structures seem helpless in preventing this kind of *regional cooperation* and *ethnic accord*.

[8]*Interfax*, 2 April 1997.

During severe downturns in the region's economies, more and more people turn to growing poppies and cannabis. The growing powers of the "Mafia network" mean that criminals are increasing their influence in political and economic decision-making throughout the region. The accumulation of revenue and weapons from the operations of these criminal networks could be a serious threat to ethnic stability in the Ferghana Valley.

Tabyshalieva points to "virtual anarchy in Tajikistan and Afghanistan stemming from the thriving narcotics trade" while speaking of the threat not only to the Ferghana Valley, but the whole Central Asian region. To give an idea about the economics of drugs, it may be noted that drug trafficking fetches the drug mafia double of Tajikistan's official budget!

The UN sanctions on the Taliban, imposed on 14 November 1999, should mean that Kabul will face greater economic hardship and would need to take greater recourse to drug trafficking. The sanctions will show gaping leaks unless the drug routes are systematically sealed, a tall order. The effectiveness and longevity of the UN sanctions will be determined by the extent to which they can curb trafficking of narcotics.

There are reports that under the garb of UN observers, the US may station its operatives in Peshawar for sealing the Afghan–Pak border. Considering the difficult terrain, the entrenched nature of trafficking with obvious local support, and the fortunes and livelihoods at stake, they have a tough task ahead.

On the other hand, Iran, which has no love lost for the Taliban, has opened its trade channels on Afghanistan's western borders. This makes good business sense and also speaks for Islamic solidarity against the American "satan". Although the Iran–Afghanistan pact is for border trade, there is little doubt that over a period this will convert into a lucrative drug trail.

Equally important is Afghanistan's border with Turkmenistan. The new situation may well facilitate an increase in drug movement, with a trade pact already in place thanks to cordial relations between Kabul and a "neutral" Ashkabad.

Whatever the efficacy of the UN sanctions, drugs and drug money, it can safely be assumed, will fuel Afghan turmoil and the resultant political instability in the region.

7

Pipelines
Pipe-dreams?

"Just Ahmed is enough," he said politely. I got the message: No more personal details.

Tall and burly, this Afghan in his mid-40s was a picture of courtesy. I had watched him come and go in the hotel's posh restaurant, always in time for his lunch and dinner. He was always dressed for business: white shirt, dark trousers and a tie. His cell-phone kept incessantly ringing. A frequent visitor to Ashkabad, he seemed to know many people, whom he met with warmth.

The black eye patch covering one eye gave him the right aura of enigma, his bald pate enhancing it. Three fingers of his right hand seemed to have been permanently crushed. His handshake was not particularly warm: a mere formality.

His lost eye? "Lost it in Kabul in 1980 during the fighting. I am a Mujahideen turned businessman."

What was his nature of business that frequently brought him to Ashkabad? He said, "I am buying and selling petroleum and gas."

It had been hinted to me earlier that he was "an important man". I knew later that he is the key man in the consortium that is trying to build the gas pipeline from Turkmenistan to Pakistan through troubled Afghanistan. He is known to be in close touch with Pakistani and Turkmen leaders and officials, not to speak of his own Taliban authorities.

"What is happening to the gas pipeline? Unocal has withdrawn", I asked.

"Unocal goes, others will come in. There is a lot of money to be made", he said matter-of-factly.

"How are the Taliban doing? One hears they have problems among them?"

"The Taliban are settling down. No, they have no problems among themselves. They are all young. Their problem is that they have never governed. But they are dedicated.

"Mullah Umar takes decisions in Kandahar. His orders are implemented. Mullah Rabbani is the *de facto* President", he volunteered.

He was beginning to look at his watch. Time was up in this short encounter. I ventured a last question: "The media outside is talking about the Taliban's treatment of women."

Looking away, he shrugged his broad shoulders and extended his arm for a final good-bye, merely saying: "You know, the Americans are bloody-minded."

Meanwhile media reports say that Greece-based Consolidated Construction Company will explore the Herat region bordering Iran for oil and gas. Disclosing this, Khudai Noor Mandarkhel, a senior advisor to the minister of mines said that a draft contract has also been submitted by the company. This was reported to be a follow-up to the visit of the Taliban Minister of Mines and Industries to Athens in early 1999. If true, a new dimension will be added to the oil politics of the region.

Surreptitiously also, a gas pipeline is being constructed on Afghan territory, a part having already been laid on the Pakistan–Afghanistan section. There is documentary evidence that a Chinese construction company, Overland, has been engaged in executing the project. The entire thing is under wraps. "It will shock the world when it becomes public. There will be a surprise announcement this December", a source claiming to be in touch with the consortium disclosed. There is, however, no confirmation of this claim.

•

Land-locked Central Asia, a region that the world almost forgot until the demise of the Soviet Union, is relatively underdeveloped. With a little more than 100 million population and an average per capita income of less than $200 per annum, it had no meaningful economic activity, other than defence-related industries.

Central Asia has vast, largely untapped natural resources, oil and gas found in Turkmenistan and oil find in Kazakhstan being prominent. Kazakhstan is able to deal fairly well with its two giant neighbours, the Russian Federation and China. But Turkmenistan by the Caspian Sea has problem exporting its gas and oil. Turkmenistan has reserves of gas estimated at anything between 1.7 and three trillion cubic metres. It is the world's second largest reserve, or at least the third largest.

In terms of proven hydrocarbon reserves Central Asia's potential is at best equivalent to that of Qatar, Oman and the UAE put together (see Table 7.1). According to *International Petroleum Encyclopedia* estimates, the proven oil reserves of the CARs constitute less than 4 per cent of the Middle East reserves and less than one per cent of the global reserves. However, the proven natural gas reserves of CARs are more than 50 per cent as compared to the Middle East and constitute about 20 per cent of the global natural gas reserves. Since gas is considered to be the fuel of the future, this gives the CARs a certain amount of strategic importance.

For that matter, Iran has the biggest natural gas deposits, estimated to be 810 billion cu ft and has also a better infrastructure for energy exports than that of the CARs. But for Iran's "rogue" state status in the West's world-view, any day global energy merchants would prefer dealing with Tehran to the CARs.

Table 7.1. Oil and Gas Reserves in CARs

Country	Proven Oil Reserves (million b/d)	Oil Production in 1997 (b/d)	Natural Gas Reserves (bcf)
Turkmenistan	546	93,000	101
Uzbekistan	300	113,000	84
Kazakhstan	5417	471,000	65
Kyrgyzstan	40	1,000	200
Tajikistan	12	1,000	530

Source: International Petroleum Encyclopedia 1998 (Okhlahoma, USA), p. 292.

The CARs can at best produce about 6–7 million barrels of oil daily, an estimate on the far higher side, and this can be achieved only with huge investments. But excess western capital is not available for investment in the land-locked CARs. With Afghanistan, Iran and to a lesser degree China, which surround Central Asia, being looked upon with suspicion by the West, free flow of western capital is not coming as it was anticipated in 1996–early 1997.

In addition, the existing oil producers are not interested in new entrants undercutting their market. Having undertaken massive developmental projects and evolved a number of welfare schemes, they already have enough problems from depressed market conditions and resultantly declining oil revenues. For instance, the swing producer, as Saudi Arabia is called in the international oil market, has been running up huge budget deficits, threatening the elaborate social welfare system it has built over the years. Iran, another major producer in the Persian Gulf, is desperately looking for greater revenues to reconstruct its war-torn economy. The troubles vexing Nigeria and Indonesia are well known.

The euphoria built around the CARs' hydrocarbons being an alternative to the Persian Gulf, it would appear, seems misplaced. The unsettled conditions in Afghanistan and Pakistan have, in addition, taken the excitement out of the proposition of MNCs to a pipeline across Afghanistan to Pakistan and later to India to export natural gas from the CARs. With thousands of small-arms available in and around Afghanistan, anybody can blow up a section of the pipeline and play havoc with the whole grid.

According to one commentator, "on a much more basic level, it would be difficult to imagine that international investors would bring billions of dollars into a project going through cruise missile attacks, to say nothing of the fighting between Taliban and its opponents—a beleaguered Northern Alliance of factions allegedly getting help from Iran and Russia." Another observer points out that in the ongoing Sunni–Shia rivalry in Pakistan, where each sect is aligned to an external power and both parties are armed to the teeth, anyone can blow up the pipeline passing through Pakistan.

Therefore, until law and order is restored no MNC will venture any large-scale investment. A day after US cruise missiles hammered Khost terrorist training camps in Afghanistan, an announcement by Unocal, the US oil giant, said on 21 August 1998:

Unocal will only participate in construction of the proposed Central Asian Gas pipeline when and if Afghanistan achieves peace and stability necessary to obtain financing from international lending agencies for this project and an established government is recognized by the UN and the US.

Unocal has even closed down its office in Ashkabad. Although work on this $2.5 billion project has not begun, Unocal is reported to have invested US$10 million in preparing feasibility reports, etc. In fact in November 1997, Unocal launched a US$900,000 programme run by the University of Nebraska at Omaha to train 137 Afghan men, mostly from the Taliban, in pipeline laying and maintenance. In addition, the Clinton administration backed this project to the hilt as that would have freed the CARs from dependence on Russia for exporting their natural gas, and avoided alternative routes across Iran to bring badly needed energy to Pakistan and India.

Umer Farooq, a leading Pakistani commentator, observes:

The consortium to lay 915 miles gas pipeline from Daulatabad (Turkmenistan) oil field up to Multan (in Pakistan) was formed in November 1997. The major shareholders in the consortium called Central Asian Gas Pipeline include:

Delta Oil Company of Saudi Arabia	15 per cent shares;
Government of Turkmenistan	7 per cent shares;
Indonesian Petroleum Limited	6.5 per cent shares;
Itochu Oil Exploration Company	5 per cent shares;
Crescent Group of Pakistan	3.5 per cent shares;
Unocal of the US, which withdrew from the project in 1998	47.5 per cent of shares

Official sources (in Islamabad) said that Bridas (Argentina) may get some percentage of left over share of Unocal.

The route of the Pakistan–Turkmenistan pipeline has been roughly identified. Officials told *The Nation* that it would pass through those areas of Afghanistan, which are under the control of Taliban Administration. The tribes from whose areas the gas pipeline will pass through will be paid royalties for the project, said an official.[1]

---

[1] *The Nation*, 7 February 1999.

Economically, Pakistan is going through dire straits, its woes worsened by economic sanctions by the US and its western allies in the wake of the May 1998 nuclear explosions by Pakistan. With a low credit rating and low recovery forecasts in the immediate future by the international credit rating agencies, the energy demand is unlikely to go up in the next 5–10 years in Pakistan. The Indo–Pak clashes in Kargil in mid-1999 further reduced the chances of Pakistan allowing its territory being used for energy exports to India. Therefore, the intended pipeline from Turkmenistan mainly for Pakistan and India has become neither economically viable nor politically feasible.

Seeking to revive the pipeline project, officials of Turkmenistan, Pakistan and Taliban held a tripartite meeting in April 1999. A joint declaration issued at the end of the meeting said, "Keeping in view the national interest of Afghan people, the participants of the Tripartite meeting have agreed that the Turkmenistan–Pakistan pipeline will have an immediate positive impact on the current situation 'on Afghanistan." Turkmen Foreign Minister, Boris Sikhmuradov, during his visit to Islamabad in January 1999, had extensive discussions with Pakistan's Petroleum Minister, Chaudhry Nisar Ali Khan, about reviving the project. An announcement at the end of the talks said, "The two sides in their talks about gas pipeline termed the project as a symbol of close Pakistan–Turkmenistan cooperation and the foundation on which future economic relations between the two countries will flourish." Sikhmuradov met representatives of the Taliban. It was announced later that experts of Pakistan, Turkmenistan and representatives of Taliban would meet in Islamabad in due course to work out modalities of commencing work on the project.

Resolved to carry on with the pipeline, Turkmenistan has shown keen interest in working closely with Pakistan for resolution of the Afghan conflict. During Sikhmuradov's meetings in Islamabad, the two countries agreed that the restoration of durable peace in Afghanistan would open up enormous possibilities and commercial cooperation between Pakistan and Turkmenistan. The two sides agreed on five points.

— The restoration of peace in Afghanistan was of utmost importance.

— Outside interference and the supply of arms to different factions in Afghanistan should be stopped completely.
— Necessary conditions should be created to facilitate the Afghans to decide among themselves a formula for durable peace. In this context meaningful dialogue should be promoted between groups which control territory in Afghanistan.
— Six-plus-two should play a supporting role towards this end.
— Pakistan, Turkmenistan and other neighbouring countries should work together to facilitate the realization of these objectives by promoting intra-Afghanistan dialogue and by sending joint missions to Afghanistan.[2]

It is thus obvious that the future of the ambitious pipeline project hangs on resolution of the Afghan conflict and cessation of any threat to the pipeline.

According to Ashkabad's diplomatic corps, Turkmenistan's main problem is that its economic progress is slower than President Supermurat Niyazov's spending spree. He does spend on the country's development and is driven by a vision of a bright future, but he also spends lavishly on building a personality cult around himself. He is running an isolationist regime that has declared neutrality as the cornerstone of its foreign policy.[3]

Niyazov's statues are fast replacing those of Lenin. He built during 1998–99, a Neutrality Tower, a monument to symbolize his country's foreign policy, bang opposite the presidential office and Parliament. On top of the tower is his statue, believed to be gold-plated. These and such other extravaganza, critics say, have placed the Turkmen economy on the brink.

"The next twelve months (till summer 2000) are going to be crucial", said a European entrepreneur involved in the gas-oil sector. If adequate oil and gas are not exported, whatever the route, "the Turkmen bubble will burst."[4]

The Turkmens have also been slow in exploiting what they already have. Oil output in mid-1999, for instance, was just 300,000–400,000 barrels daily, much less than in the Soviet era, when a million barrels was normal.

[2]Ibid.
[3]Interviews with diplomats in Ashkabad in August 1999.
[4]Ibid.

A number of gas and oil pipelines are on the anvil, ranging from dreams and drawing boards to actual construction. Only one, that connects the gas field on the Caspian Sea to Iran, has been completed. It is meant to feed Iran's domestic market.

There could be another and more pipelines taking Turkmen gas to Bandar Abbas for exports across the world. But the US has persisted in opposing any such project because of its antipathy to the clergy that rules Iran.

Turkmenistan is feverishly working to get other pipeline projects, including one that takes the gas via Turkey to Europe and another that takes it across Central Asia and China to Japan. But almost all of them have yet to take off.

A highly placed US official stationed in one of the CAR capitals, said that the "southern route" was as good as over and was most impracticable, given the political uncertainties in Afghanistan.[5]

The official was at a loss why Niyazov and his government were still stuck on this project and said that he had sought to dissuade them. He thought the Turkmen were "dangling carrots" to prospective investors. He was certain that no American multinational could convince its shareholders on the advisability of the company being involved in a project "that is going to make the Taliban prosperous". This is in the context of the Taliban's poor human rights track record and abominable treatment of women.[6]

At one stage, the Unocal "interest" along with that of Delta, a Saudi firm supposed to be owned by Prince Turki al-Faisal, the powerful intelligence chief of Saudi Arabia, and Pakistan's Fauji Foundation, was supposed to be guiding the common interest of all the three nations in Afghanistan.

The Unocal withdrawal has changed things, though its return is not being ruled out. More so, because its rival Bridas, an Argentine firm, which went to court alleging discrimination by the Turkmen authorities at the behest of Unocal, is trying to return. The Turkmen are trying to woo others, including Mobil and Exxon.

But the last word on the pipeline project has yet to come. A European hand on the job on the Caspian Sea said: "It is *when*,

[5] Interview in August 1999.
[6] Ibid.

not *if,* the project would take off through Afghanistan." It is possible, may be, over a long period. Yet, many doubt whether Turkmenistan's gambit to open the southern route will succeed.

The unlikelihood of any international capital flowing in for the Turkmenistan–Afghanistan–Pakistan pipeline in the immediate future has prompted Turkmenistan to explore alternative routes/markets vigorously. Reports in the international media indicate that Turkey is being considered as an alternative. A senior Turkish official said that with Pakistani involvement with the Taliban being so extensive, the question of peace returning to Kabul just does not arise. Others are not willing to accept Taliban–Pakistan domination, therefore the pipeline idea will fall through.[7]

Cynics also point out that the Taliban make more money through narcotics trade than they can make through transit fees of the Turkmenistan–Pakistan pipeline. The development of the region that will accompany the setting up of the pipeline may also have an adverse impact on the whole socio-economic framework, which may not be to the Taliban's liking. Neither the Pakistani elite nor the Taliban view economic development as a priority. Therefore, the urgency for setting up the pipeline is for Turkmenistan and not for the other two.

[7]Ibid.

Fig. 8.1. Ruined future of a new generation of Afghanistan

8

Pakistan
A Grandiose Agenda

Pakistan's agenda in Afghanistan has four aspects:
— quest for leadership of the Islamic world, particularly in competition with Shi'ite Iran;
— settlement of the Durand Line in its favour;
— benefit from opening the warm waters of the Arabian Sea to the land-locked CARs;
— acquiring strategic depth *vis-à-vis* its arch-enemy India by ensuring a surrogate Afghanistan.

Any hope of a resolution of the Afghan conflict received a serious setback when the Nawaz Sharif government in Pakistan was toppled in a bloodless coup. General Pervez Musharraf, Army Chief and new Chief Executive, has made it amply clear that he is determined to continue, if nothing else, Sharif's Afghanistan policy. It is well known that Musharraf and his Deputy Chief of Defence Staff, Lt Gen Abdul Aziz are ex-ISI men and Taliban sympathizers. Many observers feel that the duo, as also a majority of commanders of Pakistan Army have furthered the process of their force's "Talibanization".

While he sent clear signals right from the day he took power, Musharraf told Reuter TV in Islamabad on 7 December 1999 that there would be "no real change" in Pakistan's Afghanistan policy. He also repeated the known Pakistan line about the Taliban being the masters of their land, who ought to be recognized by the world community, and that surrender of Osama bin Laden was a matter between the US and the Taliban rulers. Musharraf also contended that Pakistan was not helping the Taliban as "we do not have the resources". At the same time, he alleged inhuman acts by Ahmed Shah Masoud's forces.

•

Well past fifty years of its creation as a separate nation from British India, a section of the Pakistani elite still entertain the notion that they are the legitimate inheritors of the Mughal empire that ruled large parts of the Indian subcontinent in the medieval era. They attempted to demonstrate this by use of force from time to time—1947–48, 1965 and 1971. On the first two occasions they tried to annex territory to expand Pakistan eastward. The rout in 1971 finally put paid to any notions of their predominance in the Indian subcontinent. A section of the Pakistani elite even started talking in terms of having to live in the shadow of a big power, India.

Refusing to accept this big power–small power syndrome in the subcontinental context, the articulation then commenced that they are part of the Islamic world/South-West Asia more than they are part of South Asia. The Islamic linkages now became almost an obsession.

Pakistan's perception that they should be automatic choice for leadership of the Islamic world rests on four factors.

— They are a nuclear weapon power.
— They have the third-largest population of Muslims (after Indonesia and India) and smaller states like Iran in the 1960s wanted to form a confederation with it.
— They have a standing army of half a million men. For some time they even went and offered protection to the custodian of the holy places of Islam, the Saudi royal family.
— They have a pool of trained manpower which can meet the requirements of the Islamic world.

The main attractions for being a predominating part of the Islamic world were:

— The oil-rich Arab countries, flush with petrodollars, were looking for investment opportunities. The elite in Islamabad

thought that Pakistan could be made into an important destination, and accelerate the nation's pace of economic development.
— The oil-rich sheikhdoms were short of trained manpower to run their modernization process. Pakistan had a pool of trained manpower which could find gainful employment.
— Pakistan then had more than 500,000-strong trained armed forces. As in the past, they could be deployed to put down trouble facing the sheikhdoms.
— En bloc backing for itself in its running feud with India.

Z.A. Bhutto, then Prime Minister, by presenting the nuclear weapon in civilizational terms, was able to convince the Islamic world's elite that the Pakistani quest for the "Islamic bomb", if it materialized, would alter the balance of power in favour of Arabs in the ongoing Arab–Israeli dispute. Bhutto bringing money in suitcases by special Pakistan Air Force aircraft is now part of the history of Pakistan's clandestine nuclear programme.[1]

However, the success of the Islamic revolution in Iran in February 1979 and the emergence of the charismatic leadership of Ayatollah Khomeini on the scene for a while dampened the Pakistani ambitions. It also created new fissures in the Islamic world, especially with the leadership of Saudi Arabia.

•

In December 1979 the Soviet Union invaded Afghanistan, an immediate neighbour of Pakistan. In the cold war political framework this unexpected development was perceived by the great powers as a chance of a lifetime to bleed the communists. The Saudi monarchy, disturbed by the emergence of Ayatollah Khomeini on the Islamic world's map, looked upon this as an opportunity to set the record right.

With the Afghan refugees pouring into Pakistan and Iran, the ruling elite in Pakistan looked upon this as a unique opportunity to demonstrate their Islamic leadership mettle. Overnight, General Ziaul Haq started organizing the refugees to fight the Red Army.

[1] See Sreedhar, *Pakistan Bomb: A Documentary Study* (New Delhi, 1988), pp. 167–98.

To mobilize the Afghan refugees, Zia and his strategists (according to Pakistani commentators, it was the US CIA) chose to tap into the Afghan religious sentiment and militarize it. According to an ISI official, "in the beginning religious terminology and symbolism was used to mobilize people against the Russians". He also refers to the fact that many Afghan leaders grew a beard, in order to establish their legitimacy, only after the "jihad" started. In fact, when the various Afghan refugees were being organized into a combined forces in 1980, Ziaul Haq was the first to use the word mujahideen at a press conference. He is reported to have chided the media for calling them refugees; and called them mujahideen waging a jihad against atheists.

This enabled General Zia to provide the much-needed ideological framework to launch the war from Pakistani soil. He successfully projected the impression that Pakistan was not participating in the cold war politics as a US ally; but as the land of the pure, Pakistan was fighting the infidels. To the regional environment already surcharged with the success of the Islamic Revolution in Iran, this reasoning looked quite acceptable.

By calling these refugees mujahideen (holy warriors) and their fight a jihad against the Red Army, Zia gave a clever twist to the subsequent developments. The US and Saudi support in terms of money, arms and mobilizing people made things easy for Zia to gain absolute control over the various Afghan tribal chieftains. Some estimates place these donations at about US$50,000 a day on an average from 1980 to 1987. This was in addition to military and economic aid from the West, especially the US.[2]

At the end of the war, Pakistan was able to build an effective infrastructure to train and arm these mujahideen. Varying estimates of the number of training institutions/centres were put out by various people: the commonly accepted figure is 80. In addition, a number of outfits were created in different parts of Afghanistan/Pakistan/Pak-occupied Kashmir to recruit cadres.

In no time, however, these mujahideen proved to be just good at hit-and-run attacks on the Red Army, and indulging in acts of terrorism and violence against innocent civilian population or patrols of the law enforcement agencies. Though the Red Army

[2]See Sreedhar and Mahendra Ved, *Afghan Turmoil: Changing Equations* (New Delhi, 1999).

did suffer casualties, they were not deterred enough to leave Afghanistan. Zia, a military man, was well aware that some two months of military training was inadequate to fight a professional army. Even though the quality of weapon systems made available to the so-called mujahideen made a quantum jump, they proved ineffective.

By the second half of the 1980s, the world started witnessing far greater professionalism in the mujahideen's campaign. Their Jalalabad offensive in the late 1980s is one example. It was then suspected that Pakistani armed forces in the garb of mujahideen were participating in the Afghan war. General Zia, who had witnessed Mukti Bahini exploits in the Indo–Pak war of 1971, tried to superimpose that model on Afghanistan. Pakistani military personnel who were initially in logistics and support role, started taking part in the guise of mujahideen. There being little noticeable difference in physical features between Afghans and Pakistani Pathans the fact could be easily covered up. In addition, induction of professional soldiers allowed the government to have a firm control over these outfits, both physically and financially.

However, there was one extraordinary development, perhaps not anticipated by the creators of the mujahideen. Since fighting the Red Army was supposed to be for an Islamic cause, volunteers from the Islamic world started landing in Pakistan. In the process dissident movements in the Islamic world found safe haven in Pakistan. By the mid-1990s mercenary forces operating from Pakistani soil indulged in acts of violence and terrorism even in far-off places like Egypt, Algeria and Sudan. Such acts made them pariahs in the international community.[3]

•

The Red Army's withdrawal in 1989, and the subsequent permutations and combinations tried by Pakistan to install a surrogate regime in Kabul, demonstrated the manipulation of the Afghan

---

[3]By mid-1996 reports started appearing in the international media that these Afghanistan-trained Arab militants were responsible for acts of violence in France, Yemen and Sudan. The Egyptian security forces claimed that they unearthed a plot to assassinate President Hosni Mubarak by Afghan-trained Arab mercenaries.

tribal leadership. This public demonstration of its clout over Afghan leaders was to demonstrate to the neighbourhood, especially India and Iran, that the pressure point they had on Islamabad through Kabul had ceased to be. Also Islamabad conveyed subtly to the rest of the Islamic world that it was in the process of incorporating Afghanistan into Pakistan. There were even subtle hints from the Pakistani leadership that a confederation of Pakistan and Afghanistan was in the offing. The notional boundary between the two countries, the Durand Line, became virtually non-existent, with free flow of men and material across the line.

The Soviet withdrawal from Afghanistan was projected as a victory of the mujahideen, and the sudden disintegration of the Soviet Union as a demonstration of how aggressors on Islam would be punished. According to one Pakistani commentator, these mujahideen started believing that they had "taken on a superpower, humiliated it and torn it apart".[4]

Even so, Pakistan's failure to install an effective government in Kabul even five years after the Soviet withdrawal generated doubts about Islamabad's capabilities to end the civil war in Afghanistan. Simultaneously, the inter-Afghan warlords' rivalry was becoming an embarrassment. At this juncture, Maj Gen Naseerullah Babar, the Pashtun Interior Minister in Benazir Bhutto's cabinet, gave a further twist to the mujahideen concept, by bringing in the Taliban movement through the students from madrasas. He makes no secret that he even trained the Taliban.[5]

The Taliban, etymologically, are supposed to be students receiving religious training based on the Quran and the Hadith, usually learned by youngsters in the predominantly rural-based and privately run madrasas on the Pak–Afghan border. These madrasas have strong linkages with Jamiat-i-Ulema-Islami (JUI), which is ideologically linked with the Deobandi school of Islam in India.

Meanwhile the emergence of the Central Asian Republics, and the international scramble for their hydrocarbon reserves, added a new dimension. The CARs being land-locked, Pakistan vied with Iran to provide them with sea outlets to export hydrocarbons.

[4] Zaigham Khan, "Inside the Mind of Holy Warrior", *The Herald*, July 1999, pp. 61–2.
[5] Cited by Khalid Mahmud, "Dealing with Taliban", *The News*, 7 September 1998.

While Iran offered them facilities across the table, peace in Afghanistan became a prerequisite for Pakistan to do so.

Hence, Naseerullah Babar's brain wave of creating a new movement, Taliban, with covert support from Pakistan, was accelerated. The JUI leader Maulana Fazlur Rehman, hitherto a lightweight in Pakistani politics, was suddenly made chairman of the National Assembly's Committee on Foreign Relations. This resulted in the Taliban acquiring a respectable spokesman to articulate their cause the world over and mobilize the needed resources. Simultaneously, from capturing Kandahar in October 1994 to the capture of Kabul in September 1996, the Taliban got a walk over, fighting only a few minor skirmishes. While fighting a serious battle, for instance for the capture of Kabul in July–August 1996, the Taliban's limitations were exposed.

In September 1996, about 2000 men of the Pakistan Army in the garb of Taliban captured Kabul. Similarly, at the time of the capture of Mazar-i-Sharif in August 1998, 3000 Pakistani troops participated in the operation.[6] Maj Gen (retd) Yashwant Dewa, a distinguished officer of the Indian Army who served in Kabul as military attaché in the 1970s, scoffs at the claim that madrasa-trained students could fight a professional army. If the strategy and tactics adopted by the Taliban in capturing Kabul were due to their training in madrasas, he declares, Pakistan should close down its military training establishment and send its armed forces personnel to these madrasas: "It is downright silly to say that madrasas on the Pak–Afghan border teach how to drive a tank or fly a MiG aircraft."

For the first time, after the Mazar-i-Sharif fiasco in May 1997 the Northern Alliance captured a large number of Pakistani PoWs. Initially the Government of Pakistan denied having any Pakistanis in Afghanistan. But when the Northern Alliance paraded these PoWs before the international media, Islamabad made a subtle shift by avowing that they were not officially sent into Afghanistan. In September 1997, the Northern Alliance submitted a

---

[6] A diplomat from one of Afghanistan's neighbouring countries emphatically told us that after the May 1997 fiasco, Pakistani soldiers in Kabul were openly cursing the Taliban's incompetence. The Pakistanis were talking openly of launching another attack at an appropriate time, he said.

158 Afghan Buzkashi

Table 8.1. Details of POWs Captured by the Northern Alliance in September 1997

A. Provinces/Regions from which the PoWs hailed	
Punjab	29
Sind	20
NWFP/Baluchistan	99
Others	
Jordan	1
Bangladesh	1
Saudi Arabia	1
POK	1
B. Age Group	
0–20 years	19
21–30 years	125
31–40 years	4
Over 40 years	4
C. Marital Status	
Married	42
Single	110
D. Occupation	
Students from madrasa	91
High School/College Students	13
Skilled workers	23
Unskilled workers	7
Store keepers	6
Unemployed youth	7
Armed Forces	1
Preachers	2
Not Available	2
E. Port of Entry into Afghanistan	
Kandahar	116
Tourkham	7
Khost	25
Bagram	1
Not Reported	3

Chart 8.1. Details of Pakistan Army Officers who Allegedly Fought in Afghanistan

Name	R/o	Remarks*
Col. Salim	Swat	ex-ISI; now retired (Rawalpindi)
Capt Zafar ul Haq	Mandi, Bahauddin, Punjab	ISI, now colonel
Lt Col Sanaulah	Swat	ex-consul Mazar and now on LPR (Peshawar)
Col Áli Hayder	Buner, Swat	ex-ISI, now retired (Islamabad)
Capt Musafir alias Gulzar	Abbottabad	officer by this name never served in Pakistan army
Major Haleem	Sanghar, Sind	ex-ISI and retired (Lahore)
Major Akbar Ali s/o Ch. Ashraaf	Shujah Abad, Multan	ex-ISI, retired and now working in Nowshera
Brig. Kifayat (Lt Col Akbar Kundi)		officer by this name has never served in the Pakistan army
Maj. Aizazullah/ Ijazulla	Nowshera, Peshawar	ex-ISI; now Lt Col AK Regt
Col Sajjad (cover name Col Mujahid)	Batagram, Hazara	ex-ISI, retired (Gujranwala)

Source: *The Nation*, 22 August 1999.
Note: *Pakistan denied this report. The clarification, as given by the Pakistani authorities about the current status of these men, is given in col. 3.

compendium of 152 Pakistani PoWs to the United Nations, under the title *"Not So Hidden Hand"* (see Table 8.1 for details). In August 1999, the Iranian press gave a list of eleven Pakistani army officers killed in Afghanistan while fighting alongside the Taliban. Denying the report, the Pakistani authorities said that these men fought alongside the mujahideen against the Red Army. Their current status as given out by the Pakistani authorities is given in Chart 8.1.

It would be seen from the details in Table 8.1 that a little over 65 per cent of the PoWs belonged to NWFP and Baluchistan provinces, abutting Afghanistan. There are also strong ethnic linkages among the frontiersmen. Interestingly, over 19 per cent of the PoWs came from Punjab and 13 per cent from Sind. There were four foreigners, from Jordan, Bangladesh, Saudi Arabia and Pak-occupied Kashmir. This pattern indicates that the number of Pakistani personnel fighting in Afghanistan had not undergone any significant change since the days of fighting the Soviet occupation forces.

Most of the PoWs were in the age group 21–30 years. The youngest was 14 years (1) and the oldest 61 years (2). The majority of the youngsters, that is less than 20 years of age, came from NWFP and Baluchistan (16), while two came from Sind, and one from Punjab. Among those over 40 years, two came from NWFP/Baluchistan, one from Sind and one was a foreigner (Bangladesh). Predictably, more than 70 per cent of the PoWs were single. There were only 4 married persons in the age group 0–20 years; all the 9 in over 30 years, and 30 from the age group 21–30 years, were married. Among the four foreigners, only the Bangladeshi was married. Almost 60 per cent of the PoWs were from madrasas. Of these, 13 each were from Punjab and Sind and the remaining 65 were from madrasas in NWFP/Baluchistan provinces. Among the high school/college students five were from Punjab, including an MBA and another engineering student and one from Sind. The lone army officer was from Baluchistan. Among the two Imams, one was from Punjab and the other from Baluchistan.

Of the PoWs, 35 entered Afghanistan in autumn (September–October) 1996; and the remaining in May 1997. All the four foreigners entered Afghanistan in summer 1997. These dates are important for two reasons. On 26–27 September 1996, Kabul was captured by the Taliban. Apparently these people were rushed to Kabul by Pakistan to assist the Taliban in consolidating their position. Similarly on 25–26 May 1997 when Mazar-i-Sharif was captured for a brief spell by the Taliban, people from Pakistan were rushed to help the Taliban. Some of those in Kabul also appear to have been rushed to Mazar-i-Sharif after the May 1997 developments. This becomes obvious as most of these PoWs were captured by the Northern Alliance in Mazar-i-Sharif, with a few from Bagram, Jabel Saraj, Salang and Charikar.

Equally interesting, more than 75 per cent of the PoWs entered

Afghanistan from Kandahar and another 17 per cent from Khost. Most of those hailing from Punjab and Sind provinces preferred to enter through Khost. It may be recalled that the international media reported about the terrorist training schools in Khost and the training methods imparted to these future "mujahideen" in these schools. Similarly, Kandahar was the place from where the Taliban started their operations. In other words, both these entry points were quite familiar to the Pakistanis. Even from details as admitted by the Pakistani authorities themselves (Chart 8.1), eight of the officers who worked in Afghanistan in course of duty, belonged to the ISI.

Sibghatullah Mujaddidi, chief of the Afghan National Liberation Front and former President, in an open letter to the Pakistan Prime Minister, Nawaz Sharif in early August 1999, pleaded:

> According to reliable sources of information and similarly in accordance with a report carried by daily *Mashriq* dated 29 July 1999 as well as the *Frontier Post* dated 30 July 1999, around 5000 Pakistanis and 400 Arab residents in Pakistan have been involved in these battles.... I, as a Muslim brother strongly urge you to issue an order for Pakistani nationals and Arabs to immediately leave Afghanistan.[7]

•

The official Pakistani explanation for Pakistani citizens messing around in Afghanistan is that the open border between the two countries "makes the people to cross the border without any official sanction". That these people are some of the overzealous religious school students is also untenable. One rational explanation would be that the government in Islamabad, to keep its options open in dealing with the various factions in Afghanistan, encouraged the madrasas to send volunteers to assist the Taliban. Another equally forceful explanation could be that the theocratic leadership in Pakistan, which could not make any dent in the nation's polity, decided to extend its influence in Afghanistan. These parties, vocal in nature, knew that the government in Islamabad could not stop them because of the ethnic linkages between Pashtuns on both sides of the Durand Line. Another

---

[7] *The Nation*, 6 August 1999.

plausible explanation could be a mixture of the two—that parties like the JUI of Fazlur Rehman did make the initial moves and the government in Islamabad found them quite useful in the furtherance of its foreign policy objectives.

Pakistan's demonstrating its nuclear weapon capability in May 1998, and the aura it created in the Islamic world, seems to have convinced its Afghanistan policy-makers that they can pursue their policy unhindered. In spite of earlier strains in Pak–Iran relations, the Iranian Foreign Minister visited Islamabad hours after the nuclear explosion to congratulate Pakistan for being the first country to acquire the "Islamic bomb". A new gleam of affection could also be seen in the eyes of the Saudis and Libyans. Islamabad, confident that it was nearer its goal of achieving its objective of leadership of the Islamic world, saw no reason to alter the course of its Afghanistan policy.

•

Thus followed the Pak–Afghan combine's assault on Mazar-i-Sharif in August 1998 and the success it managed to have in physically eliminating the opposition in Bamiyan.[8] This was preceded by the Taliban's execution of Iranian diplomats based in Mazar-i-Sharif, sending a signal to Iran that its predominance in South-West Asia was at an end. The sharp Iranian reaction made the Pak–Afghan combine retrace some of their steps.[9]

This in no way endeared the Pak–Taliban combine to others. Instead, the neighbours' position hardened. Since then there have been regular reports in the international media about regular supply of arms and ammunition by Pakistan to the Taliban. This prompted the Pak–Taliban combine to activate again Track-II diplomacy, that is actively supporting the UN peacemaking process by making correct statements. For instance it supported the Ashkabad and Tashkent peace conferences.

Simultaneously, it persuaded Turkmenistan to come out of the CARs grouping and start a dialogue with the Taliban about the

---

[8] See AFP report from Tehran, 14 September 1998.
[9] G.G. Khan, "The Enigma of Iranian Diplomats", *The Nation*, 22 October 1998.

pipeline project. It also enticed China to start dealing with the Taliban.

To sum up, Pakistan believed that the Afghan turmoil provided it a golden opportunity to neutralize the traditional unfriendly regime in Kabul. The success against the Red Army in the 1980s gave it the impression that it was close to its objective. It overlooked the fact, to quote a Pakistani commentator, that Pakistan was "artificially and dangerously empowered by the billions (of dollars) pumped in by the CIA; and their success was derivative of "American arms, American money and the CIA's ideology of the fifties". Pakistan thought of "altering the centuries old balance of power in the region" along with implementing the strategic objective of someone else.[10]

•

In the process of nurturing the Taliban, Pakistan, however, committed five tactical mistakes: (a) a narrow ethnocentric base; (b) narrow sectarian base; (c) shelter to dissident movements as a pressure point; (d) banking on narcotics production and trade; and (e) direct and complete involvement in the Taliban's military exploits.

Narrow Ethnocentric Base. To ensure their loyalty to Pakistan, only Durrani Pashtuns who have close linkages with the Pashtuns of NWFP and Baluchistan were picked for leadership of the Taliban movement. Neither Naseerullah Babar nor Maulana Fazlur Rehman foresaw the ethnocentric dynamics of Afghanistan. At one level the loyalties in Afghanistan are traditionally based on ethnicity; and this multi-ethnic society always managed affairs of the State through consensus. This ethnic equilibrium got suddenly disrupted by the Durrani Pashtuns marching into Kabul shoulder-to-shoulder with the Pakistani armed forces. This prompted the Tajiks, the Uzbeks, the Hazaras and other groups to raise the banner of revolt against the Taliban, bringing the neighbouring CARs and Iran into the picture in a substantial way.

Narrow Sectarian Base. The creators of the Taliban did not visualize the form of government that should be in place in

[10] Nasim Zehra, "Misguided Afghan Policy", *The Nation*, 17 April 1998.

Afghanistan. The Taliban's imposition of fundamentalist interpretation of Islam brought in widespread opposition from within Afghanistan and in the international community. The Pakistani recognition of the Taliban government in Kabul[11] along with Saudi Arabia and the UAE—the latter two did so at Pakistan's insistence in May 1997—brought into sharp focus the alleged Sunni/Wahabi leanings of the Taliban leadership.[12] This also eroded Pakistan's credentials as an honest broker trying to find a solution to the Afghan crisis. Pakistan's vociferous canvassing at the UN to recognize the Taliban as the official representative of Afghanistan and not the Rabbani group, in December 1998, made its leanings even clearer. Pakistan, therefore, no longer could say that it had no favourites in Afghanistan.

Shelter to Dissidents. To acquire pressure points over the major actors in the Islamic world, Pakistan allowed the Taliban to provide safe haven to various dissident movements in the Islamic world. Osama bin Laden coming to Peshawar from Khartoum and then proceeding to Kandahar, to be a personal guest of the Taliban's supreme leader Mullah Umar, brought in a totally new dimension to the Taliban movement. Most of these people were wanted in their respective countries for acts of violence and terrorism. There were allegations by the USA that people like Osama have committed acts of violence and terrorism against their citizens. In the process the Taliban and its sponsor Pakistan started being looked upon with suspicion by the international community in general and the Pak–Afghan neighbourhood in particular.

Banking on Narcotics. The near-bankrupt Pakistani economy was not able to mobilize the needed resources to sustain Afghanistan. Therefore, the narcotics trade that sustained the Pak–Afghan war with the Red Army to a certain extent and overlooked by the West, was revived in a big way. According to UN Drug Control Agency reports, in 1997–98, Taliban-controlled Afghanistan

---

[11] According to one version told to us, diplomats from Turkey, China, USA, Russia, Uzbekistan and Iran were called to the Pakistan Foreign Office on the morning of 25 May 1997 and were told that Islamabad was going to recognize the Taliban as the official government of Afghanistan that afternoon. The spokesman requested each diplomat individually to request his government to do the same.

[12] n. 10.

emerged as one of the biggest narcotics producing areas in the world. This created further reservations in the international community about the Taliban's acceptability.

Pakistan's Direct Involvement. This has proved to be Pakistan's Achilles heel. Pakistan allowed its people and armed forces to get directly involved in the Afghan civil war. Pakistan wanted to maintain strict fiscal and physical control of the movement. Without it the Afghan groups, by this time might have able to resolve their differences.

Whether it was in drafting the Constitution for Taliban-ruled Afghanistan, or reconstructing the war-torn economy or for that matter even for maintaining essential services, the Taliban are dependent on Pakistani charity. For instance, the National Highway Authority of Pakistan is constructing a number of roads, including the Jalalabad–Kabul Highway. Similarly, Peshawar telephone exchange is used for linking Afghanistan to the rest of the world.

•

The story has not ended here. By providing access to the US and Saudi Arabian intelligence agencies to the Pak–Afghan border first and later deep into Afghanistan, Islamabad has made the new elite in the post-Revolution Iran feel insecure, resulting in a realignment of forces in the vicinity. The Iranian–Russian response to this new Pakistani policy was the Rabbani–Masoud "card" and this virtually applied brakes to Pakistan's ambitions.

Instead of responding with conciliatory gestures at once to the Russo–Iranian strategy, Pakistan decided to respond to this new development by bringing in the Taliban phenomenon characterized by three Es—exclusivism, extremism and expansionism. The Taliban practised extremism in politics, exclusivism of ethnic Pashtun and expansionism of their political and military control in non-Pashtun areas of Afghanistan. In the process, Russo–Iranian suspicion of Pakistan's intentions was further strengthened and a broad-based alliance among Afghanistan's northern neighbours emerged.

Since the diplomatic clout of such a broad-based grouping is far higher than that of Pakistan, they were able to undermine the

Taliban and Pakistan at all levels—domestically, regionally and outside the region. This is obvious from the fact that even though the Taliban control two-thirds of Afghanistan, nobody wants to recognize the Taliban-led government and almost everyone treats

---

Box 8.1

Excerpts from "The Not-So-Hidden Hand"

The capture by Taliban guerrillas of the Afghan capital Kabul, however short- or long-lived, has come after two years of one of the most obnoxious interventions by one state in the affairs of another in many years ... reported in the West as an indigenous struggle, in fact Pakistan set up the Taliban as a semi-regular fighting force in 1994, recruiting the leaders from religious schools or madrassas in Afghan refugee camps in Pakistan and providing them with guns, money, fuel and technical support.... Since its creation in 1947 Pakistan has harboured the goal of dominating its northern neighbour.—*The Nation*, 11 November 1996.

[Interior Minister Naseerullah Babar] offered denials asserting that "there has been no financial or material aid to the Taliban from Pakistan". But western intelligence officials in Pakistan said the denials were a smokescreen for a policy of covert support that Mr Babar, a retired Pakistani General, had extended to the Taliban ... [that] apart from ammunition and fuel, included the deployment at crucial junctures of Pakistani military advisers. The advisers were easy to hide, since they were almost all ethnic Pashtuns [like] an overwhelming majority of the Taliban.—*New York Times*, 31 December 1996.

Among [the captured Taliban] are 37 who concede they are Pakistani citizens ... [their] road to Afghanistan was smoothed by the Jamiat Ulema Islami (JUI), a Pakistani religious party.... Pakistani authorities know exactly what is going on; JUI leader Maulawi Fazlur Rahman was a member of Benazir Bhutto's ousted government ... [who] worked closely with ... Naseerullah Babar, Bhutto's pointman on Afghanistan.... [Pakistan's spy service] ISI has links with Pakistani religious parties that provide volunteers for jihad in both Kashmir and Afghanistan. "It is part of a privatization of an enterprise earlier run by ISI for the Kashmir conflict", says a western source.—*Asiaweek*, 29 November 1996.

The 26 men sit in grim isolation.... They are Pakistanis captured while fighting against the forces of the Afghan government that

the Taliban as an international pariah. Even the Taliban's overt/covert supporters like the Saudis and the Americans, have started distancing themselves from them. By mid-1999 it became clear to everybody that Pakistan itself has to look after its offspring,

> was driven from the capital by the Taliban.... Khalid Mohammad Zia, 22, was a member of an Islamic paramilitary unit ... in Pakistan's Punjab province. He says his unit was under the control of the ISI.... He was transported across the border by Pakistani military vehicles and ... received orders and money from the senior Pakistani officer in Kabul....—*Time*, 4 November 1996.
>
> .... no Afghan force, government or opposition has ever carried out such a swift and complex series of operations over such a wide operational area. That semi-literate Afghan mullahs could have been capable of such planning and execution defies belief ... circumstantial evidence points strongly toward Pakistani involvement at the planning level and reliable reports of cross-border logistics support and Pashto-speaking ex-Pakistani military personnel operating on the ground suggest Islamabad's support was not confined to the map room.—*Jane's Intelligence Review*, November 1996.
>
> ... all-out Pakistani backing for the Taliban ... was not difficult to deliver. As former Pakistani General Mirza Aslam Beg observed, "their origin is in Pakistan, their bases are in Pakistan".... On 29 September, a BBC correspondent in Kabul reported that aid workers has recognised Pakistani army officers within the Taliban occupation force. This independent confirmation ... suggests that the fall of Kabul should be seen not as a revolt of society against the state, but rather as the culmination of a creeping Pakistani invasion of its neighbour.—*The World Today* (Royal Institute of International Affairs), November 1996.
>
> By the late summer of 1994, arms began flowing through [Pakistan Interior Minister] Babar's JUI back-channel to the Taliban.... Mysteriously well-funded, the Taliban were also happy to pay off local commanders.... They were now being supported logistically and financially not just by Babar but also by the Pakistani ISI.... On the ground, Pakistani nationals were involved at two levels. First, ex-Frontier Corps personnel from Pakistan's Pashtun belt ... were in key staff positions. Second, hundreds of Pakistani fundamentalist volunteers were eager for some hands-on Jihad in Afghanistan....—*Soldier of Fortune*, May 1997.

the Taliban, and no one would give a helping hand. For instance, in January 1998, while meeting Pakistani officials, Saudi Crown Prince Turki al-Faisal was clear that the Taliban had pushed themselves into a corner both politically and diplomatically. He observed to his Pakistani hosts: "You take the lead in persuading Taliban to change their extreme positions and we will support you."[13]

This unfortunate state of affairs on the Afghan front is largely due to the bipolar nature of Pakistan's decision-making process until Nawaz Sharif's ouster. At one level, there was an elected government headed by a Prime Minister. He was advocating Pakistan's disengagement from Afghanistan as early as possible and bringing a combined approach and collaboration with neighbours. He was personally travelling to various capitals of the neighbouring countries to fine-tune Pakistan's policy with that of others.

While nobody would disagree with the ousted Pakistani Prime Minister's assessment, everybody was sceptical because they were aware of the limitations on his sphere of activity. In July 1998, a diplomat from Central Asia observed: "Poor Nawaz Sharif, from June 1997, he was trying to do something on the Afghan front. His foreign office, like in the past, at the last minute, the milk was spilled and the whole policy was given up. I don't think now he is any longer interested."

The armed forces of Pakistan, with their clout, set their own and different agenda for resolving the Afghan issue. In the final analysis, as always, the armed forces' view prevailed. As typical of the armed forces anywhere in the world, Pakistani armed forces are not visionaries and lack political acumen. Any undermining of the Taliban at this stage or later is being perceived by the Pakistani armed forces as undermining their own position within the polity. There were also regular reports in the Pakistani media that it was Islamabad, the ISI in particular, which pushed the Taliban into an agreement with General Abdul Malik Pehalwan in May 1997 that finally ended in a fiasco.

One could also argue that Pakistan, having been isolated

---

[13]Nasim Zehra, "Ball is in Taliban's Court", *The Nation*, 23 February 1998. This Saudi stand was regularly repeated in the subsequent months.

regionally, is following a dual policy, diplomacy on one hand to win over the neighbours; and military solution to clinch the issues as quickly as possible. This, however, is highly unlikely for two reasons. With different people at different points of time, the Pakistani foreign office expressed its inability to translate the policy of political leadership into reality. In fact, the sudden inflexibility of the Taliban to various proposals is attributed more to their closeness to the armed forces than to the political leadership. This becomes obvious from the fact that no meeting ever took place between Mullah Umar and Nawaz Sharif, at least not reported in the media. If so, how could Mullah Umar, who is the politico-spiritual head of the Taliban, garner support from Pakistan without the consent of the government in power in Islamabad?

To further illustrate this point, in the intra-Afghan dialogue, Foreign Secretary Shamshad Ahmad met Mullah Umar on 28 December 1997 at Kandahar and obtained his consent for intra-Afghan dialogue. Pakistan's diplomatic effort then went into top gear to convene an ulema meeting. When the actual meeting was convened, the Taliban tried to change the agenda and dilly-dallied at the talks. From where does the Taliban draw the strength to behave in this fashion is a puzzle to every Afghanistan watcher.

Some clues are provided in commentaries of writers like Ahmed Rashid, Ikram Ullah and others. Writing on the eve of the Defence Committee of the Cabinet (it may be noted that the DCC is the highest foreign policy body in which the President, the Prime Minister, the Foreign, Finance and Interior Ministers, the three service chiefs and the Director General of the ISI participate) in early 1998, Ahmed Rashid observed:

The backlash of Pakistan's pro-Taliban foreign policy in Afghanistan has antagonized every neighbouring state. Iran remains belligerently opposed to Pakistan's Afghan policy; the Central Asians feel the same way and are deeply alienated and annoyed with Pakistan. Russia remains antagonistic and has stepped up links with India. Many Muslim states are equally frustrated with Pakistan, and there was virtually no support for Pakistan's pro-Taliban stance at the OIC summit in Tehran last year.

Moreover, Pakistan's western allies, in particular the US and Europe, are deeply frustrated at the ISI's unwillingness to introduce opposition factions from Afghanistan in diplomatic fray. Apparently the ISI strongly opposed the recent visit of ex-President Burhanuddin Rabbani [December 1997], head of the anti-Taliban alliance to Islamabad. The ISI's objections were overruled by the Army chief. Pakistan's attempts to serve as a pipeline route to Central Asian energy have been indefinitely deferred. Islamabad tries to convince the world that the Taliban will be better managers of a gas pipeline than a broad-based government.

Meanwhile, Pakistan's initiative to call a meeting of the Afghan Ulemas has virtually collapsed. The Taliban's rather staunch preconditions have ensured that the attempt would lead to oblivion. The Taliban insist that the opposition alliance must nominate their ulema first and the Taliban would then have the discretion of approving and in a more likely scenario, rejecting them. The Taliban also refuse to sit with the Shia Ulema of the Hazaras. The Taliban further insist that the ulema's decision would be binding, ignoring the fact that it would be impossible for the political and military leaders of the anti-Taliban alliance to abdicate their powers in favour of the ulema.[14]

Rahimullah Yusufzai makes this point by citing the example of Rabbani's visit to Islamabad. According to him:

Taliban's refusal to allow a Pakistani plane to fly across their territory to bring Rabbani to Islamabad, and, later attacking Rabbani's home province Badakhshan, when Rabbani was in Islamabad, are all indicative of the displeasure of the people at the ground level.... The Badakhshan province adventure may have been blessed by certain elements in the ISI, who felt uneasy with the government's moves to befriend Prof. Rabbani and his Northern Alliance at the expense of the Taliban.[15]

In these circumstances, what is it that the Pakistani armed forces want from Afghanistan? One answer could be that they would like to incorporate or maintain a friendly government in Kabul; and shift the Pak–Afghan border from the present Durand Line to the Hindukush mountains. Their argument could be that during the past several years, the Durand Line has virtually vanished, which neither side is respecting in any fashion. There is free movement of people and goods and materials both sides of the border. Besides, neither the Taliban nor the Northern Alliance is in a position to capture the entire country; and in the existing circumstances, balkanization of Afghanistan looks unavoidable. Over a period of time when tempers cool down, if the various groups agree to rejoin, they can do so.

[14] Ahmed Rashid, "Drifting Along", *The Herald,* February 1998.
[15] "Pakistan Opens Peace Front", *The Nation,* 5 January 1998.

Chart 8.2. Pakistan's Support to the Taliban in the Summer Offensive of 1998 against the Northern Alliance

---

- Some Taliban units comprised 25 to 50 per cent Pakistan personnel. Reports suggest that 1700 Pakistani personnel participated in the operations along with a total of 8,000 to 10,000 Taliban militias
- Pak Regulars from unidentified units of 11 and 12 Corps (regiments identified are Punjab and Sindh)
- Military personnel (Pishin Scouts, Khyber Rifles and Chitras Scouts)
- Ex-servicemen
- Activists of Jamaat-i-Ulema-Ittehad JUI(F), Sipah-i-Sahaba and Harkat-ul-Ansar
- Unidentified artillery and armoured units
- 400 Nissan pick-up vans supplied by Pakistan
- Two Pakistan garrison in around Kabul.
- PAF pilots participated in aerial bombardment of Bamiyan, Mazar-i-Sharif and Kunduz airfields
- Helicopters from PAF and Army Aviation Units for movement of reinforcements and logistic suply
- Airbases identified in Pakistan for providing support to the Taliban:
    - Samungli   17 Squadron (F-6), 23 Squadron (F-6); 10 and 27 Army Aviation Corps
    - Kamra   14 Squadron (F-7P), 15 Squadron (F-7P), 25 Squadron (Mirage III)
    - Peshawar   16 Squadron (A-5), 26 Squadron (A-5), 9 Army Aviation Squadron

---

Source: Collated from various published inputs.

There is some merit in this argument. The Pakistani armed forces, who invested men, money and materials for twenty years have not done so for any altruistic reasons. They wanted to resolve their problems on the western borders once and for all. Above all, they want to redeem their honour sullied in the December 1971 Indo–Pak war.

•

While the political leadership looks upon the idea of Pakistan becoming a gateway to Central Asia as a high priority, the armed forces appear to be giving it lower priority than to resolving the Pak–Afghan border problem. They perceive that if the status quo is maintained for some time longer, Afghanistan's northern neighbours would need to accept the ground reality. Until such

172 *Afghan Buzkashi*

time they, through the Taliban, should prepare for a long-drawn-out guarding of the tense borders.

Putting forth the ethnic argument, the then Foreign Minister of Pakistan, Gohar Ayub Khan pointed out that

two provinces of Pakistan which are adjacent to Afghanistan are populated by the Pushtuns, an ethnic group that is a major one in Pakistan. This fact reveals our responsibilities and priorities in Afghanistan.

Both Burhanuddin Rabbani and his Defence Minister Ahmed Shah Masoud belong to the Tajik minority which constitute 13 per cent population of Afghanistan. Mr Karim Khalili, leader of Hizb-ul-Wahdat party belongs to the Hazara minority which forms 10 per cent and General Abdul Rashid Dostum belongs to the Uzbek minority which constitutes 7 per cent of Afghanistan's population.[16]

The exiled government of Afghanistan disputes these statistics. No ethnic group, it contends, constitutes more than 37 per cent of the total population. "Raising the population's configuration by Ayub, who is himself a Pashtun, is meant to fuel the flames of ethnic strife and to destabilize the Afghan polity", says Masood Khalili, ambassador of the Rabbani government in New Delhi.[17]

Gohar Ayub also told *Al Ahram*: "Pakistan, in the event of a confrontation with India, is in need of strategic depth. We always believe that the presence of a friendly government in Kabul would suffice in providing such strategic depth for us."

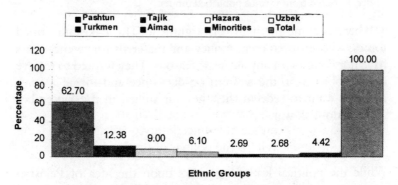

Chart 8.3. Ethnic Composition of Afghanistan
Source: Based on a survey by the Wak Foundation for Afghanistan, 1991–96

[16]In an interview to Ebrahim Sameh, editor of *Al Ahram* (30 June 1998).
[17]In an interview with the authors in June 1999.

However, there are two dangers in this logic. First, the Pakistani quest to redraw the map in this part of the world should take cognizance of the fact that 95 per cent of the population in the NWFP province of Pakistan are also Pashtuns. And the Taliban, whatever may be their efforts to make it a broad-based movement, have largely remained a Pashtun movement. In other words, an attempt is being made to extend the Pashtun homeland concept.[18]

Already, just renaming the NWFP as Pakhtunkhwa has drawn fire from the other ethic groups in Pakistan. The NWFP Provincial Assembly passed a resolution to this effect, and almost all the major regional parties in the Assembly supported the move. In other words, people with a vision among the Pashtuns are looking for an opportunity to create a homeland for themselves, which they missed out on during the turbulent years of the freedom struggle in the Indian subcontinent. Whether such a homeland of Pashtuns would remain a part of Pakistan or declare itself a separate nation-state is too early to say.[19]

The Taliban phenomenon itself could turn out to be a whirlwind that Pakistan reaps in the long run. With the quality of Pakistan's polity deteriorating in recent years (1989–99) there is a clamour for an alternative political system. Some have already started arguing that the Taliban is one alternative. A success story in Afghanistan, seen as first driving out the Red Army, and then establishing a theocratic State, would enhance its acceptability greatly. The sectarian violence and the mushrooming of madrasas all over Pakistan could question the very foundations on which Pakistan was established as a nation-state. Will Pakistan be able to withstand such an onslaught?

Certainly, both Pakistan and Afghanistan are entering the new millennium with considerable uncertainty of their own making. It does not augur well for the polities of the Indian subcontinent and South-West Asia.

---

[18]Rizwan Querishi, "Just Cause", *The Herald*, March 1998, p. 65.
[19]For a better understanding of the Pashtun phenomenon in Pak–Afghan politics see Olaf Caroe, *The Pathans* (Karachi, 1983).

9

Iran
Wary Coexistence

During the Soviet invasion of Afghanistan, Iran was for eight years preoccupied with a war which Iraq had launched to wrest the Shatt al-Arab waterway from it. Iranian policy was therefore necessarily confined to avoiding a spillover of the Afghan turmoil. The Iranian support to the Afghan refugees' fight was minimal. When the Soviets withdrew in 1989, Iran, busy reconstructing its war-torn economy, assumed that Pakistan could find a way out to the feuds of Afghan warlords, bring the various factions to the conference table and work out an amicable solution. The Pakistani game of musical chairs with various factional leaders of Afghanistan was watched with concern, but Iran went along nevertheless. Till 1992–93, Iran lent its advocacy to most of Afghanistan's neighbours to the effect that:

— Afghanistan's territorial integrity must be preserved; and
— a broad-based government must be formed in Afghanistan, where all the major ethnic tribes in the country must be represented.

The Taliban's appearance on the scene in 1994, however, made the Iranians cognizant that their strategic objectives were at variance with those of Pakistan. In the Iranian view, the Taliban movement was created by Pakistan in collaboration with Saudi Arabia and the US with three specific objectives:

— From the US perspective, a movement like the Taliban could

quickly wrap up the infighting in Afghanistan and facilitate finding an outlet to the sea via Afghanistan and Pakistan for the hydrocarbons being explored in the CARs by the American oil companies. The Taliban would also be a tool for the US to sustain its policy of containment of Iran.
— For the Saudis it was the chance of the century to reassert their leadership of the Islamic world, considerably eroded by the Islamic Revolution in Iran. This Iranian success had placed Shia Islam on a higher pedestal than the Wahabi Sunnism of Saudi Arabia. To neutralize the rise of Shi'ism, developments in Iran's next-door neighbour, Afghanistan, provided a golden opportunity.
— For Pakistan a trans–Afghan–Pakistan oil pipeline would offer unlimited opportunities; it would also change the geopolitics of the region because investments by western multinational corporations would make Islamabad an alternative to Iran to reach the CARs markets.

Developments in Afghanistan since 1995 strengthened these Iranian perceptions. The Taliban's capture of Kabul in September 1996, followed by their aggressive postures all around to capture the rest of the area, necessitated some quick rethinking by Iran. Three priorities emerged:

— how to contain the Taliban;
— how to keep Afghanistan's territorial integrity and form a broad-based government; and
— how to prevent the international community from recognizing the Taliban government.

•

As a first step to meet these new priorities, Iran decided to arm the other ethnic groups. According to various estimates, Iranian arms aid to these groups was something like $100 million.

According to a Pakistani commentator,[1] the fall of Mazar-i-Sharif exposed the scale of Iranian involvement. Two Iranian C-130s packed with military equipment were seized at Mazar-i-

---

[1] A. Siddique, "Iran's Afghan Debacle", *The Nation*, 23 August 1998.

Sharif airport, besides huge caches of sophisticated small-arms and ammunition which were abandoned by the Iranian-sponsored Hizb-i-Wahdat militia. The Taliban also captured thirty-five military trailers along with Iranian military drivers. The trailers were part of an Iranian convoy that had taken the overland trip from Iran through Turkmenistan to bring vast supplies for the anti-Taliban forces in their last-ditch battle in Mazar-i-Sharif. The commentary added that the Iranians had pumped in over $3 billion worth of military equipment and cash to sustain the anti-Taliban Northern Alliance. To sustain the Alliance, the Iranians had established an air bridge which extended from Tehran and Mashad to Mazar-i-Sharif, Bamiyan and Kulyab in Tajikistan. While supporting the Alliance over 400 flights plied between Iran and Northern Alliance during the past twelve months alone. Iran's scope of involvement in Afghanistan was not restricted to political manipulations aimed at forging unity among anti-Taliban forces and provision of military and logistic sustenance, but also entailed provision of military advice, guidance and liaison through the presence of officers and personnel of the Iranian Revolutionary Guard. To help manage the numerical superiority of the Taliban, Iran also trained and raised a corps of 7000 Afghan refugees in the Iranian hinterland to fight against the Taliban.

Pakistani accounts also allege that there is Russo-Iranian collaboration in rearming anti-Taliban forces. These accounts point out that the 130 Scud missiles along with launchers and other arms and ammunition captured in Mazar-i-Sharif are a clear indication of it. They also point out that Russians are supporting Ahmed Shah Masoud in Panjshir Valley. Masoud's fighter aircraft are positioned in Takhar province, close to Badakhshan province where he maintains an overland supply route from Tajikistan through Ishkamish border. The Russians are also sustaining Masoud's forces in the North Eastern Province from the Kulyab airbase in Tajikistan. After the fall of Mazar-i-Sharif in the first week of August 1998, Russian First Deputy Foreign Minister Boris Rostukhov and Chief of Staff of the Russian Armed Forces, Anatoly Kvahin, reached Dushanbe on 19 August 1998, to take stock of the situation.[2]

[2]Ibid.

In October 1998, there was a much-publicized "seizure" at Osh in Kyrgyzstan of a trainload of arms and ammunition meant for Ahmed Shah Masoud. Intelligence sources say the Russians were also party to this transaction.

Thus eighteen wagons were readied at Mashad with 500 tonnes of armament and 200 tonnes of sugar and wheat flour. Sources said Iran had checked with the governments concerned, apparently without disclosing the content of the consignment. The train passed through Sarakash, Turkmenistan, through Uzbek and Tajik territories to Osh in Kyrgyzstan.

Things went by plan and the Iranian Foreign Minister sent a message to Bishkek, capital of Kyrgyzstan, that the train was on its way. This was, however, an open fax message, which alerted the US. The satellites monitored the train's movements. On the ground too, monitoring was stepped up. The 200-odd Peace Corps workers located in Kyrgyzstan were activated.

A drama unfolded once the train reached Osh. Ruth Pojman, Programme and Research Specialist of International Organization of Migration (IOM), suspected to be a top CIA operative, leaked the information about the train to the media. She telephoned A. Karabekov, editor of *Vicharny Bishkek*, an eveninger. The two met at a Bishkek restaurant on the evening of 9 October when she told him that there were sixteen wagons (Of the eighteen that had originally started at Mashad, one reached later and one was offloaded by the Uzbeks while it was on their territory, who possibly sold off the military consignment). The editor sent a team to Osh to investigate.

The team worked on the "story". The local KGB man received a handsome bribe so that he would allow the reporter and the photographer access to the train, intelligence sources say.

The eveninger came out with an exposé on 12 October and followed it up the next day. The reporter cited top officials of the Kyrgyz government and representatives of some of the neighbouring countries. The Iranian envoy to Bishkek was also there with two Afghan translators. There was a representative of Masoud and quite significantly, two deputies of Dostum. It is well known that the Iranians have been investing in Dostum, as they had done in the past.

The exposé caused an international stink. The Kyrgyz had to

do a lot of explaining to the Russians, Uzbeks, Tajiks and Turkmens, besides Iran. A senior Kyrgyz minister had to visit their capitals, particularly Moscow. The National Assembly Speaker was sent to Tehran and to Tashkent, since everyone down the line got exposed in this aborted attempt to bolster Masoud's forces.

Intelligence sources believe the US did not approve of this Masoud–Iran tie-up in which several CARs cooperated. No matter who lost and who gained from this, the basic purpose of Masoud not getting timely help was served and the Shias in Hazarajat were butchered by the Taliban soldiers.

Detailed accounts of Iranian intervention in the Pakistani press may similarly be intended to tell the world community that Pakistan is not alone in indulging in the whole exercise. It is acknowledged that in August 1998, Iran was also playing host to an array of Afghan warlords, including Gulbuddin Hikmatyar and Abdul Malik Pehalwan. However, there are notable differences between Pakistani and Iranian involvement in the Afghan civil war.

•

After the Soviet withdrawal in 1989, initially it was left to Pakistan by all the other regional players to sort out the mess in Kabul. But Pakistan instead of playing an honest broker, tried to install a government favourable to itself. The Pakistani leadership's public and private pronouncements to this effect totally eroded their credibility as an honest broker. The speed with which Pakistan changed its favourites among the Afghan warlords further alienated almost the entire Afghan leadership. Pakistan made no attempt to build up a regional consensus on finding an acceptable leadership in Afghanistan. The creation of the Taliban in September 1994 by the Pakistani leadership made Pakistani intentions further suspect.

Since the other neighbours of Afghanistan also subscribe to this Iranian assessment of the Afghan situation, they readily joined the Iranian effort to contain the Taliban. That placed Iran, Uzbekistan, Turkmenistan, Tajikistan and Russia on one side, with Pakistan on the other. This also enabled Iran to mobilize international opinion in not recognizing the Taliban as the legitimate rulers of Afghanistan. In all international forums, whether it was the Organization of Islamic Conference (OIC), the Non-Aligned Movement or the UN, Burhanuddin Rabbani's government was considered the official representative of Afghanistan.

While the Taliban's is primarily a Pashtun-dominated movement, other principal ethnic groups like the Tajiks, Uzbeks and Hazaras organized themselves into a broad front under an umbrella organization called the Northern Alliance. The Alliance offered stiff resistance to the Taliban in May 1997, when the latter made an all-out assault on Mazar-i-Sharif. In the bloody battle that ensued during the three days 26–28 May 1997, the Taliban suffered heavy casualties, estimated at around 3000–4000. The Iranian strategy had paid dividends. Since then, Iran has tried to keep the initiative or at least play an active role as much as Pakistan does, in finding a way out to the complex Afghan civil war.

Meanwhile, the sudden glut in the oil market prompted American and European multinationals to postpone their investments in the CARs reserves of energy source materials. Even companies like Unocal, which had made significant investment in Afghanistan, announced temporary deferral of investment. Afghanistan, therefore, became a low-key issue for the great powers, who from 1988–89 showed readiness to go along with the local players' perceptions.

An additional factor in the changing perceptions was the victory in Iran of a government generally seen as moderate in the May 1997 elections. President Khattami's call soon after the elections for dialogue and cooperation of the diverse civilizations of the world was received with unusual warmth in the western hemisphere. The first concession the latter made was to acknowledge that Afghanistan is Iran's backyard and that Iranian strategic concerns must be taken into account. In this the aspirations of Iran and its other regional allies were given priority over those of Pakistan and the Taliban. This crucial factor prompted the West not to recognize the Taliban even though they occupied 90 per cent of the country. The Taliban and Pakistan thus got sufficiently isolated.

Khattami's leadership also brought in an element of wariness in the Iranian foreign policy. The reconstruction of the war-ravaged economy was not moving fast enough. Also, Iran was emerging slowly from its global isolation and did not want to disturb the equilibrium painstakingly crafted over a decade. In the process, Iran overlooked the fact that the differences within the Northern Alliance partners were deep rooted, with each trying to upstage the others. In May 1997, Dostum's troops were not able to fight the Taliban; and initially a section of Dostum's men turned against him and joined hands with the Taliban. Finally it was left to the Hazaras and Hizb-i-Wahdat men to challenge the Taliban and launch a counter-offensive. Similarly, the speed with which the Taliban moved and routed the Northern Alliance by September 1998, took Iran off guard.

•

After the fall of Mazar-i-Sharif to the Taliban on 8 August 1998, and the imminent fall of Bamiyan province was foreseen, Iran announced that ten of its diplomats based in the Iranian consulate in Mazar-i-Sharif along with an IRNA corespondent were missing.

On 5 September 1998 Radio Tehran announced:

Iran will in no way allow its nationals to be in the Taliban's captivity and witness this group's offensive behaviour. Iran has tried under the UN Charter under article 35 to attract the attention of the world community, especially the UN Security Council.[3]

This Iranian outburst surprised many. The statement added that "now completing this process, Iran reserves the right based on chapter 7, especially article 51 of the Charter to adopt necessary measures of legitimate defence."

A puzzling factor, according to a Pakistani commentator, is that by deputing so many personnel in Afghanistan, Iran was running a needless risk:

What continues to perplex is the Iranian failure to explain its compulsions for placing its personnel in certain harm's way and its lack of acknowledgement of responsibility for having participated in the ruthless killing

[3]IRNA Wire Services, 6 September 1998.

fields of Afghanistan. The presence of nine diplomats in a consulate is an abnormally high number, especially when it happens to be a war zone.... Therefore reports which assert that apart from Naseer Rigi, the acting head of Mazar mission, all the remaining staffers either belonged to Iranian Revolutionary Guard Corps or were operators of "Italaat" (Iran's premier intelligence outfit) who were stationed at Mazar to look after and coordinate politico-military affairs of Northern Alliance.[4]

Reacting quickly to the warning from Iran, in an interview to an Iranian newspaper *Abrar,* Wakil Ahmed Muttawakil, a senior leader of the Taliban, said, "the possibility of them being killed is very strong. Within the next week we will try to find the bodies of the dead diplomats." If the search failed the Taliban would launch a joint probe with Iran and Pakistan to find the missing Iranian diplomats, he said.

Simultaneously, Iran mobilized 70,000 of its elite Revolutionary Guards to the Iran–Afghanistan border and announced conducting of "military exercises". According to media reports Iranian troop concentration was at Islam Qila and Zaranz in Nimroz province.[5] Meanwhile, the US State Department issued a statement to the effect that it had repeatedly called upon "Afghanistan's neighbours to refrain from taking any action that could further enlarge or inflame the conflict. We call upon Afghanistan's neighbours to respect its borders." Obviously, the US was urging restraint by Iran. Any conflict between Tehran and Kabul could drag in the neighbours also and make peace efforts that much difficult. Also, during President Bill Clinton's visit to Moscow, the Americans made it amply clear that they would not approve of anyone presuming the US attack on Afghanistan on 20 August 1998 to be a precedent for others to take similar action.

Another version of the events says that feeling the tension on the domestic front, and angry at the defiant tone of the Taliban, the Iranians were raring to go. But hours before they were supposed to enter Herat for a clinical operation, the US launched its missile strike on the Taliban in order to get Osama bin Laden.

[4] See n. 1.
[5] IRNA Wire Services, 7 September 1998. Also see *New York Times,* 10 September 1998.

Joining any US-led initiative, or launching parallel action that would go to help the US standpoint would have cost Iran seriously at home and in the Islamic world community. Also in the Islamic world, since the US target was Osama, and the missiles were landing on an Islamic country, Iran could not be seen joining the "Satan" in attacking an Islamic neighbour.

If this version is right, the US pre-empted an Iranian initiative to reach help to Ahmed Shah Masoud. There is a perception that had Masoud acted in tandem with an Iranian invasion, a Taliban rout was certain.

Whatever may have been the reasons for the Iranians not going to war with Afghanistan by early September 1998, the Iranians were on a diplomatic offensive, which seems to have had the desired effect. On 6 September 1998 the Iranian Foreign Ministry spokesman, Mahmud Mohammad, said that Tehran would try all the diplomatic channels to get the Iranian diplomatic staff back. On the same day, the *Tehran Times* published a statement by Iran's supreme spiritual leader, Ayatollah Ali Khamenei, that Iran would not enter into a military confrontation with the Taliban. A few hours later the Taliban offered to release 45 Iranians as a goodwill gesture. This was followed by a statement the next day by the head of Iran's Expediency Council, Ali Akbar Hashemi Rafsanjani, that "the government and National Security Council are trying to remove the problem as soon as possible with *prudence and in a calculated way*" (emphasis added).

Seeing the positive reaction from Iran, on 8 September the US State Department spokesman, James P. Rubin said that significant number of Iranian troops, who were despatched to the border with Afghanistan, completed their exercises but were none the less deployed there. He said that the US was unable to confirm reports that several Iranians, including diplomatic staff at an Iranian consulate, had been missing since the Taliban fighters captured the city and might have been killed. "Now the Taliban is the dominant force in Afghanistan." Rubin also said that the Taliban were holding the diplomatic staff in violation of international law.

On 10 September, the Taliban officially announced that nine out of the eleven missing Iranians had been killed by their forces at the time of the capture of Mazar-i-Sharif on 8 August 1998; and they were approaching the UN for mediation in handing over the bodies to Tehran.⁶ In reaction, Iran called for:

— an official apology from the Taliban;
— arrest and punishment of the killers of the diplomats; and
— unconditional release of the remaining Iranians held in Kandahar.

Over the next two days Iran made three significant moves. One, an IRNA report quoting officials said that "the responsibility for martyrdom rests on the Taliban militia and the government of Pakistan, which had assured us of their safety".⁷ By bringing the Pakistan factor out in the public Iran made it clear that it was not willing to go along with Islamabad's perception on Afghanistan.⁸ Two, Iran demanded extradition of the persons responsible for the killing of Iranian diplomats. And three, a cabinet minister was quoted by IRNA as saying, "Iran reserves the right to take action for the blood of its children in Afghanistan". This was accompanied by an announcement by Brigadier General Abdol-Ali Pourshas, Commander of the Army Ground Forces, that the second phase of the military exercises, Zolfaqar-2, involving about 200,000 troops, would start on 23 September 1998. The exercise would cover an area of 50,000 sq km, from southern Khorrasan province to north of Zahedan, the main town in Sistan-Baluchistan province.⁹

These Iranian moves were accompanied by the Taliban allowing Iran to airlift bodies of the killed Iranian diplomats from Mazar-i-Sharif on 14 September.

Simultaneously, Iran also moved the UN Security Council for taking necessary action for the "war crimes" committed by the Taliban. Acting on this Iranian request, the Security Council condemned the slaying of Iranian diplomats in Afghanistan and

⁶Voice of America, 10 September 1998.
⁷IRNA, 11 September 1998. Also see AFP despatch from Tehran, 10 September 1998.
⁸Ibid.
⁹IRNA, 12 September 1998. Also see Afshin Valineja's despatch on AP Wire Services, 10 September 1998.

called for speedy investigation to bring the perpetrators to justice. Russia[10] and France[11] in separate statements condemned the killings but asked the neighbours to find a way out through negotiations. The Chinese issued a bland statement condemning war in Afghanistan. A *Xinhua* statement said, "We express our deep regret on the death of the Iranian diplomats and our sympathy and solicitude to the relatives of the victims."

•

The sequence of events clearly indicates that Iran has succeeded in mobilizing international public opinion against the Taliban and Pakistan. This to some extent applied the brakes to the Taliban getting recognized by the international community. The next Iranian step would be how to sustain this anti-Taliban sentiment; and how to force the Taliban to come to the conference table and accommodate other ethnic groups in forming a broad-based government. Here Iran would have four options.

Option one: Direct intervention by surgically striking at various Taliban concentrations. If it weakens the Taliban, Iran can invite the leadership of the other ethnic groups to continue the fight. Military analysts, however, rule out this option because of the terrain. The Iranian armed forces are not trained in mountain warfare to any significant extent. One Taliban sympathizer told us that Iran got a good briefing from the British and the Russians on this, about how difficult it is to fight the Afghans in the mountains.

Option two: Continue the guerrilla war on the entire Iran–Afghanistan border and Afghanistan–CARs border by offering safe haven to anti-Taliban forces. This will be expensive.

Option three: Wait for winter, when the Taliban forces will be hard put to maintain their supply lines from the south to the forward areas in the north and west. At that time, the reorganized anti-Taliban forces can be encouraged to attack.

Option four: Continue the coercive diplomacy and tie the Taliban forces to the Iran–Afghanistan border. At the same time

[10] AFP report of 12 September 1998.
[11] See AFP report on 11 September 1998.

encourage anti-Taliban forces to open new fronts to partly capture lost territory.

Developments of the entire quarter August–October 1998 indicate that Iran set Option Four in motion and achieved remarkable success in terms of isolating the Taliban and Pakistan. One reason why Iran has chosen the diplomatic course is the realization—and Iran is not the only one in the region thinking this way—that the Taliban have settled down in Kabul, keeping control of a vast territory for three years.

"The Taliban have the advantage they ask whatever they want, but that is not the solution", observed S. Mehdi Miraboutalebi, Iran's ambassador to Turkmenistan during an interview at Ashkabad on 27 July 1999. But he was categorical: "Even if the Taliban take over the whole of Afghanistan peace cannot come. Nobody can run that country alone. All must participate in the governance."

He confirmed that of the four options before it, Iran had chosen the diplomatic course. "I do not think military response is the solution." He pointed out that at the six-plus-two meeting in Tashkent, the Taliban had been identified. "I don't think any country around the world can condemn us for our role in the events after the fall of Mazar-i-Sharif." At the Tashkent conference, Iran played a positive role in conjunction with the Central Asians and Russians to counter the Pakistan–Taliban–Turkmen moves.

Although there has been a thaw in the US–Iran relationship, Iran continues to nurse reservations about "foreign influence" in Afghan affairs. The Tashkent conference was clearly the result of combined moves by the US and Russia. Miraboutalebi, without naming anyone in particular, said, "The meeting was only for a show. Somebody else is taking decisions." Of the Taliban he said, "You know who is helping them."

Meanwhile, Iran is hosting a million refugees from Afghanistan. While it has been helping the Northern Alliance, it has kept the refugees in its territory free from any role. This is important since the territory in Afghanistan abutting the Iranian border is in Taliban hands. Iran has to cross this territory to reach the Shias in central Afghanistan.

Also, the fall of Mazar-i-Sharif and the subsequent consolidation of their position by the Taliban in Afghanistan has prompted Iran to take a fresh look at the whole question of dealing with the Taliban. According to a group of intellectuals from Iran with whom we talked in January 1999, Tehran has opened up its channels of communication with the Taliban.[12] In November 1999 it was suddenly announced by Iran that the border between the two had been opened and trade would resume. An Iranian Foreign Ministry spokesman also disclosed that the Iranian consulate in Herat would start functioning normally.[13]

[12]Tehran still seems to be adamant about not dealing with the Taliban officially. According to an editorial in *Iran News* (3 February 1999), the representative of the Taliban regime in Islamabad, Molavi Saeid-ur Rehman Mottaqi recently announced that the Taliban were keen to forge ties with the Islamic Republic of Iran, but added that he did not know why the Iranian leaders were not eager to do so. Mottaqi also acknowledged some of the mistakes of the Taliban, especially the one in Mazar-i-Sharif, and said "we are ready to make up for the mistakes...." As of now, it would appear that the first condition for any official contact by Tehran with the Taliban is the apprehension and punishment of the killers of Iranian diplomats. Only then would talks with the Taliban as a member of a broad-based coalition be possible.

[13]The spokesman told Radio news channel Payam that Iran opened a border point with Taliban-ruled Afghanistan on 21 November to enable trade between the two countries. Afghan businessmen might engage in trade with the Iranian provinces of Khorrasan in the north-east and Sistan-Baluchistan in the south-east near Herat. The spokesman also confirmed an Afghan Islamic Press Agency report that former Iranian consul-general in Herat Reza Moushadi met Herat governor Mullah Khairulla Khairkhwa. Saying that there was no change in Iran's policy towards the Taliban, he also stressed that reopening of border trade was not violation of UN Security Council sanctions against Afghanistan.—Deutsche Presse Agentur report from Tehran on 22 November 1999. See *Indian Express* (New Delhi), 23 November 1999.

10

The Taliban "Revolution"
A Contrast to the Iranian Revolution

The Taliban's capture of Mazar-i-Sharif on 8 August 1998, and their announcement that they are in effective control of 90 per cent of Afghan territory have induced many Pakistani commentators to declare the Taliban to be a greater revolution than Ayatollah Khomeini's Islamic Revolution in Iran in 1979. The note of jubilation in this comparison is understandable. There is, however, also an unstated objective of undermining, subtly, the Iran factor in the Islamic world. A former Chief of Staff of the Pakistan Army, General Mirza Aslam Beg, for instance, has observed that the past two decades have witnessed historic transformation of great magnitude in the two neighbouring countries of Pakistan—Iran and Afghanistan. Both have emerged successful after the revolution, uprooting the power structure and dismantling the age-old systems, thus producing reverberations across the borders.[1] The point has also been made earlier (see Chapter 9) that Pakistani commentators have also been giving a detailed account of Iranian involvement in Afghanistan, especially in terms of aid to the Northern Alliance.

To what extent are the Islamic Revolution in Iran and the Taliban movement in Afghanistan comparable?

It has been a common belief among many political scientists in the second half of the twentieth century that the process of modernization would by the very nature of things bring in an

---

[1]"The two Revolutions", *The Nation*, 4 April 1998.

element of secularism in the perceptions of nation-states. They also believed that the importance of religion would decline to the level of being an individual's private affair and the State would have nothing to do with it. In fact religion as an ideology lost its relevance. The success of the Islamic Resolution in Iran forced everyone to rethink on this entire proposition. It is generally conceded by Persian Gulf watchers that the Islamic Revolution in Iran put paid to this belief.

The Islamic Revolution in Iran was the outcome of three factors. These were: (a) the Shah of Iran's keen promotion of western cultural values in Iran; (b) the Shah's turning Iran into a surrogate of the US; and (c) the charisma of Ayatollah Khomeini.

Invasion of Western Cultural Values. In the name of modernization, the Shah of Iran allowed the invasion of western culture and values into the country, to the extent of downgrading the 2500-year-old Iranian civilization and culture. In this clash of cultures, many sensible Iranians like Ayatollah Khomeini felt that Iranian culture is far superior to that of the West. Accepting the finer points of western culture and assimilating them in the Persian milieu would be acceptable, but wholesale cultural invasion from the West, which uprooted the traditional Persian social values was to be resisted. The speed with which this process of modernization was thrust upon Iranian society say, from 1964 to 1976, brought in a clash civilizations, rather than a dialogue. Western political scientists placed this phenomenon in too simplistic terms as tradition-versus-modernity. They crusaded to discredit the Islamic Revolution in Iran, but failed. The overweening view of the West that they are right and others wrong was confounded.

Surrogate State. In accelerating the modernization of Iran the Shah made Iran a surrogate of extra-regional powers, which the traditional leadership of the Iranian society resented. The latter's perception of development, in both historical and civilizational terms, placed Iran on a higher pedestal than the three-and-a-half centuries old US civilization was willing to concede to their country in the international system in general and the Persian Gulf in particular. Pre-eminence in the region is Iran's by right, both in terms of history and geography. The largest country in the region in population, it also greatly influenced the rest of the present-day Persian Gulf states at different points of history.

Losing perspective, the western media debased the whole debate to the level that a woman wearing traditional Persian *chador* is primitive and the skirt is modern!

Khomeini's Charisma. Being himself a savant of Islam, and his teachings being integral to international Islamic theology, Ayatollah Khomeini carried authority among the Islamic clergy as well as he did among the masses. His political acumen enabled him to confront the Shah at both theoretical and realpolitik level. Even the Shah's regime, known for its repressive ways, could not deal with him more harshly than exiling him.

A shrewd strategist, Khomeini understood that the Shah's oppressive regime could be toppled only by the sword of Islam. Like Gandhi's non-violence and Ho Chi Minh's liberation struggle, Khomeini was able to translate his understanding of Islam into a political philosophy to overthrow the Shah's regime. This social engineering experiment proved unique in contemporary Islamic history.

Having overthrown the Shah, Khomeini ensured that a liberal, progressive Islam, in tune with modern-day governance, was in place. He provided a written constitution to Iran and created the needed institutional framework to thwart any efforts to undermine it. He ensured that the Iranian State came first and also that other religious minorities were not persecuted in the name of Islam.

Even more important, Ayatollah Khomeini was not indebted to any outside power. His success was entirely due to the people's endorsement of his policies. A quick learner and a man with vision for Iran, he was able to correct his mistakes and made Iran a factor in the international order. This disturbed the traditional equilibrium in the Islamic world and undermined the position of countries like Saudi Arabia which, being the custodian of the holiest places of Islam, enjoyed a predominant position.

All this prompted the world community to look upon the Islamic Revolution in Iran as an internal matter of that country. No one questioned its legitimacy, and its membership of international organizations like the UN or even in the OIC remained intact. In 1998, the OIC held its conference in Tehran, and Iran was elected as its President.

•

Developments in Afghanistan, on the other hand, appear to be an antithesis of the Islamic Revolution in Iran. When the Soviet Union invaded Afghanistan in December 1979, the Afghans fled and took shelter mainly in Iran and Pakistan. The Taliban chief Mullah Umar was among them. The Afghan refugees were persuaded to fight the Red Army by three major powers, Pakistan, Saudi Arabia and the US. The ideological framework was provided by General Ziaul Haq, then President of Pakistan. Monetary help was given by Saudi Arabia and arms by the US and its allies. In fact, it was Ziaul Haq who coined the term mujahideen for the Afghan refugees, and for their fight against the Red Army the term jihad to save Islam. Otherwise, Islam in the traditional Afghan context is more liberal and a handiwork of sufi saints.

All the three external players in the Afghan turmoil had their independent agenda—the US in terms of Cold War politics (bleeding the Red Army); the Saudis to re-establish their predominance in the Islamic world and checkmate Iranian ascendancy after the Islamic Revolution; and Pakistan to resolve the vexed question of the Durand Line between the two countries and subtly stake its claims for leadership of the Islamic world.

After the Soviet withdrawal from Afghanistan in 1989, it became a question of who should take over the spoils of office in Kabul. The US withdrew from the scene since its objective was achieved by 1988–89. The others too played a game of musical chairs to install a leader amenable to them who would pursue their policies, but failed.

In this backdrop, the Taliban were created by collecting a group of middle-level Afghan refugees. Mullah Umar, the Taliban supremo, has closeted himself in Kandahar, and not Kabul, and directs the Taliban's campaign to capture power. He never led the men from the front. What entitles him to be called amirul momineen has not been explained. He receives mostly Pakistani visitors and none else. Even the officials from the US have to deal with his second-in-command. At every stage, Pakistan from behind the scenes provided the brains to the Taliban. When Urdu-speaking Taliban soldiers were spotted by the international media and UN agencies and workers after the fall of Kabul in September 1996, it was ensured that no such person was around in August 1998 at the time of the capture of Mazar-i-Sharif.

From time to time, the Pakistani citizens captured by the opponents of the Taliban; and their families trekking down to the prison camps to plead with the leaders concerned to release them, was well documented by the Pakistani media and others. Some foreign news agencies were even able to name the officers and their ranks when Kabul was captured by the Taliban in September 1996. The Pakistani military officers and politicians bringing back mementos of Kabul National Museum was also documented by the international media. The Taliban also sought the help of Jamiat-i-Ulema-Islami of Fazlur Rehman to help them draft a constitution for Afghanistan.

In other words, unlike the Islamic Revolution in Iran, which is totally indigenous and never allowed any external involvement, the Taliban movement is out and out a movement of external origins. It is a movement with an agenda decided by others for Afghanistan and at a later stage for the rest of the Islamic world.

In his lifetime, the Pakistanis were not able to undermine Ayatollah Khomeini's pre-eminence in the Islamic world. Even diehard Islamists like General Ziaul Haq refused to oblige the Saudi demand for such an action. Only from 1994, when the Taliban movement was started, the sectarian factor was given a twist and brought to the forefront—that the Islamic revolution in Iran was a Shia revolution only. The massacre of Shias by Sunnis started rather intensely from the beginning of the 1990s in Pakistan. This was followed by specific targeting of Iranian citizens from around 1995. The culmination was the massacre of Shias in Bamiyan province in September 1998. The Taliban movement thus left no one in doubt that it was a Sunni movement dominated by Pashtuns.

In contrast, in Iran in the mid-1980s, at the height of Iran's war with Iraq, some overzealous Revolutionary Guards misbehaved with Iranian minorities. When this was brought to the notice of Ayatollah Khomeini, the authorities were chided and minority communities were assured full protection.

•

The turning-point in the Iranian revolution of 1978–79 was the Iranian air force joining Ayatollah Khomeini some time in

December 1978–January 1979. That proved crucial. When the oil workers joined the movement, and Iranian crude oil production stopped, the issue was clinched. Less than a fortnight later, Ayatollah Khomeini triumphantly returned to Tehran from Paris.

While group after group of Iranian society joined Ayatollah Khomeini's Islamic Revolution, voluntarily, the same cannot be said about Mullah Umar's Taliban. While very few groups joined the Taliban voluntarily, the majority were bought over by the money donated by extra-regional powers and/or money generated by drug trafficking or were forced to join after pitched battles.

The Taliban leadership, after the initial success with capturing territory, quickly coopted warlords into their movement by purchasing them or invoking their tribal loyalties. And as a first principle the Taliban disarmed their new entrants. As the Taliban's success story started unfolding throughout 1995 and 1996, especially in mid-1996 the disgruntled elements in Najibullah's party cadres and men in uniform started joining the Taliban ranks. Whether the Pakistani armed forces provided the needed inputs in this strategy or not is beside the point here (evidence shows that they did, including military support). However, this proved short-lived. The Taliban had not anticipated that their adversaries would organize effectively against them. Rabbani, Dostum, Masoud and Khalis joined together and got help from outside powers. The massacre of the Taliban in May 1997 in Mazar-i-Sharif showed their adversaries' strength. It took the Taliban more than a year to get militarily prepared to defeat the alliance and capture their strongholds. In other words, what Ayatollah Khomeini achieved in less than six months, if we take the Jalal square incident in September 1978 as the beginning of the Iranian Revolution, the Taliban took almost four years to capture 90 per cent of the area. This prompted one Afghan to comment that this was achieved "by killings and more killings" and "ethnic cleansing". This long time brought in a number of new variables to the forefront and spoiled the Taliban show.

There are, however, certain commonalities at the macro level between the Taliban movement and the Islamic Revolution in Iran. Foremost would be the religious factor. Both are headed by politico-religious leaders, and the Islamic clergy plays a predominant role. The ideological framework in which one operated, and the other does currently, is Islam. Like Ayatollah Khomeini, Mullah Umar (or his sponsors) too used religion as a primary instrument to mobilize people to achieve a particular political objective. Both started with a literal interpretation of the religion. One might even see a certain similarity in the treatment meted out to women immediately after the Revolution in Iran and now in Afghanistan. The leadership in both countries perceived that any moderation would dilute their Islamic moral authority. Some would argue that if the Taliban consolidate their position, they will also start moderating their policies towards women.

In both revolutions, in the initial phases, especially the lower level leadership of the movement wanted to export their ideology to other countries.

The Islamic Revolution in Iran was against the oppressive regime of the Shah, whose policies were perceived to be undermining the Iranian spirit. In the peculiar circumstances in which Iran was placed before the Revolution, a movement like Gandhi's non-violence or violent communist variety to overthrow the Shah would have been defeated easily. Therefore Ayatollah Khomeini using religion as a potent weapon to achieve his objective came as a surprise and the ruling elite were not clear how to deal with it. The Taliban were against feudalism and exploitation by the tribal warlords of Afghanistan. Here too any other means would have been easily defeated. In fact the permutations and combinations tried before the arrival of the Taliban by their sponsors have amply demonstrated that factional fights will not end in Afghanistan.

While the great powers were upset by the success of the Iranian revolution as it altered the power equilibrium within the region and to their disadvantage, they collaborated to a certain extent with the Taliban movement up to a point of time. The Iranian revolution defied the dictates of the great powers and went ahead with consolidating its revolution. The Taliban, the instant they were disowned by the great powers, started looking around for ways and means of getting on their right side.

Two other interesting similarities between the two movements are: The Iranian Revolution was first welcomed by the Hizbullah of Lebanon. The Iranian linkages with the Hizbullah were a major point of controversy in the early 1980s. Similarly, the Taliban's linkages with Osama bin Laden's Al-Quaide emerged as a major issue in the international security system. Equally interesting is that the US decided to impose economic sanctions on both revolutions. Like containing Iran in the 1980s and 1990s, containing the Taliban became a major foreign policy plank of the US in the 1990s.

•

This comparison and contrast between the two leads one to suspect that the Taliban movement may not be able to sustain itself long enough if its pariah status continues. In fact, even after its occupation of almost the entire Afghanistan, the international community is not willing to bestow recognition on it. The Iranian revolution did not face this problem since the international community looked upon it as an internal affair of Iran.

Why this duplicity? Among other things, the international community apparently feels that the Taliban movement is not indigenous, as it was made out to be, with even the credentials of the leadership in doubt. The ethnic cleansing resorted by the Taliban raised many fundamental questions about their motives in the long run. Above all, the Taliban's top leadership is not willing to come out in the open to put across its viewpoint. Their public relations outfit, Pakistan, enjoys much less credibility. The clumsiness with which it handled the whole Afghan drama during the past decade has led everyone to suspect that it is not a simple civil war.

Ayatollah Khomeini succeeded in projecting Islamic revolution as good for Iran; in the process the international community was made to accept that he was fighting for Iranian nationalism and civilization. The Taliban, on the other hand, managed to project themselves as religious zealots who believe in the subsect of their religion and not the Afghan spirit and nationalism and civilization. That is why one finds priceless Kabul National Museum art objects in the houses of Pakistani generals in Islamabad. The Taliban talk in terms of destroying historical monuments like the thousand-year-old Buddha's statues in Bamiyan. Also the Taliban's talking of the need for poppy cultivation and Osama bin Laden as an honoured guest of the Taliban do not evoke sympathy or comfort for the international community.

11

Saudi Arabia
Challenges from Within

Saudi Arabia's trouble comes mainly from the need to assert its claim to be the temporal kingdom guarding the heritage of Islam, against those who have the clout to question it. At one time it was Ayatollah Khomeini's revolution in Iran and its fallout on the Islamic world. When they were about to tackle it, their association with extra-regional powers for security emerged and ossified into an al-Saud–US-specific phenomenon. The outcome, entirely unexpected by the protagonists, is the phenomenon of Osama bin Laden, born a Saudi but for many years operating from Afghanistan.

The success of Khomeini's Islamic Revolution in Iran in February 1979 posed a direct challenge to Saudi predominance in the Islamic world. Khomeini's initial target was the Saudi monarchy, "stooges of Satan", along with the USA, "the Satan". It was the first time since World War II that somebody had questioned publicly the Saudi monarchy's credentials to be the custodian of the holy places of Islam. Interestingly enough, many Muslims endorsed Khomeini's criticism, and Khomeini was emerging as a pre-eminent leader of the Islamic world. Thus cornered, the Saudi monarchy was looking for avenues to preserve its position in the Islamic world, and undermine Khomeini.

•

Amidst Iran's escalating tirade against the Saudi monarchy, there came about the seizure of Ka'bah at Mecca by a former theology student, Junayman bin Mohammad bin Seif al-Oteibi. Oteibi's cause was disenchantment with the way Islam was being interpreted in his native kingdom. The episode occurred on 20 November 1979, just seven months after the Iranian Revolution.

Oteibi, a student of the Islamic University in Medina in the early 1970s, dropped out in 1973—he was 22 then—after clashing repeatedly with his teachers over their interpretation of the application of Islamic law to everyday life. In 1974, he started a movement to enquire into, what he termed, the "condition of the Muslims". He was joined in this by several other theology students, Mohammad bin Abdullah al-Qahtani being the most important. Together they rented a house in Medina and began to gather a following. Oteibi was arrested several times and questioned by the authorities; but the ulema, the scholars and elderly religious leaders who give counsel on the applications of Islamic law to the state, came to his rescue.[1]

Oteibi managed to recruit some members of the National Guard, an important force of some 30,000 Bedouin soldiers who mainly look after internal security. For a while he moved freely between Saudi Arabia and Kuwait, eluding their security officials. He wrote extensively on the interpretation of Islamic law and religion and, by the end of 1979, twelve of his essays had been published. In his most important work, a 37-page monograph entitled "Rule, Allegiance and Obedience", he observed that the Khalifa or leader of the Islamic people must be a Muslim *chosen by the people* and must uphold the religion. "Yet", he wrote, "we are living today under an imposed royalty where it is not the Muslims who choose the Khalifa. The rulers have been imposed on the ruled, and disapproval of the Muslims does not result in removing the monarchy." It appears from his other writings that he also had strong reservations about Christians, Jews and Shi'ites, whom he refers to as outlaws in relation to Islam. He also rejected all Islamic groups that did not adhere to the most fundamental application of the Koran, that of the Wahabi movement in Saudi Arabia. He rejected education as a manipulation of the masses by the rulers. His sharpest sting was reserved for the royal family—

---

[1]Citations to the Oteibi episode from Sreedhar, *Gulf: Quest for Security* (New Delhi, 1983).

as betraying Islamic ideals, as being corrupt, and as having abused the people's trust. The royal family's relationship with the religious establishment was based on deception, he said (see Box 11.1).

In 1975 Oteibi went into hiding to escape the authorities. He remained a fugitive, moving around several Saudi cities, recruiting followers, and hiding among his tribe, the Oteiba, or his supporters, whenever the heat of the chase was on. His following came from all the five major tribes in Saudi Arabia, from non-Saudi students in the Medina University, from immigrant workers, and in Kuwait and Qatar. Those beheaded after the recapture of the mosque included ten Egyptians, six South Yemenis, three Kuwaitis and one each from North Yemen, Sudan and Iraq.

According to a confession allegedly made by Oteibi after the capture of the Ka'bah, the concept of Mahdi dawned upon him in early 1979 in a dream. Qahtani was the man designated by Oteibi as the awaited Mahdi, and whom all Muslims must obey. However, according to some Kuwaiti scholars who were in regular contact with both Oteibi and Qahtani:

> there was never any talk of a mystical envoy from God, as the Saudis have claimed. Their premise was that the present Saudi rulers had forfeited their role as leaders of Islam, that a new leader was needed more as a symbol and rallying point for the revolt against the Saudi family rather than someone with divine powers. It was a political move with Islamic foundations.

Soon, Oteibi decided he must resort to an armed revolt to bring down the dynasty.

•

The seizure of the Ka'bah by about 500 armed men began on 20 November 1979 at 5.30 a.m. local time, immediately after morning prayers. Seizing the microphone, their leaders declared one of their own to be the new leader of the Muslim nation, denounced the Saudi royal family headed by King Khalid, and urged the 40,000 worshippers either to join them or leave in peace. Then they sealed all the doors and spread throughout the Ka'bah, placing snipers on minarets and roofs. According to Khalid al-Hassan, chief of the PLO in Kuwait, a tape-recorded version of Oteibi's statements shows that they talked about commissions paid to royal princes on business deals, of the drinking of alcohol and the smuggling of spirits by members of the royal family, of the need to select rulers who adhere to the religion, and of the general climate of moral collapse in the kingdom.

Saudi troops mounted their assault on the mosque on 21 November, a day after its seizure. They blasted one of the doors with plastic explosives, but retreated when they met heavy fire from the rebels. According to the official version, during the first three days, Oteibi's men used a lot of firepower, shooting at targets or at random. Many outside observers felt, however, that the government response was confused and disorganized. Regular army men were mixed with National Guard soldiers and other security officials, and there was little coordination. The fighting continued till 4 December, when finally Oteibi's men surrendered. Official

---

Box 11.1
Excerpts from Junayman bin Mohammad bin Seif al-Oteibi's Writings

Today the Muslims are not united in the choice of Imam. Each nation has its own ruler. They rule as opportunists. While showing their allegiance to Islam they support infidels and outlaws. Some of them ally themselves and make peace with the Jews. Others ally themselves and make peace with the Communists. Still others ally themselves with the Christians and give sanctuary to the Shi'ites, who have rejected the faith....

All Muslims are living under imposed rulers who do not uphold the religion. We owe obedience only to those who lead by God's book. Those who lead the Muslims with differing laws and systems and who only take from religion what suits them have no claim on our obedience and their mandate to rule is nil.

Ever since the rule of King Abdel Aziz (Ibn Saud) has settled down in the peninsula, you find that people have become ignorant of the ways of Islam. Those with poor insight and awareness see some good in the Islamic rule, but they fail to see what it hides in the way of suspending the struggle for Islam (jihad), in the alliance with Christians and in the pursuit of worldly things. Our belief is that the continued rule (of those leaders) is a destruction of God's

estimates placed the casualties on the government side at 127 soldiers dead, including 12 officers, and more than 300 wounded.

Oteibi's movement is still reported to enjoy considerable support throughout the Gulf region, and even as far as Egypt, where adherence to Islam is strong. According to a Kuwaiti, who met Oteibi many times, Oteibi saw himself as the initiator of a revolt by all Muslims of the Arabian peninsula. He added: "He told me the first time I met him: 'I am a Muslim who happens to be born in this place they named Saudi Arabia. But the message is to challenge all these rulers who have no rights of obedience upon us.' He was talking about other governments in the peninsula." Thus Oteibi's objections to the Saudi ruling elite were similar to those put forward by Ayatollah Khomeini then and to a certain extent by Osama bin Laden from 1996.

In the wake of the Oteibi episode, Prince Fawaz Ibn Abdel

---

religion even if they pretend to uphold Islam. We ask God to relieve us of them all.

The best and most obvious example (of the deception by the rulers) is the founder of their state, King Abdul Aziz and the tribal elders who share his power, who are in agreement and in support of his policies or silent about his wrongdoings. He called upon the Ikhwans, may God rest their souls, to support him on the basis of the Holy Quran and the tenets of the religion as the Imam of all Muslims. They fought for him, spread the faith and opened the country for him. But as soon as his power was established and as soon as he secured what he wanted, he allied himself with the Christians and stopped jihad outside the peninsula.

Anyone with eyesight can see today how they represent religion as a form of humiliation, insult and mockery. These rulers have subjected Muslims to their interests and made religion into a way of acquiring their materialistic interests. They have brought upon the Muslims all evil and corruption. Those who seek degrees from the universities do not mean to uphold the religion. They mean to secure a job, acquire material wealth, to increase their possessions of real estate, cars and clothes. Education is not a way of serving God, but a way for (the rulers) to fill jobs and to use people.

(Originally in Arabic; translated and published by the *New York Times*, 23 February 1980.)

Aziz, half-brother of then King Khalid and governor of Mecca where the Ka'bah is located, resigned on "health grounds"; also retired were General Assad Abdel Aziz al-Zuhair, commander of the Air Force, General Ali Majid Qaddani, a top official in the Defence Ministry, and Major Fawzi al-Awfi, commander of the Public Security Forces (National Police). Simultaneously, the application of Islamic law was also tightened. There is now more vigilance in enforcing the prohibition on the employment of women; and newspapers have been told not to publish women's pictures or to black out their faces. Religious programming on the radio and television has been intensified. In early March 1980, the government announced the preliminary details of the proposed Third Five Year Plan which, *inter alia,* envisaged an investment of more than US$200 billion to improve agriculture, mining and complete infrastructural facilities started under the previous plan. This extraordinary reaction from the ruling elite was evidence that the ruling family can be challenged on the platform of religion; and it is vulnerable on this point.

The Ka'bah episode also demonstrated that there is fairly widespread discontent among the Saudi religious leadership: throughout his difficult times during 1975–78, Oteibi received patronage; and his following included all the five major tribes in Saudi Arabia. Oteibi's teachings have also brought legitimacy, in terms of Quranic teachings, for revolting against the ruler. His refrain that the Saudi royal family has betrayed Islamic ideals, is corrupt and has abused the people's trust, and the acceptance of his convictions by a section of the Saudi people shows that, as in Iran, Saudi Arabia is also susceptible to an Islamic upsurge, provided it has a charismatic leadership. Interestingly, despite five years of intensive training by US personnel, government forces could not promptly smother this minor upheaval involving 500 armed men. Also, events of later years have shown that Saudi counter-measures to avoid a recurrence of similar incidents by increasing investment and strict Islamization have not paid enough dividends.

•

The Oteibi episode left a profound impact on the Saudi monarchy's threat perceptions.

Just a month after the Oteibi episode, the Soviets invaded Afghanistan. In the perception of the Saudi ruling elite, this was a unique opportunity to re-establish their predominance in the Islamic world; and also to curb the Ayatollah Khomeini's influence in Iran's neighbourhood. Through liberal doses of financial aid, running into millions of US dollars, they supported the US–Pakistani efforts to organize the Afghan refugees in Pakistan to fight the Red Army. Pakistan being a Sunni-majority state and its allegiance to the Saudi monarchy being total, facilitated the Saudis' involvement. In addition, the Saudi endorsement of Pakistan's Islamic ideological orientation provided the much-needed legitimacy to the Afghan jihad.

It is also believed that the Red Army's invasion of Afghanistan, an Islamic country, was looked upon by Saudi Arabia initially as a direct challenge to the entire neighbouring Arab world. The region was just recovering from the traumatic experience of the socialist ideology of Nasser and Iraq–Soviet interactions. As almost always, the Saudis wholeheartedly collaborated with the US for defeating the Red Army. Saudi and other Arab volunteers were sent to Afghanistan to fight along with Afghan mujahideen; and in 1988[2] they sent people like Osama bin Laden, a member of an influential family in Saudi Arabia, to celebrate the victory over the Red Army.

For the Saudis, Afghanistan was to be a convenient, and permanent, pressure point on Iran. Like all the other parties involved in supporting the Afghan refugees-turned-mujahideen, the Saudis operated through Pakistan to work out a *modus vivendi* among the various Afghan factions. But the situation became grotesque when, in the subsequent four years Pakistan failed to get a stable government installed in Kabul. The Pakistani scheme of liquidating every opponent of their nominee or making him run for dear life revived the old Afghan warlords' feuds.

The Saudis initially recognized the interim government formed in Afghanistan after the Red Army's withdrawal. Later they often

---

[2]There are conflicting versions as regards when Osama bin Laden first appeared on the Afghan scene. Some accounts say he was there in 1984, some others say in 1986. One diplomat, who was physically present at Jiddah airport, told us it was the second half of 1988.

publicly distanced themselves from the Taliban by declaring the Taliban's emergence as an "internal development" in Afghanistan. After the capture of Kabul in September 1996, and Mazar-i-Sharif for two days in May 1997, the Saudis recognized posthaste the Taliban government as the official government of Afghanistan. We were told by an Arab diplomat close to the Saudi royal family that they recognized the Taliban only at Pakistani persuasion. However, the Taliban's subsequent failure to consolidate their position and their extra-territorial designs considerably alienated the Taliban from the Saudis.

Saudi Arabia's initial strategic interests, say from 1992, in developments in Afghanistan may be summarized as:

— religious-theological interests, in terms of spreading Wahabi Sunni Islam;
— extending the Saudi sphere of influence in the Iranian neighbourhood, where Tehran was perceived as emerging as a major challenger;
— checkmating Iranian pre-eminence in the Persian Gulf permanently;
— geo-economic interests, in terms of tapping the hydrocarbon reserves through the Delta oil company, in which members of the Saudi royal family have financial interests.[3]

•

While the Red Army was still in Afghanistan, the Saudis instigated another neighbour of Iran, Saddam Hussein's Iraq, to revive the settled dispute of Shatt al-Arab waterway. There is enough evidence that the Saudis lavishly funded Saddam Hussein to commence hostilities against Iran in the fall of 1980. The next eight years saw a systematic wrecking of Iran's economic infrastructure; and Iran's energies were focused on fighting Iraq's aggression. This Saudi tactical move clipped the wings of the new regime in Tehran. Also, Khomeini's tirade shifted its target from Saudi Arabia's ruling family to Iraq.[4] Once again, the Saudi ruling family

---

[3] See Citha D. Maass, "Afghan Conflict: External Involvement", *Central Asian Survey*, 1 March 1999.

[4] See Sreedhar, *Iraq–Iran War* (New Delhi, 1985), esp. ch. 1.

had made its money power work to neutralize a potential threat. In the bargain, it got its major adversaries in the Persian Gulf to slug it out.

Throughout the 1980s, Iran attempted to discredit the Saudi regime, including causing disturbances during the Haj by Iranian pilgrims. Interestingly enough, the Iranian protests were the same as those of Oteibi and his followers—anti–al-Saud and anti-US. There were, at the same time, reports of increased clandestine activity in the country against the ruling family. The Saudis seem to have concluded simplistically that the escalating dissident movement was of Iran's doing. The outside world knew, though, that Saudi dissident leaders like Salman bin Fashd al-Aouda and Mohammad al-Masari had nothing to do with Iran.

By the time the Soviets withdrew from Kabul, the war with Iraq had completely drained out Iran. In addition, Khomeini's demise in 1989 removed the rallying-point for those who could question the Saudi leadership. Suddenly there was a vacuum in the camp of opponents of the Saudi royal family. Nevertheless, the vulnerability of al-Saud family and its total dependence on the US also became glaringly public.

The Saudis, however, had themselves laid the foundation for the emergence of hard-core Islamic radicals. Strangely, the Taliban's ascendancy in Afghanistan in 1995–96 coincided with increased terrorism and violence in Saudi Arabia. The Taliban's September 1995 ultimatum to the Rabbani government in Kabul to surrender or face attack, was accompanied by two bomb blasts in a mosque in the town of Qubah 500 kilometres southwest of Riyadh in October 1995, killing eight persons.[5] In the subsequent month, on 13 November 1995 two car bomb explosions in Riyadh destroyed a building housing US military personnel who assist in the training of the Saudi National Guard, whose prime duty is to protect the royal family. Five Americans and two Indians were killed and over sixty persons, most Americans, were injured.[6]

[5]*The Telegraph* (Calcutta), 14 November 1995. For a comprehensive account of terrorism and violence in Saudi Arabia, see P.B. Sinha, "Terrorism Strikes at Saudi Arabia", *Strategic Analysis* (New Delhi), September 1996, pp. 946–9.
[6]*Times of India* (New Delhi), 2 June 1996.

Again on 26 June 1996, a massive tanker-truck bomb explosion outside a housing complex of the King Abdul Aziz airbase at Al-Khobar near the port city of Dhahran in the eastern province killed 19 Americans and injured nearly 400 people, including 105 Americans, 147 Saudi nationals, 118 Bangladeshis and some Egyptians, Jordanians, Filipinos and Indonesians.[7]

These are the five thousand-plus Afghanistan-trained Arabs, popularly known as Afghani Arabs, floating around in the Arab world. Battle-trained and well equipped, they have strong ideological moorings. They want to see a pure Islamic state established in their countries. Sacrificing worldly comforts, some of them have started radical movements for replacing the existing order. Osama is just one among them.[8] In the process, the Saudi dissident movement has acquired an ideology and a framework which cannot be easily challenged. The Taliban expressing extraterritorial ambitions has added a new dimension to the phenomenon.

•

Meanwhile, the thaw in Iran–Saudi relations has given a new thrust to the Saudi stance on Afghanistan. Acknowledging Iranian sensitivities about the developments in Afghanistan, the Saudis began to bring down their own involvement. It must have dawned on the Saudis that in the event of a major upheaval in the Islamic world due to the Afghan Arabs, the first target would be the Arab world, and not Iran.

With the Taliban's failure to consolidate their position quickly even after their capture of Kabul, and the Saudi involvement in Kabul's affairs becoming public gave an excuse to Saudi Arabia to retrace some of its steps, like recalling its ambassador from Kabul and asking the Taliban emissary in Riyadh to pack up in autumn 1998. The Saudis have no answer to the allegation that they are a covert party to cross-border terrorism, anathema to its supporters in the US.

With leaders of Saudi dissident movements getting safe haven

---

[7]*Indian Express* (New Delhi), 28 June 1996.
[8]Sinha makes this point in his article "Terrorism Strikes", see n. 5.

in Taliban-controlled Afghanistan, combined with the reported Taliban assistance to wage a war against the Saudi royal family, the Saudis have been compelled to hastily reappraise their policy towards Iran and Afghanistan. The Saudis were also struggling with falling oil revenues through 1998 due to low prices, which has cooled their interest in exploring hydrocarbon reserves in the CARs and marketing them.

In these changed circumstances, the Saudis were trying to get Saudi dissidents out of Afghanistan double-quick. They also have a problem how to keep their influence in the region, after having substantially tarnished it with their covert support to the Taliban.

The visit of President Khattami of Iran to Saudi Arabia in May 1999 has gone a long way in narrowing Iran–Saudi differences. It has also brought about a qualitative change in the Saudi perception of its involvement in Afghanistan. The Saudis are now bringing pressure on Pakistan to withdraw its covert support to the Taliban to compel it to come to the conference table to form a broad-based government.[9]

The dilemma for the Saudis is that failure in installing a broad-based government in Afghanistan, acceptable to all the ethnic groups, would blot their credibility as leaders of the Islamic world. But to have a broad-based government, the hard-liners among the Taliban, especially the Kandahar coterie of Mullah Umar, who believe that they have the guns and the muscle on their side, need to be neutralized. Whether Riyadh has clout enough to get Pakistan to stop extending military help to the Taliban remains to be seen. Simultaneously, the Arab dissident movements getting strong backing from the Taliban will need to be dismantled.

A new dimension has been added to the scenario by the sudden change of regime in Islamabad on 12 October 1999. With the sympathy and support of the new rulers in Islamabad to the Taliban and Arab fugitives being well known, the Saudi ruling elite have indeed been placed in a cleft.

---

[9]For an excellent analysis of Saudi–Iran relations, see Turki al-Humad, "Saudi Stances", *Asharq al-Awsat*, 5 September 1999, p. 9.

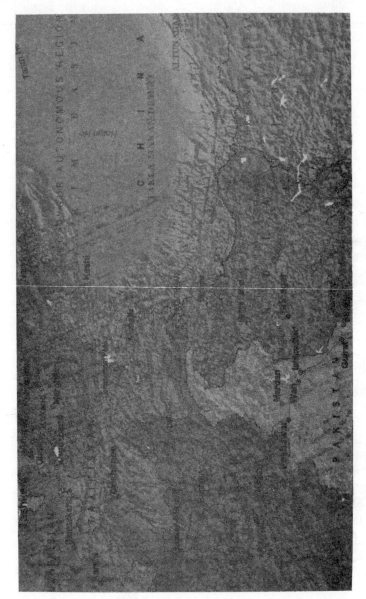

Map 12.1. The link between Afghanistan and the Xinjiang Uygur Autonomous Region

12

China
Playing for Advantage

The fact of the support of the People's Republic of China to the Afghan resistance movement against the occupying Red Army in the 1980s is well documented. The PRC then collaborated with the West, supplying arms and ammunition and extending covert diplomatic support to the Afghan resistance movement. The then Sino–Soviet rivalry was one of the reasons for this policy. After the Red Army's withdrawal in 1989, the Chinese were reportedly selling arms and ammunition to the warring factions in Afghanistan.

After the advent of the Taliban until 1998, the Chinese attitude towards the movement was overt indifference. Beijing refused to condemn the Taliban's actions—whether religious extremism, the treatment meted out to women or the harbouring of radical Islamic militia in their occupied territory. The Chinese leadership was content to mouth platitudes like "peace should return to Afghanistan" or "a broad-based government should be formed in Afghanistan".[1] For instance, Shen Guofeng, the Chinese Deputy Permanent representative at the UN, said:

Afghanistan is a multi-ethnic country, its ethnic problems have had their profound historical background and outside forces' intervention has further complicated its domestic problems. The military advances which one faction has made over the past several months have not

---

[1] See, for instance, "Dialogue on Hot Topic" column by Jiang Anquan in *Renmin Ribao*, 8 October 1996. FBIS-CHI-96-205.

solved the problems. China maintains all military advances are temporary and cannot help solve the problems. The Afghan conflicts can only be settled by all factions through peace talks under UN aegis.[2]

Similarly, Foreign Ministry spokesman Zhu Bang Zao said on 8 August 1999: "China sincerely hopes that parties in the conflict pay close attention to national interests, cease fire as soon as possible and seek a proper, peaceful settlement of the issue through negotiations."[3] Zhu said China regretted the recent escalation of fighting between the Taliban and the opposition.

During the July 1999 UN-sponsored peace talks in Tashkent, China urged the international community to create a conducive atmosphere in Afghanistan for negotiations and urged the warring Afghan factions to sink their differences. The international community should try to create a conducive environment for settling the Afghan issue, Vice Foreign Minister Yang Wenchang, who led the Chinese side, said. Yang voiced Beijing's hope that a stable Afghan government would be formed in Kabul at an early date.[4]

Against this backdrop, in the semi-official Chinese interaction with the Taliban, even overlooking Iranian objections to the Taliban, it would appear from Pakistani media reports that Islamabad played a major role. Apparently, in the Chinese assessment, the Taliban are going to be recognized in due course by all the neighbours and they should not lag behind. The Pakistani calculations would have been that if one of the permanent members of the UN Security Council like the PRC started dealing with the Taliban it was only a matter of time before others followed suit. It might also be that the PRC would like to establish its presence in Afghanistan much before others, especially before the US steps in in a big way.

If the PRC can pull off the Turkmenistan–Afghanistan–Pakistan gas pipeline it can score a major victory *vis-à-vis* the West and also gain a firm foothold in the CARs. Some commentators have also argued that the slowdown in the quantum of foreign investments and the negative vibrations in the Chinese economy prompted the

---

[2]Shen Guofeng urges Afghan Factions to Resume Talks. Official News Service for Overseas Chinese (Beijing), 9 December 1998.
[3]*Times of India* (New Delhi), 9 August 1999.
[4]Ibid.

authorities to look around for alternatives. They believe that like the narcotics traffickers from the Golden Triangle who use Chinese banks to launder their money, Taliban-generated narcotics money is finding its way through Xinjiang Autonomous Region.[5]

The first non-official delegation of the PRC consisting of about fourteen members, including scientists and People's Liberation Army personnel, visited Kandahar, Khost and other places in December 1998 ostensibly to examine the unexploded cruise missiles fired by the US in August that year. A seven-point understanding was reached between the delegation and the Taliban. In terms of this understanding, China with its vast experience with Russian military hardware will train Taliban military personnel in the operation and maintenance of captured military equipment of Russian origin. This includes training Taliban pilots in flying the MiG aircraft. In addition, China agreed to provide $10 million assistance for repair of some major highways and airfields damaged during the Afghan civil war. The Chinese also promised to equip the 25,000-strong Taliban Army in the next twelve months.[6]

In return, the Taliban are reported to have promised not to give any further training to Muslim militants from Xinjiang in any form either in Pakistan or in Afghanistan. The Taliban are also reported to have agreed to maintain the madrasas (religious schools) and places of worship in the Xinjiang province. By mid-July 1999 there were reports that some 22 MiG aircraft had become operational for the Taliban, the fact being generally attributed to some quick work done by the Chinese to enable the Taliban to launch their offensive against Ahmed Shah Masoud's forces in late July.[7]

A four-member Chinese business delegation which included one woman, and again described as non-official and private, visited Kabul and signed a trade agreement on 28 January 1999 with the Taliban. The delegation held detailed talks with the Taliban authorities in Kabul, including political matters like the opening

[5] See Deepak Arora's report in the *National Herald*, 7 February 1999.
[6] See idem, 31 December 1998. Some interesting points were made by Aziz ud-din Ahmad, "Afghan Policy and its Defenders", *The Nation*, 24 September 1998.
[7] Ibid.

of a non-official Chinese embassy in Kabul. The two sides came to an understanding on resuming trade links between the two countries and starting cargo flights between Kabul and Urumqi at the earliest.[8] The date and time for the inauguration of such flights is, however, yet to be finalized. In this connection, the Chinese authorities have suggested repairing the Kabul and Kandahar airports runways and also some complexes for storage of goods to be exchanged between the two countries.[9]

The Chinese government in principle agreed to export electronics, cosmetics, textiles, tyres and other rubber materials to Afghanistan through its cargo. In return, Afghanistan would export gems, carpets and rugs, dry fruits and wool and woollen products to China. In the light of such understanding, the Chinese authorities agreed to tap the mineral potential of Afghanistan and for this purpose, China is likely to establish some factories. The Chinese authorities have also agreed to extend cooperation to the Afghan government in rebuilding and reconstruction of the war-affected country.

In early July 1999 again, there were reports that China and the Taliban had reached certain important agreements, including one on defence cooperation. These reports also observed that some of the earlier contracts given to Turkmenistan had now been shifted to China; and China would invest shortly in producing gas cylinders.[10] A Chinese construction company, Overland, is also engaged in constructing portions of the gas pipeline that is supposed to run from Turkmenistan, through Afghanistan, to Pakistan.

•

In historical perspective, the PRC's flirtation with the Taliban is not unusual. The PRC has always supported radical elements in countries in the immediate neighbourhood with which it had land boundaries. Maoist China extended support to the radical

---

[8] See Sreedhar, "China, Taliban and India", *Deccan Chronicle* (Hyderabad), 9 April 1999.

[9] See Shamim Shahid's despatch from Peshawar in *The Nation*, 25 February 1999.

[10] Summary of World Broadcasts, FE/3577/A/1, 3 July 1999.

elements in North Korea, northeast India, Vietnam and Laos. The support was rationalized on ideological and politico-strategic grounds. In nearby Cambodia, dictators like Pol Pot were also extended support on the same considerations. It may be argued that none of these movements, basically political movements based on an ideology, is comparable with the Taliban, a supposedly religious movement. Even conceding this point, the fact remains that the Taliban is a political movement based on Islamic ideology. Its authors and leadership claim that the movement was started to end the exploitation of Afghan feudal lords.

In the post-Mao period, the closest one can think is the PRC's support to SLOC in Myanmar, again another country with a close land border with the PRC. The latter's sudden announcement in 1988 of $1.8 billion military aid to the military junta in Myanmar astonished the rest of the world.

The pattern of Chinese behaviour with its immediate small neighbours seems to be to have "in-depth" and "brotherly" relations irrespective of the ideological orientation of the regime in power. The Chinese attitude towards the Taliban would appear to be on these lines. Their primary concern seems to be to have secure borders.

•

Diplomatic sources say China is worried that any flare-up in the fighting in Afghanistan may spill over into its own volatile Xinjiang Uygur region in the northwest, already facing a spurt in religious fundamentalism.[11] Beijing is aware of the threat posed by the export of religious fundamentalism from countries such as Pakistan and that has kept the Chinese authorities on permanent vigil in the strategic northwest region.

According to a Pakistani report, among the 25,000 Muslim militants trained in Pakistan, there were many Uygurs. There were also reports in 1992 of Islamic uprisings in the town of Baren in Xinjiang autonomous region, in which 22 persons were killed. After this uprising China closed its road links with Pakistan for a considerable period of time.

[11] Interview in Bishkek, July 1999.

The Chinese have a serious problem with Uygur Muslims in the post-Soviet period, which they have sought to deal with both on the domestic front and with the neighbours. The events in Afghanistan in the 1990s have had a profound impact on the Central Asians, including the large numbers of Uygurs living as minorities in Kyrgyzstan, Kazakhstan and Uzbekistan. The Chinese have had bilateral pacts with the post-Soviet governments in the CARs to keep a check on the Uygurs who had contacts with their counterparts in the Xinjiang autonomous region.

With the Taliban too, the Chinese have used the December 1998 defence pact to have information on minorities. Similarly, when Kyrgyz President Askar Akayev was in Beijing in 1998, he was told by the Beijing leadership to keep the Uygurs in check. This was followed by a visit to Bishkek by Qian Qichen, then Chinese Foreign Minister, in June 1999. Although the ostensible reason was to announce a US$3 million grant, the real issue was information on Uygurs. The two governments think the Uygur activity is being fanned by Saudi Arabian money funnelled through Turkey. There have been reports that after gathering information from the CARs, the Beijing authorities have tracked down the Uygur youths and persecuted them.

Beijing uses economic leverage with the CARs, giving them grants and undertaking repair and construction of their roads and other infrastructure. A similar tactic has been extended to the Taliban. But the Chinese, while importing steel from Kazakhstan and engaging in trade with Kyrgyzstan are also aware that the CARs are being utilized by the US and Europe. The CIA has a strong presence among the Chinese-speaking minorities. The US also woos the media in the CARs, taking large numbers of them on conducted tours. This helped the US during the Chinese nuclear test at Lop Nor when the media in the CARs, particularly in Kyrgyzstan, took a strong anti-China line on this issue.

The US has installed a sophisticated electronic observation facility at Naryn in Kyrgyzstan, at 4000 metres height, to keep a watch on Lop Nor. The Americans are supposed to be sharing data on nuclear radiation with the Kyrgyz, but the latter have no way to analyse it or take any counter measures.

The actual Uygur population in the CARs is difficult to assess. The official figures are far removed from the facts on ground, according to most independent sources. A major reason is the high degree of migration. Fear of persecution also prompts many Uygurs to declare themselves as Kazakhs or Kyrgyz. The Uygur population in Kyrgyzstan is officially 70,000, but actually could be double that. The Uygur population in Kazakhstan, though declining and officially 200,000, is estimated at a million.

According to Professor Ibrahimov Israil Mamunovich, Dean of Uygur Faculty, the world's only university faculty at Bishkek exclusively studying Uygurs, 25 per cent of Uygurs in the Soviet Union died during communist purges. Traders were killed on suspicion of being intelligence conduits. In the post-Soviet period some have done well as traders. But a large section of population enters their local nationality as Uzbek, or Kyrgyz or Kazakh, instead of Uygur even now. A large majority of the world's Uygur population lives in the Xinjiang autonomous region. The official figure for this is seven million, but it is actually 20 million, according to Mamunovich.[12]

The Uygurs have had an ancient culture that coexisted with the Chinese, Mamunovich says. They took to Buddhism before the Chinese and were in touch with India through their monks. The Turkish links were established much later, when the Karakhanis State was established. Around the eighth or ninth century, the Uygurs ceased to be nomadic and settled down. They developed a rich folk culture and literature distinct from the Chinese. Indeed, the first translation of Buddhist literature into Chinese was by Uygurs. The Uygurs also got buffeted in the conflict between Mahayana and Hinayana streams of Buddhism. In the twelfth century they embraced Islam.

"This is my version, but it is true", said Mamunovich. "The Chinese were also Buddhist, and should have assimilated the Uygurs, but they did not. The Uygurs have a broader approach to history, but have suffered." The Chinese conquered the Uygurs after a long struggle in the early eighteenth century. The conquest meant the end of the Uygur state that covered the present-day Yarkand, Khata and Turfan in Mongolia, Tibet and Kashmir along the Great Silk Route.

In the eighteenth century, the Mongolian state of Jungar was

[12]Ibid.

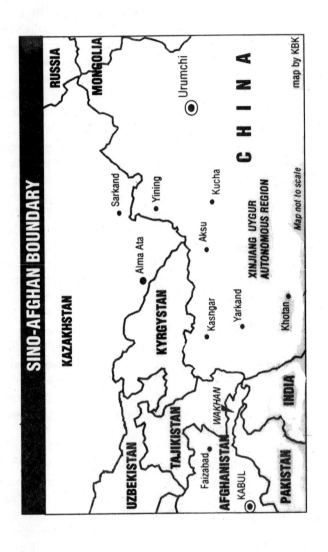

Map 12.2. China–Afghanistan Boundary

established. But by the end of the century, Uygurs became dependent upon the Manchus. In 1759, the Chinese conquest of Uygurs was complete. The resistance began only in the nineteenth century. Over 400 rebellions took place against the Chinese.

In 1866, a new state was established by Yaqub Beg. The Eastern Turkestan Uygur Republic was established in 1933. Between 1944 and 1949, 4000 Uygurs were liquidated in a joint action by Moscow and Beijing. In 1949, the head of the Uygur republic was killed in an air-crash in the Altai mountains. Travelling with him were all his ministers. "It was a carefully planned action to curb any move at independence." This was the time the communists took over in China. Mamunovich asserts that the conspiracy by which the entire government was eliminated was proved subsequently, but there are still doubts whether the air crash occurred at Alma Ata (now Almaty), according to one version, or near Moscow, according to another. "We have no access to records of that period and cannot prove it conclusively."

Mamunovich, an Uygur born and brought up in a village near Issy Kool in Kyrgyzstan, says Uygurs are the key to understanding the history of Central Asia, "since everyone is keen to revive the Great Silk Route". Although Sunni Muslims for the past nine hundred years, Uygurs retain the "Indo-Buddhist culture that permits diversity". Mamunovich said Uygurs respect Nehru and Tagore and during the Soviet era, were exposed to Indian cinema.

The Uygurs have been struggling to retain their identity both in and outside China. Stray attempts to form a government-in-exile have failed. Uygur organizations have semi-legal status in the CIS. Chinese pressure on the CAR governments has ensured that Uygurs do not form legitimate bodies. The "unity centre" in Bishkek is a social body and not a political organization.

Mamunovich is emphatic that the Uygurs are not Wahabis. He termed it the result of "Chinese influence". There were Wahabi groups active among the Uzbeks, Kyrgyz and Tajiks, but the authorities CARs have been particularly harsh on the Uygurs, he alleged.

Mamunovich agreed that "some" Uygur youths had gone to the Kashmir state in India to fight for Pakistan, but was at pains to explain that they were driven by religious, and not any anti-Indian sentiment. They were taken to learn theology, some to

Iran and some to Pakistan. Sunni youths were heading for Iran to know what the Shia stream of Islam was. If the youths were trained in handling arms, "they might use it against the Chinese, but unfortunately, they got involved in Kashmir".

Mamunovich spoke of the Uygurs fighting like the Jews for a homeland of their own. Scattered in different countries, they are facing the wrath of both Moscow and Beijing. "Every time there are signs of turmoil in China, we see prospects of control loosening. Our only hope is that we gain from the internal contradictions within China."

The Uygurs have been left behind compared to the Tibetans, whose cause has been taken up by the world community. Mamunovich said that the Tibetan and Uygur "interests coincide" but was noncommittal on any collaboration between the two fighting the Chinese. A major Uygur leader, Erkin Alaptagin, who was active in organizing dissidence among the Uygurs, is now in Japan. The Tibet and Uygur cooperation "continues", but Mamunovich was not clear at what level it was taking place.

Until the 1990s, the PRC was not overtly worried about the resurgence of militant Islam after the Iranian revolution in 1979. From 1992–93, especially after the disintegration of the Soviet Union, there were regular reports that a small group of Muslims from Uygur community in the Xinjiang had started asserting their independent identity. Out of the Xinjiang population of 16.89 million, Uygur Muslims constitute around 40 to 50 per cent. The group of Xinjiang province–based Muslims in collaboration with radical Muslim outfits in and around West Asia revived the demand for Eastern Turkestan. Supporters of the Eastern Turkestan Movement (ETM) can be seen in the rank and file of the Taliban in Afghanistan, Hizbullah in Lebanon and Hizbul Mujahideen, a Pakistan-based outfit operating mostly in Jammu and Kashmir. Some of these Uygur are also getting their religious education in the seminaries of Pakistan and Egypt. There seems to be a positive correlation between the Taliban's ascendancy and Uygur Muslim uprisings in Xinjiang. For instance the success of the Taliban through the beginning of 1996 resulted in increased militant activity by Uygur Muslims. Consequently, in a major crackdown by the Xinjiang authorities in June 1996, 2773 people were arrested and more than 600 guns were seized.[13] In another incident on 7 February 1997, 25 Uygur Muslims were shot dead by the Chinese forces and 55 Chinese civilians and police were beaten to death by the Uygurs.[14]

Following a crackdown in Bishkek, Osh and Jalalabad in May 1998, the Kyrgyz authorities detained several youths and seized documents, video material and photographs that they found "inflammatory". They maintain that the material and the youths' activities aimed at spreading fundamentalism. At the time of the interview, the youths were still in detention, without trial.

According to media reports, the Islamabad-based sponsor of ETM and President of the Asian Muslims Human Rights Bureau, Abdul Rasul, is determined to raise the issue wherever he can. His family along with other Chinese Muslims migrated to Pakistan from Xinjiang some time in 1967 and acquired Pakistani nationality. Rasul claims to have met Osama bin Laden in Khost province of Afghanistan in the first week of October 1998 and "he had promised to help the Muslims of China". After launching the Asian Muslim Human Rights Bureau on 2 October 1998, Rasul also claims to have met Ali Musa, chief of the commando wing of the Lebanon-based Hizbullah in Tehran, the Dalai Lama, spiritual leader of Tibet in New Delhi, and leaders of the Taliban including Mohammad Nibe Muhammadi, former chief of the Jihadi group in Afghanistan.[15]

Subsequently, at a press conference in November 1998, Abdul Rasul also made some interesting observations. According to him "the Chinese government on 24 October (1998) decided not to allow the Muslims of Xinjiang province to perform pilgrimage (Haj) this year". For the Muslims of Xinjiang, pilgrimage is very expensive, costing about Rs (P) 400,000. He believes that this is because the pilgrims would be inspired by other Muslims of the world during the Haj season. The Chinese government

---

[13]Cited in P.B. Sinha, "Islamic Militancy and Separatism in Xinjiang", *Strategic Analysis* (New Delhi), June 1997, pp. 451–9.

[14]Moonis Ahmar, "Ethnic Assertion in Xinjiang", *The News,* 6 March 1997.

[15]See Nafees Takkar's report in *The Nation,* 24 November 1998. Also see Tayyeba Kayani, "The Dark Side of the Afghan Situation", *The Nation,* 4 October 1998.

had resorted to racial elimination, restricting Muslims from having more than one child per family, which was against the spirit of Islam. He also disclosed that China barred Muslims under 18 years of age from entering mosques.[16]

The immediate demand of the Uygurs seems to be 10 per cent share in the resources of the Xinjiang province for its Muslim population, religious freedom, equality in the allocation of jobs, stopping the ethnic cleansing and settlement of non-Muslim Chinese nationals in Xinjiang region. The leadership of the Uygurs outside PRC assert at regular intervals that their ultimate aim is an independent Eastern Turkestan.

•

For the unemployed Uygur Muslim youths, a six-month contract for US$20,000 to wage a "jihad", be it Kargil, Kabul or Dagestan, is an attractive proposition when compared to the average US$25 salary if they were employed. They get enrolled in Xinjiang, where they are targeted for their religious beliefs and political opposition to Beijing. They also come from the neighbouring CARs of Kazakhstan and Kyrgyzstan, where their activities are under constant watch by the authorities, ostensibly under Chinese pressure. A score of them were killed in the Pakistan-launched incursion in the Kargil sector in India in mid-1999, and the matter was taken up with the Chinese.

Authoritative reports in Bishkek say Pakistan's ISI's representatives recruit these youths either as tourists or students. They also travel as Hajis, and once the pilgrimage is over, they disappear. Once the journey begins, the youths' parents receive the money. "In the Central Asian context, this is big money. So, even if the son does not return home, the family is well off", said an Asian diplomat who has been monitoring these movements. They travel on passports of different Islamic nationalities, which can be procured at a price. Fake Turkish passports have been seized by authorities in Bishkek and in neighbouring Kazakhstan. The money comes from Saudi Arabia. They travel either by their respective national airliners or by AeroAsia, a private airline

[16]Ibid.

registered in Pakistan. After training in handling arms, these youths are dispatched for "jihad."

"Unfortunately, some Turkish-speaking youths have joined Pakistan's campaign against India's Kashmir", Mamunovich said. He regretted this departure from "the aura of mysticism" in the way the Uygurs practise Islam. The number was a hundred in 1997. It went up sharply after some returned home in Bishkek to tell their stories. But the whereabouts of the others are not known. "It is the same story as that of young girls from Central Asia who go to West Asia for jobs and end up in brothels", said a diplomat.

A top Kyrgyz government functionary, speaking strictly off the record, confirmed that "several" youths had travelled in recent months to Pakistan and Afghanistan to become "mercenaries". But he maintained that this was "not a trend", adding: "Uygurs have their own preoccupations."

•

Evidently, the Xinjiang Muslims started gaining inspiration from developments in the neighbouring Islamic countries. The Chinese authorities have time and again tried to suppress the Uygur Muslim agitation through the law-and-order machinery of the state. This met with limited success only. In a simplistic fashion, at one point of time, especially in the mid-1980s, the Chinese courted Saudi Arabia, the custodian of the Islamic holy places, to placate the Uygur Muslims. In fact the Chinese went a step further by selling CSS-II missiles to Saudi Arabia in 1988. There were reports that the Saudi King's emissaries were allowed to freely distribute the Holy Book among the faithfuls in Xinjiang and renovate some mosques. This, however, failed to pacify the Uygur Muslims.

With the Taliban movement providing the needed ideological support, some jihadi groups indulged in violence and terrorist activities at regular intervals. By mid-1998, it no longer remained a local law-and-order problem. The Uygur were getting the needed international publicity and human rights activists in the West started taking cognizance of the problems faced by the Uygur.

Simultaneously, the Taliban's efforts to gain recognition from the US, and the concessions it was willing to make, must have sounded alarm bells in Beijing. If the Taliban were willing to intensify their activities at the instance of the US with Uygurs, the issue could get murky, and even snarl up with the Afghan imbroglio. Apparently, the PRC is worried over the extensive US contacts with the Taliban; and hence the variety of lines of communications it has opened, without formally recognizing the Taliban government.[17]

---

[17]According to some commentators, the Chinese policy towards Afghanistan and the Central Asian Republics is governed more by fears of western domination in their backyard. See Richard Sokolsky and Janya Charlick-Paley, *NATO and Caspian Security: A Mission Too Far* (Project Air Force, Rand, Washington, 1999), pp. 35–9.

13

Central Asian Republics
"Back of the Beyond" Under Siege

For Central Asia—hitherto variously nicknamed Tartary and Back of the Beyond—the twentieth century unfolded with new ideas threatening its people's pastoral, nomadic lives. The Bolshevik upheaval quaked the region. For seven decades-plus, it was part of the mighty Soviet empire—molly-coddled where it suited larger Soviet designs, neglected otherwise.

Central Asia was badly affected by the Afghan war when its men and material got sacrificed for a full decade (1979–89). It was scarred by the time Moscow withdrew and those of its men who did not become cannon fodder returned home.

Even as the region recovering from the backlash of the Afghan war, the USSR itself split up, rendering the republics of Central Asia independent—and orphan—politically, economically and socially. A major change for the five new nations was that "God" was freed. They could practise their faith—or whatever faith they wished to. But with that also came an overdose of Islam they had never known before.

"Suddenly, we in Central Asia want to be believers, whatever it means", said Anara Tabyshalieva, director of the Kyrgyz Institute of Regional Studies. Speaking in Bishkek, she was reflecting on the urges of millions of Central Asians who have emerged from seven decades of communist rule hardly a decade ago and are still in transition. The end of communist controls has brought a cultural shock to a people who were by and large innocent of the activist aspects of religion. The somewhat unsettled atmosphere makes the region a happy hunting-ground for highly motivated clergy of various faiths, armed with holy books and, more to the point, oodles of money. A region trying to find its feet in its new avatar as independent republics, Central Asia has plenty of reasons to wish to immunize itself from fundamentalist Islamic blasts from Afghanistan across the borders.

Alcohol is not taboo in Central Asia. It is even consumed ceremonially by those who bid farewell to those setting out on the Haj pilgrimage. Also, pork is eaten in many of the CARs. Even though Islam is becoming more and more a faith practised in the workaday life, the approach remains secular. Regimes like that of Islam Karimov in Uzbekistan see an element of threat to the nation's fabric from imported fundamentalism, and have consciously sought to promote secular ways of life. A law enacted in 1998, for instance, forbids anyone but a priest to sport a flowing beard. There is also a ban on women covering their face with *hezab,* but one comes across women donning it regardless.

•

The Central Asian republics were carved out haphazardly during the Stalinist era, unmindful of the divisions caused among the nationalities. Thus the ancient cultural centres of Samarkand, Khiva and Bukhara, that had been part of Tajikistan for centuries, were transferred by a presidential decree to Uzbekistan. Uzbekistan also benefited from another Stalinist decision when some 100,000 square kilometres of territory was transferred to it from Kazakhstan.

Thus, there are large populations of Uzbeks in Tajikistan and Tajiks in Uzbekistan. Turkmen inhabit parts of Tajikistan and Uzbekistan. The Kyrgyz population in eastern Uzbekistan caused economic problems for the latter in July 1999 by buying up goods available in the open market. Much of the intertribal conflict in the region today can be traced to the fact that the entire Central Asia is multi-ethnic, but stands divided along unnatural borders. There is also no sign of these being redrawn, absent the overriding presence of the Soviet Union. The CARs have themselves agreed that their borders would not be altered. The

Almaty Declaration of 1991 states that "the administrative borders of the former Soviet Union are not subject to change".

Simple in their ways, Central Asians are still waking up to the "cruel" world outside, which is complex and articulate. Used to a controlled system for seven decades under the Soviet dispensation, they are still in the process of learning the capitalist ways. They have yet to adapt to new ways, enacting liberal laws and procedures. Still inward looking, they are wary of change. The Russian language remains the *lingua franca*. Local languages, some of them rich and cultured, lack the vocabulary required for the pursuit of business and science. Although people of Russian origin are depleting in numbers and are generally held down, with a vengeance, there is no way they can be kept away from many key positions. The Russians man most of the business, tourism and trade and entertainment industry. Asians have been slow, and shy, at adapting "Christian" ways. Russians are treated as adversaries, and new governments tend to fan anti-Russian feelings as their own way of inculcating their local brands of nationalism.

Being land-locked, the CARs have the problem of communication and getting across to the outside world. In each of the CARs, the standard of living is falling constantly. Some like Tajikistan are not even viable economies. Overwhelmingly Muslims, save Tajikistan they are also Turkic in their cultural mores. At the same time they are multi-ethnic and multi-tribal, with tribal norms and nomadic instincts still guiding their reflexes. They lack a yearning for an independent identity, not having worked for the freedom that they have acquired and not having suffered any social and political churning. Privately, they miss the Soviet ways, especially the largeness that sheltered their lives, the social security, the free education and health care, subsidized food and housing. They are left to fend for themselves, but they enjoy personal liberty, which on the surface at least, is a matter of pride and satisfaction. The pangs of migration and separation are still felt in the cities. In the rural areas, it was the Khan earlier, replaced by the local party secretary, now replaced by the local bureaucrat or the boss at the workplace.

The social transformation has meant a beginning of the need to believe. It was Lenin and the Communist party earlier, today it is some God or the other. The population was Muslim in

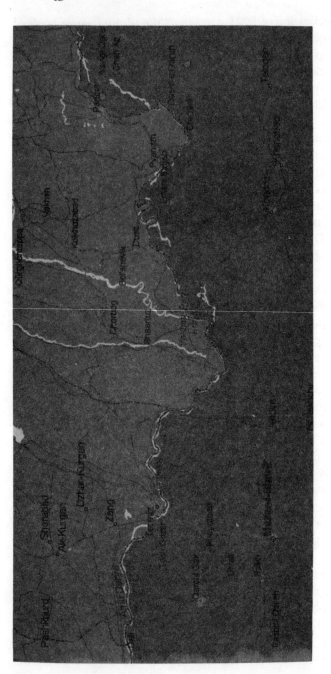

Map 13.1. The CARs–Afghan border

name, tribal and nomadic in reality. The Muslim clergy being officially appointed during the Soviet era, care had been taken to keep them away from religious rituals and divisive ideas. The result was a high level of literacy and man–woman equality. In the modern sense, Central Asians are secular because they did not know what it was to be non-secular. All this is changing with the advent of foreign clergy, money, religious literature and the lure of going abroad.

Politically, the Central Asians are still at a nascent stage. The former communist leaders have changed labels to become democratic leaders. They are elected presidents, having parliaments, variously called *Ulus, Majlis* and *Jirga*. But they are all uniformly presidential systems with the chief executive enjoying overriding powers. They have moved from one-party to multi-party rule, but the opposition is held at bay, often harassed and termed antinational. Suppression of democracy and even personal liberty is frequent, with isolationist Turkmenistan an extreme example of a presidential dictatorship with a strong personality cult thrown in. Tajikistan in the neighbourhood is plagued by civil war inspired and fed from across the border.

•

In neighbouring Afghanistan, the avowed aim of the Taliban, whose political and military clout is not a matter to be discounted, has been to spread the Wahabi school of Islam. Disclaimers from Kabul that the Taliban would not cross the Afghan borders have not calmed Central Asia's fears.

By and large, Central Asians do not think there is a conventional military threat from Afghanistan. An Uzbek scholar gave three reasons, some with significant riders, why the threat from the Taliban was not military. First, it does not help the Taliban to cross the Amu Darya. They are totally preoccupied with the resistance at home. Second, the history of the region shows that while people have moved southward for trade, climatic, or even political reasons, Pashtuns never had military interests in Central Asia. There have been kinships, but no conquests. Third, there are major differences, cultural, economic and political, between the Uzbeks, Tajiks and Turkmens settled in Afghanistan on the one hand and their countrymen back home. A major difference is that while the former have been exposed to radicalization of Islam, the latter have been free from it.

A significant rider to the first point about discounting a military threat from Afghanistan is that Uzbekistan was for long smug about the role of a buffer played by Dostum. His departure has made them realize that the Taliban, right on the banks of the Amu Darya on some locations, could pose a military threat. Dostum's role is now expected to be played by Ahmed Shah Masoud. After the six-plus-two conference in Tashkent in July 1999, the Uzbeks hastened to assure Masoud that they would support his endeavour and that they would not back any other rival forces.

Said the Uzbek scholar: "Uzbekistan has more soldiers, jets and weapons to meet a military threat on the border. But we cannot deal with the guerrillas attacking at will, establishing sanctuaries and causing subversion."

Officially, none of the CARs complains of "a border problem" with Afghanistan. Indeed, Turkmenistan's Foreign Minister Boris Sikhmuradov in an interview boasted of "warm relations" and "a peaceful border" with Afghanistan, while comparing the situation with that on the India–Pakistan border.[1] The reality is that cross-border migration, an age-old phenomenon, has accentuated in recent years in the form of political refugees, smuggling, arms and drugs.

The regimes in the region, whether the czars and the Soviets in the past or the present-day governments, if not the entire people, have been clear about shunning radical ideas. Post-Soviet regimes in Uzbekistan and Tajikistan in particular have launched drives against radical elements.

The Afghan turmoil has constantly sent refugees across to the CARs. For instance, Uzbekistan received a hundred thousand refugees from 1992, a large number of them political, in the wake of changes in Afghanistan and another hundred thousand from Tajikistan, which was in turmoil immediately after independence. Many of them have become citizens over a period. There are 8000 refugees officially registered with the UNHCR in Uzbekistan. Over a thousand are "mandate refugees"—refugees

[1] See *Mainstream*, 6 November 1999, pp. 25–6.

from political persecution. Many of them are supporters of the Najibullah regime and moved over during 1992–93. They are settled in Tashkent and other major towns like Samarkand and Bukhara, according to Frank Remus, in charge of the UNHCR office in Tashkent.

Tajikistan has a constant flow of Afghan refugees. Turkmenistan also has a significant refugee problem, from Afghanistan and from Tajikistan, although Turkmenistan does not officially accept that it has a refugee problem. For almost three years, the UNHCR has been repatriating Tajik migrants, an estimated 2000, from Turkmenistan.

The break-up of the Soviet Union led to nine million people changing their country of residence, most of them Russians. In Tajikistan, the Russian migration was as high as 70 per cent of the migration. Political persecution in China also forced the Uygurs to move to Karakalpak in Uzbekistan and to Osh in Kyrgyzstan. The migration has led to the development of NGO culture, with 169 bodies active in various fields. There are large American NGOs that specialize in setting up small, national-level NGOs to carry out specific programmes.

Uzbekistan does not want to be seen as a country readily accepting refugees. It has refused to settle the isolated camps, causing a running dispute with the UNHCR. Besides the cost of setting up such camps, the Uzbeks think once they set up camps, it would encourage greater influx. The present arrangement allows the refugees to buy or rent houses and live with families and take up jobs. But it does not permit them to buy land, which is with the State, and does not grant citizenship rights.

There is, however, a glaring lacuna in the Uzbek policy. Keeping refugees in isolated camps could help the authorities check their activities and prevent the spread of fundamentalism. This makes sense anywhere, in any situation. But allowing the refugees to go where they please and mix with the local population could lend itself to activities the State would not desire.

The CARs, though, keep the refugees under surveillance. The UNHCR says it has no reports of crime of political nature from among refugees.

Religious trouble has had a tendency to turn inter-ethnic and there have been instances of Russians being targeted for violence.

Tajikistan is facing a threat of narco-terrorism, although it is not entirely driven by religion and has its roots in ethnic imbalances. Turkmenistan is trying hard to shut itself from these threats, partly by living in isolation and the rest by buying peace and forging trade links with the Taliban. If there is indeed a threat to Turkmenistan from Afghanistan, it is being explained in terms of the new nation's policy of neutrality which does not exclude supping with the source of the threat.

Uzbekistan, the most populous CAR, faces the threat directly in the mushrooming growth of political parties and groups who draw inspiration from the Taliban in Kabul or their mentors, the Islamist parties in Pakistan. Ironically, the worst affected are ancient seats of learning: Samarkand, Khiva and Bukhara. Also affected in the neighbouring Kyrgyzstan is Osh, home of universities and institutes.

They all constitute the ancient and culturally rich Ferghana Valley. Namanghan in this region has had a spurt in the Wahabi movement. Its police chief was hanged outside the police station by extremists in 1997, an incident that goaded Karimov's administration to take strong action.

In the years immediately after independence the CARs adopted an open-door policy and allowed religious groups and bodies to come in from Turkey, Iran, Pakistan and Saudi Arabia. For five years, they even hobnobbed with Islamic nations in the name of religious solidarity, but changed tack once they realized that this was fomenting destabilizing fundamentalism. Groups like those active in Uzbekistan work for money and religion, and are not even keen to share power. They keep away from electoral politics.

While trying to keep the fundamentalists at bay, with varying degrees of success, the CARs have thought it prudent not to stop the religious activities *per se*. Kyrgyzstan, which had fewer than ten mosques at independence, has over two thousand now, mostly in the south, built with funds from Saudi Arabia, other Islamic countries, and Turkey. Turkmenistan is also witnessing a boom in building mosques, or rebuilding of those that had fallen into disuse during the communist era, ostensibly with foreign money, but also with a lot of own money.

Anara Tabyshalieva spoke of the need for "modern Islam" for

the CARs. The concept is still vague, she admits, but defines it thus: an Islam that would be suitable to accommodate western capitalist ideas akin to the US, Germany or Japan, not India or Pakistan, certainly not Saudi Arabia, not even Turkey." Secondly, it should take into account the gender equality to which CARs have got used during the communist era. Half the work force in the CARs is of women. The Central Asian woman is not ready to don a purdah or *chador*.

"Our attitudes are still nomadic and free. And then we had the Soviet legacy", Tabyshalieva explains the Central Asians' social norms. Independence has not meant a great change since "we have no traditions to build on, as our best thinkers were killed or purged during the Soviet era and many quit after the break-up".

She painted this scenario in the context of how missionaries—Protestants from the US, South Korea and Western Europe; Jehovah's Witnesses of different nationalities, Shia clergy from Iran and Sunni from Turkey, Saudi Arabia, Pakistan and elsewhere and Bahais came to Central Asia. They converted members of a predominantly Sunni Muslim society to their faiths. In Kyrgyzstan, they targeted women. The priests, who continue with the task, deliberately say they do not keep any records. They are also cagey about the sources of funds, except that they claim they receive donations.

Christian and Shia Muslim members in predominantly Sunni Muslim households caused their own tensions. They were all adding to the large-scale influx of Sunni clergy. "Jamaatis and Tablighis from India to Turkey thronged the CARs before the respective governments, seeing a clear threat, acted to curb them. They have sought to stem the tide of Islam's 'modernization'", notes Ahmed Rashid in *The Resurgence of Central Asia: Islam or Nationalism?*

Thus it was that Uzbekistan forbade Protestant priests, expelled Turkish teachers, closed Saudi Arabian schools when it found religious teaching was giving rise to fundamentalism. President Islam Karimov connected the bomb blasts that very nearly killed him and his entire cabinet on 16 February 1998, to Islamist militants trained in Pakistan and expelled several Pak nationals. Tashkent also lodged a formal protest with Islamabad for the role of people trained in Pakistan in fomenting trouble. Karimov made this point just on the eve of a summit-level dialogue with the US.

As Ahmed Rashid notes, "the CARs have had little exposure to Islamic politics and political activism and ideas generated in the rest of the Islamic world. But in 1992, Tajikistan and Ferghana Valley witnessed religious backlash, mainly because of being close to Afghanistan." He also notes that the then Soviet President Gorbachev's *Perestroika* helped the process in that people learnt to bypass the "official" religion and set up their own mosques.

... arrivals of funds, Korans, literature and mollahs from Saudi Arabia, Iran and Pakistan spread their respective versions of Islam.

The vacuum created by the lack of leadership from official Islamic hierarchy allowed fundamentalist groups to proliferate. The growing involvement of outside powers increased as Wahabi groups from Saudi Arabia, Islamic Revolutionary Guards and some Sunni fundamentalist parties in Pakistan took advantage of unprecedented political opportunities.

Rashid further says: "The West, especially the US, first encouraged the use of Islam to undermine communism in Central Asia." He quotes Anthony Bevins in "British Plot Aimed at Destabilising Soviets" (*The Independent*, 26 February 1990):

In the 1920s, the British in India supported the Basmadis with guns and money. In 1939, the British infiltrated agents from Afghanistan and India to whip up Islamic feelings in Central Asia. Fitzroy Maclean, a British diplomat and secret agent, advised his government in a secret memo in October 1939 that Central Asia should be destabilized through mullahs in order to prevent Russians from invading Turkey and Iran, and even as Germany fought Britain.

As for the Americans, Rashid says: "CIA funded Afghan Mujahideen to smuggle in Korans, tapes, money and weapons to Islamic groups in Uzbekistan and Tajikistan." He also notes the radical change in the West's line after ensuring the collapse of communism. "At US signals, CAR leaders began indulging in rhetoric against fundamentalism—to be friendly to West and to World Bank and IMF. This smothered the moderate content of Islam."

Having said all this, Rashid, in his book published in 1994, but still fairly relevant, gives a set of reasons why Islamic fundamentalism cannot succeed in the CARs. The majority of the people are Hanafi Sunnis and will not easily embrace the Wahabi line; Central Asia is divided on ethnic lines and fundamentalist parties cannot succeed in uniting them. "CARs have a high literacy level, a secular social growth, a free-market economy, consumerism encouraged by new rulers—all militate against Islamic fundamentalism and puritanical ways." Also, he notes that the CARs have been a home to Sufism, "which survived centuries of tribal, nomadic culture and 70 years of communism. Sufism is an amalgam of Buddhist and Shaman Christian beliefs and preaches tolerance—which is the antithesis of the Wahabi school."

He concludes: "To presuppose that narrow nationalism or fundamentalism will win the political battle in Central Asia is to underestimate the deep wells of heritage and experience that these ancient people have drawn on."

Whatever may be the final outcome, and one hopes that Rashid's conclusion is right, the CARs regimes have had to curb activities of the fundamentalists on the one hand, project heroes of their own on the other and occasionally take anti-Russia or anti-West postures. In some cases, opposition parties have been dealt with harshly on the ground that they are fomenting fundamentalism when the real opposition may be purely political.

As Rashid, himself a Pakistani, points out, Pakistan's role in this matter has been questionable. The governments of Benazir Bhutto and Nawaz Sharif in the early 1990s wanted close trade links with Central Asia and also to impress the US of Pakistan's strategic importance. While they encouraged businessmen to visit Central Asia, the fundamentalist Jamaat-i-Islami wanted an Islamic revolution. Its chief, Qazi Hussain Ahmed called upon the Pakistan government to "counter US imperialism and new world order by using Central Asia for a continued fight" and wanted Pakistan to provide "Islamic guidance rather than economic aid". Pakistan's efforts to follow this dual route disturbed the CARs leadership. In March 1993, the foreign ministers of Uzbekistan and Tajikistan directly accused the Jamaat of arming and training Muslim radicals from their people. Jamaat and Gulbuddin Hikmatyar were training large numbers of Central Asian Muslims in Pakistan camps by 1992. The Jamaat helped the Islamic Renaissance Party in Uzbekistan and Tajikistan to establish links with Arab Islamic groups and later, Osama bin Laden.

Contact with militancy, or failure to curb it, has cost the CARs image and money. For instance, extremism has affected tourism in Uzbekistan. British tourist groups visiting Ferghana Valley reported negatively about their experiences, which had a negative effect for some time.

Uzbekistan closed its border with Afghanistan to prevent infiltration, causing in its wake inter-border problems with other neighbours. Kyrgyzstan, on the other hand, has not taken specific measures. Frequent movement of militant groups is reported to be taking place through Tajikistan and Kyrgyzstan, and in between, through the turbulent southern Uzbekistan.

President Boris Yeltsin of Russia has also blamed the Islamic militants for the trouble in Dagestan and the blast in a building in Moscow on 12 September 1999. "It is time to recognize that terrorism has become an international problem", Prime Minister Vladimir Putin told Parliament on 15 September 1999.

An indication of the Central Asian unease at terrorism of the Taliban variety spreading its tentacles all around it can be had from the observations of Kyrgyz President Askar Akayev. On a state visit to Germany in mid-September 1999, when he met Chancellor Schroeder, Akayev said: "The present events could lead to the disintegration of Russia, just as the developments of 1991 led to the dissolution of the Soviet Union." Such an event, he said, would have "catastrophic results" for Eastern Europe and Central Asia. "This could lead to a terrible and endless civil war similar to what we have seen in Afghanistan for the past decade." Akayev said the West needed to recognize the threat from Islamic extremists and provide defensive aid to Moscow. "The terrorists are clearly getting support from abroad."

The drug trafficking is causing its own problems among the population of the CARs, exacerbating ethnic differences and fomenting Islamist extremism. Interestingly, the drug runners meticulously avoid these areas, while affecting the economic and political lives of their people. The Uzbeks in the adjacent Ferghana Valley have been experiencing fundamentalist resurgence. The

Uzbeks also have running battles with the Kyrgyz population of the southern region, which is threatening to rise in revolt against the "northern" regime in Bishkek.

Political turmoil in southern Kyrgyzstan and in adjacent Uzbekistan has led to the regimes in Tashkent and Bishkek conducting regular crackdowns against the "fundamentalists". A religious party, "Hizbi-at-Tahry", formed in Uzbekistan, has come up to oppose the government in Tashkent. Its stated objective is to establish a "Caliphate" in Namanghan and Ferghana. Media reports in Tashkent and Bishkek say the party gets its funds and support from Kabul. "The inspiration is Arabic", Orozbek Moldaliyev, Director, Bureau of International Trade and Security, Bishkek, said in an interview.

•

For the CARs abutting Afghanistan, safe borders have become essential, not only for their territorial sovereignty and economic well-being, but for political survival itself. Hence, the need for border management, which is a new and expensive phenomenon. They are in the process of setting up or reorganizing their border guards. Turkmenistan has raised a force of about 10,000 and Uzbekistan is raising an even larger force, separating it from its army, since it has major borders with several CARs. By comparison, Kyrgyzstan is not even planning to set up a force to guard its porous border with Tajikistan.

These forces require funds, equipment and training. The US is among those training them, driven as it is by the desire to see them managing their own borders effectively against the movement of men, arms and drugs. Top officials, from both Russia and the US stationed in these countries confirm that besides training, they also provide equipment. "We supply even handcuffs", said a US official, to stress the point that they are beginning from scratch. But it is strictly non-lethal. "Short of arming them, we are having to kit them fully", he said.

The US is also engaged in setting up a communication network along Uzbek–Afghan border. Fifty jeeps and a number of drug-smelling dogs were supplied in mid-1999.

With the US deeply involved in helping Uzbekistan set up its border guards, it is not surprising that these guards don uniforms, complete with large hats, like the Texas Rangers!

There is unanimity among Central Asian scholars, as also watchers of the Central Asian scene, that the societies have turned religious, but not turned fundamentalist, yet. But it is entirely possible in future, with the flow of drugs, money, and ideas brought by those who study Islamic theology in confrontation with other faiths and those spreading fundamentalism by exhorting the youth to take to arms in the name of religion, on payment of handsome amounts to their families.

14

Peace Initiatives
Till Now, a Mirage

They met in Tashkent, Uzbekistan, on 19–20 July 1999. The Afghans talked at each other, rather than to each other, with others in attendance playing to their respective national agendas. The Afghans agreed to disagree on just about everything except the bare minimum: the exchange of prisoners of war.

Representatives of the main participants obliquely admitted, a week after the talks ended, to anticipated failure. The two-decades old Afghan conflict cannot be solved overnight, they said. There are no instant solutions.

Tashkent was basically a reiteration of concern by parties, including the Taliban who signed the final declaration, at the alarming growth in drug traffic and the corollary arms running that threatened to perpetuate the armed conflict.

Fighting broke out within a week of the Tashkent conclave. It was clear from the way Kabul launched its offensive on 27 July, capturing Kapisa and Parwan provinces, and the determined counter-attack by forces loyal to Ahmed Shah Masoud, recapturing these provinces, that both sides meeting at Tashkent were actually keeping their powder dry.

Pakistan's large-scale involvement this time was unconcealed and determined. In this round of fighting, for the first time Pakistan army committed personnel, estimated at between 5000 and 25,000, heavy-arms including guns, and ammunition and vehicles. According to the Afghan Chargé d'Affaires in Tashkent, intercepted messages clearly indicated that the Pakistan Air Force combat planes operated from Peshawar, and not Jalalabad, which is not operational for combat role. This use of air power and artillery—and the heavy casualties, an estimated 1200 killed on both sides—showed that Pakistan also was preparing for this offensive in anticipation of failure at Tashkent.[1]

The Pakiştan–Taliban operation, aided by an estimated 300 Arab mercenaries, came immediately after the Pakistanis were forced to vacate their aggression in the Kargil sector in India's Kashmir region. Units of the Northern Light Infantry (NLI), which were in evidence in Kargil, were now seen in Kabul. A senior Pakistani journalist said that he had seen in Kabul the "same persons" who had been in the thick of Kargil operations. According to a Masoud aide in Dushanbe, Arab mercenaries were shifted from Kargil to Afghanistan after being told that this was another theatre of "jihad" as Ahmed Shah Masoud's forces were fighting "with Indian help". The cause of jihad was complete when the mercenaries were told that Russia had also committed troops, like Indians, to fight the Taliban.

•

While fighting in Afghanistan goes on intermittently, talks are resorted to by mutual convenience to sort out very limited objectives. Exchange of prisoners of war is one of the points of mutual convenience. Alternatively, there has to be someone keen and willing to play the mediator.

A month after the Tashkent talks, a conclave was held in Dushanbe, capital of Tajikistan, on 19 August 1999. The talks were Pakistan-brokered, and the Masoud-led side rejected Pakistan's mediation. The Pakistani team, which included Pakistan's envoy to Kabul, Aziz Ahmed Khan, left Dushanbe on way to Kandahar, the Taliban headquarters, possibly with some proposals for the Taliban leadership. Interior Minister and special envoy Rustam Shah Muhamand led Pakistan's team.

Masood Khalili, the Afghan envoy in New Delhi owing allegiance to President Burhanuddin Rabbani, described the Pakistani

---

[1]Interview in Tashkent, August 1999.

efforts at playing the mediator as "attempts to confuse the situation". He pointed to the impending UN General Assembly session and said that Pakistan wanted to convey the impression that it is acceptable to both the warring sides in Afghanistan and would be able to broker a resolution. These talks were at best posturing by Pakistan and the Taliban in time for the UN General Assembly session and obviously, under US pressure on Pakistan to disengage itself from the fighting in Afghanistan.

Tashkent was the first occasion when both sides in the fighting met formally in the presence of their immediate neighbours—Pakistan, Iran, Turkmenistan, Uzbekistan, Tajikistan and China—and two major powers, the USA and Russia, with supervision by the UN. Previous meetings at New York, Islamabad and Ashkabad had mostly been bilateral, without a structured agenda.

At Tashkent, Turkmenistan, which manages to conceal its close ties with the Kabul regime under the garb of its policy of neutrality, declined to sign the final document. Pakistan, too, did not wish to sign it and told Turkmenistan so. But at the last minute, it went along and signed, without informing the Turkmen delegation of its intentions. The last-minute about-turn by Pakistan was attributed to US pressure.

Karl Inderfurth, the Assistant Secretary of State, headed the US delegation. He talked formally during the conference, and on the sidelines of the conference informally, with all delegates, putting forth the US viewpoint.

The US and Russia, it would appear, had set their hearts on a formal meeting of Afghanistan's immediate neighbours in their presence. A decision appears to have been taken in April 1999 by the two to organize talks to forestall resumption of summer-time fighting. Uzbekistan, considered dependable by both, was prepared to host the meet.

And although both Washington and Moscow were agreed on the timing and Tashkent as the venue, the Russians privately questioned the timing of the meeting by hindsight, betraying reservations over a prominent American role in an area that has been a Russian backyard (and Soviet graveyard!). A senior Russian diplomat, present at Tashkent, said the conference was ill-timed. It should have been in winter, when in snow-bound Afghanistan, the Afghan contestants rest their guns and are in a better mood to talk. "To call them during spring or summer was being naïve.", he said. If the parties concerned had waited for ten years of bloodshed, what was the harm in waiting one more season, he asked. The decision to hold talks "as soon as possible" was taken at New York in October 1998, he said, and should have been followed up during the winter itself. Independent sources, however, question this claim. They insist that the six-plus-two meeting was decided not before April 1999.[2]

Pakistan had sought to throw a spanner in the works by conveying to the US and Russians that the Taliban would not agree to attend and hence, holding a conference was pointless. But the Americans told Pakistan that the conference would be held, regardless.

When the Taliban arrived, although several hours late, there was "relief and pleasant surprise in all quarters", said an Indian diplomat monitoring the conference. It was a higher level of representation in that while others met at the level of Minister of State for Foreign Affairs, Amir Khan Muttaqi is his government's Information Minister enjoying cabinet status. Clearly, Pakistan had used its good offices to persuade the Taliban to attend.

Earlier, Uzbek Foreign Minister Kamilov had visited each capital to invite the six-plus-two. In Kandahar to seek Taliban participation, he received first a rejection from Mullah Umar and then a noncommittal response. Uzbek diplomats later said that the Taliban agreed only after Pakistan Foreign Minister Sartaj Aziz spoke to Mullah Umar.[3]

Pakistan's representative Murshid sought to break the six-plus-two meeting by bringing in the Islamic angle during a two-hour separate meeting with the two Afghan factions. He was understood to have pleaded with Muttaqi and Rabbani's Minister of State for Foreign Affairs, Dr Abdullah that it was best to keep the "White Man" out and resolve the dispute among the Muslims.

Abdullah and Muttaqi met directly for two hours separately. According to sources, Abdullah heard out Muttaqi, who did much of the speaking, and neither side made any commitment. At this meeting, Muttaqi profusely praised Ahmed Shah Masoud as a "patriot" whose reputation ought to be safeguarded. "He must

---

[2]Interview in August 1999.
[3]Diplomatic sources in Tashkent who wish to remain anonymous.

join us", said Muttaqi to Abdullah, emphasizing that sooner or later, the Afghans must come together for the greater good.

But, in keeping with the Taliban approach of speaking from a position of strength, Muttaqi told Abdullah that even if Masoud joined, the question of Afghan leadership did not arise. The Taliban would welcome Masoud, but their Amir was Mullah Umar.[4]

Turkmenistan, which sees itself as a competitor to Uzbekistan, was put out by the choice of Tashkent as the venue. The US government had made it clear to the Turkmens that it wanted to see the talks through, though President Niyazov demurred.

At the end of the talks, while refusing to sign the final declaration, the Turkmen side stressed that it would continue to cooperate with any future peace process. The point was sought to be made that the exclusion from signing was a formal, and one-time, position. Turkmen Foreign Minister Boris Sikhmuradov said in the course of an interview that his country was committed to complete cooperation with the United Nations and had conveyed this to the UN Secretary-General's special envoy, Lakhdar Brahimi.

In reality, the Turkmen side was upset at the Taliban being singled out in the Tashkent Declaration for criticism for drug trafficking and spread of terrorism, despite its urging against such references. Russian and American diplomats agreed that the hand of not only Taliban, but also Pakistan, was discernible behind the Turkmen postures.

Sikhmuradov explained the Turkmen position thus:

We decided not to sign because there are two parties to the dispute and to condemn one of them is wrong. It was a very delicate matter. The Afghans are wise enough to sort out their problems, provided there is no negative influence, at least from outside. We wanted a common platform and have been saying so for the last seven years.

Going to Tashkent was counter-productive. But I would say it was neither a setback, nor a movement forward. Its idea was brilliant, but its implementation was not. The time has come to stop dividing Afghans into factions, tribes, etc. They are hostages of international negligence. Everyone knows how the crisis was aggravated.[5]

[4]Ibid.
[5]Interview in Ashkabad, July 1999.

Fig. 14.1. In its peace initiatives in Afghanistan, the UN at the receiving end
Courtesy: Frontier Post, 27 July 1999.

In his welcome address at the conference, Uzbek President Islam Karimov lashed out at the Taliban, accusing it of initiating and encouraging drug trafficking and using its earnings for spreading terrorism. Karimov was also concerned about the "summertime ritual" of resumed fighting. This set the tone of the conference.

Tashkent was the venue for exchange of views and some plain speaking, according to some participants in the talks. For instance, in what is described as the first direct contact at ministerial level, Inderfurth told Muttaqi that "Pakistanis and Arabs" have been using Afghan soil for training youths in acts of terrorism and made it clear: "We will fight terrorism."[6]

Immediately after the conference, Ahmed Shah Masoud arrived at the venue, causing a flutter. The Turkmen expressed resentment at this sudden appearance, citing Masoud's "failure" to respond to their invitations in the past. The Uzbeks urged the Turkmens not to make an issue of it and promised that Masoud would visit Ashkabad at a later stage—possibly a vain presumption, since Ashkabad's position *vis-à-vis* Masoud and the Taliban is well known.

Quite obviously, Masoud's appearance was an Uzbek coup. President Karimov's inaugural address had made reference to him alone as the party opposed to the Taliban. It meant Uzbek acceptance—many say a grudging one—of Masoud as the sole resistance leader, now that the principal man that Uzbekistan supported, General Abdul Rashid Dostum, is not on the scene.

This Uzbek reference has been interpreted in Central Asian circles variously as the relegation of President Rabbani as a marginal force in Afghan politics. However, despite the differences Masoud has with Rabbani, he is not seeking to raise the leadership issue at this juncture. For one, the Afghanistan seat in the United Nations is in the name of the government headed by Rabbani. Any talk of a change in leadership would jeopardize this, besides injecting needless controversy into the ranks of the Afghan resistance.

---

[6]This US willingness to talk openly about the Taliban–Pakistan nexus and the latter's defiance of US assertions surprised the diplomatic community in Tashkent. According to one diplomat, the United States' direct snub to Pakistan/Taliban failed to have the desired effect.

Masoud's meeting with Inderfurth, reportedly the first ever, was an opportunity for him to brief the latter on the situation in Afghanistan, emphasizing that the "Afghan tragedy" was thanks to Pakistan's "direct interference". The moment this ceased, the Afghan problem would be resolved. Masoud was understood to have urged that the US use its good offices with Pakistan to restrain it. Afghan people were tired of bloodletting and could not go on indefinitely, he pleaded.[7]

Inderfurth agreed in principle, but emphasized that it would be difficult for the US to meet all the expectations. US influence within Pakistan was limited, he pointed out. A clear indicator of this limitation was the fact that Pakistan was not cooperating in the surrender of Osama bin Laden.

Inderfurth also emphasized that the US could not pressurize Pakistan to the extent that this could lead to Pakistan's disintegration. Anything short of this, the US would seek to keep Pakistan's activities in Afghanistan under check.[8]

Inderfurth assured, according to Masoud aides, that President Rabbani's government would not be jettisoned and that it would remain the government recognized as the member of the United Nations General Assembly. The US position on this would not change and the question of UN membership, if and when raised by any party, would not be allowed to be put to vote.

Inderfurth's point about the US not wanting to precipitate things leading to a possible disintegration of Pakistan needs to be read in the context of the Taliban's role. In the event of a military defeat, the Taliban would have nowhere else to go but Pakistan, and this would in turn destabilize Pakistan's Pashtun-speaking areas. This is already evident from the way Nawaz Sharif was removed from power by the Pakistani army when the former just started the process of dismantling the terrorist apparatus on the Pak–Afghan border.

•

Among the CARs, each one, being a new nation, has sought to play a role as mediator in the Afghan imbroglio as part of an

---

[7] Diplomatic sources in Tashkent.
[8] Ibid.

effort to gain recognition. Pre-emption of problems emanating from Afghanistan has been another motivating factor. Even those who do not have a direct border with Afghanistan have played mediators and promoters of peace with varying degrees of success.

Tashkent has been the venue of numerous contacts, official and unofficial. Tajikistan and Turkmenistan have also played hosts to the two warring sides—Tajikistan to the Rabbani faction and Turkmenistan to the Taliban and their allies. A round of talks at Ashkabad preceded the Tashkent meet. Dushanbe followed Tashkent.

If Ashkabad had the cooperation of Pakistan and the Taliban, Dushanbe has acted at the prompting of the Rabbani alliance. Almaty, the Kazakh capital too hosted the first meeting at Moscow's instance in end-1996. Tashkent had the goodwill of both the US and Russia and the others went along.

Kyrgyzstan, a tiny CAR tucked away between Uzbekistan, Kazakhstan and China, has acted often to give itself a profile in Central Asia and the region. In April 1997, Bishkek took the initiative at Moscow's instance. Its then Foreign Minister, Rosa Otunbayeva, proposed Bishkek as the venue for an international conference on Afghanistan under UN auspices—a non-event till date. But it has given Kyrgyzstan something to speak of in the regional fora. The ground was first prepared by Otunbayeva meeting the UN Secretary-General's special envoy on Afghanistan, Lakhdar Brahimi. Bishkek also hosted the inter-Tajik dialogue in May 1997 and paved the way for the final Moscow agreement in June that year. Kyrgyz President Askar Akayev wrote to select heads of governments, particularly to all neighbours of Afghanistan and to India, China, the US, Japan and Germany. India, China and Russia supported the initiative. The US said it had no objection, but did not say a firm Yes. Japan was lukewarm in its response, being itself keen to host a meeting, which it did in late 1997. Pakistan disagreed on the venue. The idea did not take off.[9]

The Kyrgyz, nevertheless, succeeded in getting the warring factions to hold informal talks. A special cell was constituted in President Akayev's office, headed by an experienced official who had been KGB chief of Kyrgyzstan till 1991. This official went

[9] Diplomatic sources in Bishkek.

about establishing contact with all parties, including the Taliban. Thus, a Taliban representative based in Karachi and a Rabbani aide met in Bishkek in end-1997. The trend picked up and the Taliban's deputy foreign minister visited Bishkek unofficially. Reportedly, Dostum also paid a secret visit to Bishkek. Representatives of Masoud, Hikmatyar and Karim Khalili were also among the important visitors.[10]

Playing host to them was Kyrgyz Deputy Foreign Minister Irfan Abdulayev, a former Soviet diplomat who had earlier worked in China and had returned to the Russian foreign office in Moscow till 1996 before opting for Kyrgyzstan. In 1997, he joined President Akayev's administration as First Director of the First Political Department, before becoming one of the three deputy foreign ministers in charge of political relations. The post gave him leverage to talk to various Afghan sides and also visit Tehran and Islamabad.

Abdulayev was also in New Delhi, where he was received well. India acted positively to the Kyrgyz initiative. Finally, four CARs, but not Turkmenistan, which had declared its "neutrality", met in Dushanbe in October 1998. The Kyrgyz initiative was endorsed and this was conveyed to Brahimi.

The Kyrgyz proposal met with subtle opposition from Pakistan, although Pakistan's deputy foreign minister Mohammad Sadiq Khan Kanju toured Tashkent, Bishkek and Almaty in November 1998. At each of these capitals, Kanju pleaded for recognition for the Taliban regime but the response everywhere was noncommittal.

The Kyrgyz hoped to hammer out some kind of agreement by early 1998, but this floundered, and finally fell through after the fall of Mazar-i-Sharif and Herat. The Kyrgyz then took recourse to the October 1996 Almaty Declaration that called upon all sides to cease hostilities and hold talks. Nevertheless, for all the good work done, the Kyrgyz earned the goodwill of most sides. President Rabbani visited Bishkek in May 1999. Kyrgyzstan is host to a number of Afghans whose political leanings are with Masoud.

The variety of peace initiatives from Afghanistan's immediate

[10]Ibid.

neighbours in the past two years have all had the blessing of the United Nations. Curiously, all these peace initiatives have come either on the eve of a major offensive by the Taliban or after the event.

•

The new role that the US had adopted since early 1998 as a peace broker in the Afghan cauldron is being attributed to a number reasons. These include:

— The toughening posture adopted by the European, Islamic and CARs allies of the US towards the Taliban. The US policy of covertly being soft on the Taliban was a negative element in the United States' relations with Russia and the CARs, which wanted the Taliban tamed and contained.
— The role of US women groups who have galvanized into an effective lobby and signature campaign with the US administration. The Secretary of State, Madeleine Albright in late 1997, after a visit to Taliban-controlled areas observed that the Taliban's attitude to women is "despicable".
— The widely publicized US oil companies' interest in building an oil pipeline from the CARs via Afghanistan and Pakistan. Apparently, by 1998 the US concluded that Pakistan-dominated Taliban cannot resolve the Afghan issue amicably; and that unless the Taliban and all other ethnic groups work together, no solution can be achieved to the Afghan problem.
— The Taliban's giving shelter to Osama bin Laden. The fact of Osama, allegedly responsible for bombing the US military targets in Saudi Arabia, offering prayers along with Mullah Umar irked the Clinton administration.
— Growing rapprochement since mid-1997 between the US and Iran has been an important factor necessitating Washington's reappraisal of its Afghan policy. For the first time US and Iranian officials sat face to face and discussed the issue during the six-plus-two conference on Afghanistan in early 1997 in New York.

In April 1998, the Clinton administration sent William Richardson, a senior diplomat, as a special envoy to Pakistan and

Afghanistan. Purportedly, Richardson's main agenda was to assess the situation in the region and report back whether conditions were favourable for a possible visit by President Clinton to South Asia in the last quarter of 1998. Afghanistan and Kashmir were the two main issues. After detailed discussion in Islamabad, Richardson flew to Kabul to meet the Taliban leaders and leaders of the Northern Alliance in Shebergen. On return to Islamabad, Richardson announced a nine-point agreement on the intra-Afghan front.

— Immediate cease-fire between the Taliban and the Northern Alliance.
— Intra-Afghan talks under UN and OIC auspices on or before 27 April 1998, the 20th anniversary of the Afghan revolution.
— Holding of the next round of intra-Afghan dialogue in Japan.
— Initiating of exchange of PoWs by both sides as early as possible.
— Agreement not to allow Afghan soil to be used for terrorist activity.
— Banning of the cultivation of poppy from the next harvesting season.
— Lifting by the Taliban of the blockade of Hazarajat.
— Agreement to respect women's rights.
— Agreement to allow the UN and other developmental agencies to resume their operations unhindered.[11]

In Islamabad, Richardson gave the impression that he had finally managed to break the ice; and intra-Afghan dialogue would bring the Afghanistan issue out of the prevailing impasse. To quote Ahmed Rashid,

For a few hours it appeared that the agenda for the Islamabad talks would include many of these controversial issues—that is until Taliban started backtracking. "The agreement is very important, but there is no specific talks proposal for the Islamabad meeting", said Taliban spokesman Wakil Ahmad Muttawakil, minutes after Richardson left Kabul. In Kandahar, Mullah Umar, the spiritual leader of Taliban, whom Richardson had not met said there was no such broad agenda for the talks. In fact using the traditional Afghan chicanery the Taliban said yes

---

[11] Ikramullah, "Intra-Afghan Dialogue: A Victory Pakistan's Foreign Policy", *The Nation*, 23 April 1998.

to most of Richardson's wish-list but when once he was out of sight, had narrowed down the talks agenda to discuss only formation of a council of Ulema from both sides which in turn would set up a commission for actual settlement. The assessment by most diplomatic observers was that these are just talks about talks and the Taliban want to buy time because they are under increasing international pressure to ease up on their hard line.[12]

Whatever may have been the reservations regarding agreement between Richardson and the Afghan factions, the contestants in the Afghan civil war met at a conference convened by the UN and OIC in Islamabad on 26 April 1998. The following ground rules were agreed upon for this round of talks.

— The UN and the OIC could co-chair the Steering Committee.
— Dari and Pashtu would be the official language of the talks.
— At the conclusion of every session, only the co-chairmen would make the statement approved by the talks.
— Decisions of the steering committee would be made by consensus. Absent lack of consensus, the issue would be referred to the leaders of the respective parties or would be kept pending for future talks.
— The steering committee would complete the work in three to five days.[13]

Pakistan's then Foreign Minister Gohar Ayub played host at the talks held at Punjab House in Islamabad. In the talks, the Richardson agenda was jettisoned. Just before the talks commenced, the leader of the Taliban delegation, Wakil Ahmed, made it clear that the Taliban did not have any formula other than the

[12]Ahmed Rashid, "Pakistan, Taliban Engage US on Afghanistan", *The Nation*, 21 April 1998.
[13]Umer Farooq, "Afghan Groups Arrive at 5 point Agreement", *The Nation*, 27 April 1998. It must be noted that Nawaz Sharif made a number of visits to various capitals in the CARs and Iran in mid-1997 to mobilize public opinion for a peace conference between the Taliban and the Northern Alliance. In fact in October 1997 Mullah Rabbani visited Islamabad and agreed to talk to the opposition on two conditons: the talks must be held in Islamabad; and all factions must be present. Then Burhanuddin Rabbani visited Islamabad in December 1997. This was followed by Pakistan's Foreign Secretary Shamshad Ahmed's visit to Kandahar on 28 December 1997.— *The News*, 18 October 1997; *The Nation*, 2 January 1998. Ikramullah, "Fate of Ulema Meet Hangs in Balance", *The Nation*, 4 January 1998.

Ulema Commission. The talks would be symbolic only, if the ulema, who would take part in the talks, were not recognized ones. Mullah Umar's message, read out at the meeting, said:

> For many years, political dialogue has been going on aimed at finding a solution to the Afghan conflict, but so far it has not brought about any positive result. Afghanistan is a land of Muslim people and therefore nothing else can bring about such a result except the decision adopted in accordance with the law of Almighty Allah.

He reaffirmed that except an Islamic decision by the ulema, there could be no other formula to settle the dispute.

In this backdrop, the discussions came to a stalemate on the first day itself. Rabbani's side proposed a cease-fire, followed by convening of a Shura-i-Ulema at a later date. The Taliban delegation insisted on the choice of delegates who would represent both sides. It boiled down to the definition of who the "ulema" should be. While the Rabbani government was for anyone educated, the Taliban insisted that only the religious clergy could be termed "ulema".

To resolve the issue, the co-chairpersons proposed two alternatives. The first was to let an international panel decide who was qualified to sit on the commission, wherein the panel's decision would be binding. The second proposal was to create an advisory body for the purpose. The Taliban accepted the first proposal only, the Northern Alliance rejected both.[14]

On the fourth day in Islamabad, the two co-chairpersons and the Pakistan government made another proposal. Under the new solution both parties agreed to the establishment of a joint commission of Ulema. Each side would appoint twenty men to the commission, with neither side having power to veto the other's nominee. The ulema would be entrusted with negotiating a lasting settlement of the Afghan conflict and their decisions would be guided by the principles of the Islamic sharia; and any settlement reached by the commission would be binding on all sides.

It was an ingenious mechanism. By disallowing veto on membership, the agreement allowed the Northern Alliance to install its most important men in the Ulema Commission, people who might have little or no background as authentic Ulema. On the

---

[14] Ali F. Zaidi, "Talking to the Enemy", *The Herald*, May 1998, pp. 61–2.

other hand, by adding the provision that the commission's deliberations and decisions should be in keeping with Sharia the Taliban's demand for a solution based on the principle of Islamic law and tradition was also met.

According to one commentator, while the Northern Alliance was jubilant about the final decision, the Taliban described it as a great sacrifice on their part.[15]

•

The Taliban's reluctance to honour the accord reached in April 1998, was soon followed by a massive summer offensive in July–August 1998. Their spectacular success in capturing almost the entire northern region minus Panjshir Valley, eliminated the entire opposition except that of Ahmed Shah Masoud. The ethnic cleansing that followed in Mazar-i-Sharif and Bamiyan provinces brought in a totally new dimension to the ground realities. At an informal meeting in February 1999, both the Taliban and anti-Taliban forces made some contacts. Again the UN intervened and brought both parties together in Ashkabad (Turkmenistan) in mid-March 1999. The Taliban side was represented by a three-man delegation headed by Wakil Ahmed Muttawakil; and the anti-Taliban forces by a four-man delegation headed by Mohammad Younis Qanouni. After a marathon session lasting over four hours, both sides agreed to the following:

— release 20 prisoners each as soon as possible through the ICRC (Intentional Committee of the Red Cross);
— form a shared executive, shared legislature and shared judiciary;
— continue talks in order to address remaining issues and to implement decisions already reached; and
— hold the next round of talks preferably inside Afghanistan at a mutually agreed place.

Qanouni remarked at the end of talks: "We have had talks and negotiations in the past. This is the first time we have been able to create an atmosphere of trust and take a step towards political

[15]Ibid.

solution to the Afghan crisis". Muttawakil, leader of the Taliban delegation, was also upbeat saying that a permanent cease-fire would automatically follow any establishment of shared power structure.[16] The next day, however, Radio Kabul reported that the Taliban and opposition forces had accepted just for talks on a power-sharing formula. "So far there has been no agreement on the proposed broad-based government", the radio said. Muttawakil was quoted by the radio as saying, "We will discuss broad-based government and some other issues later in Afghanistan".[17] Apparently, the Taliban leadership under Mullah Umar had decided that they have the capacity and staying power to defeat the anti-Taliban forces militarily and did not need to think in terms of sharing power.

•

Three months later on the sidelines of the six-plus-two meeting, the Taliban and anti-Taliban forces met again in Tashkent. While the Tashkent declaration adopted the usual resolution of forming a broad-based multi-ethnic government constituted through political negotiations among the Afghan parties, the dialogue among the warring groups ended in a stalemate. According to one report, other than a pledge not to block foreign humanitarian assistance from reaching each other's territory, both sides wasted one more opportunity to resolve their differences.[18]

All this indicates that peace is still elusive to Afghanistan. The Taliban firmly believe that they can find a military solution to the problem; and the international community is needlessly hostile to them. But the process of softening the Taliban is on. The UN sanctions and the developments in Pakistan in October 1999 had a somewhat sobering effect on the Taliban leadership. With sanctions on, the Taliban cannot expect unlimited support from Pakistan. As a Taliban sympathizer told us, their first problem would be petroleum, oil and lubricants. The sympathizers in the Arab world can no longer supply them on a continuous basis.

---

[16]Umer Farooq, "Pakistan a Key Factor", *The Nation*, 15 March 1999.
[17]Ibid.
[18]Afrasiab Khattak, "Failure of Tashkent Talks", *Frontier Post*, 25 July 1999.

According to him, the Taliban had no POL storage capacity beyond 3000 barrels and one reason for losing the summer 1999 offensive was POL shortage. Similar is the case on other fronts. The sheer economic compulsions may force Mullah Umar to find a way out.

Afghanistan's irony is that those who are talking peace are also the principal suppliers of arms, which encourage a hard-line stance among the warring factions. The Taliban use talks only for posturing and buying time. They simply do not want to share power. The opposition, weak on the ground, but having support on the diplomatic front, finds talks convenient, albeit on its own terms.

Would a weakened Taliban begin to talk to a relatively stronger opposition? A military way could well be support and strengthening of Masoud, sufficient to inflict severe defeats on the Taliban to get them to talk. By itself, a peace initiative seems less likely to succeed given the Afghan abhorrence to talking. Only pressures from the international community can work—but only up to a point. But since Afghanistan is not a European nation, there is a marked absence of urgency. The efforts are more likely to remain seasonal—in fits and starts.

Meanwhile, as has been happening each year, the winter of 1999, with little scope for fighting, revived activity on the diplomatic front. King Zahir Shah, the 85-year-old deposed monarch, initiated moves to convene a Jirga or even a Loya Jirga (grand assembly) of Afghan representatives. In this he is being aided by his hosts, the Italian government, indicating a possible European Union initiative, with tacit support from the United States. Nothing of note emerged from this effort. But significantly, the King kept out both the Taliban and the Northern Alliance representatives.

While this is a continuous, long process, there are no prospects of the two contending sides coming to terms, at least for the time being.

15

What Next?
A New Pashtunistan, Perhaps?

No matter that the world refuses to recognize their government, and no matter that the Islamic Front for Deliverance of Afghanistan (IFDA) led by Ahmed Shah Masoud is offering them a stiff fight, the Taliban look like they are here to stay. On the other hand, even if, hypothetically, the Taliban were to vanquish Masoud and gain absolute control of the territory, there will still be no peace in Afghanistan. Even Vietnam-style carpet bombing cannot get Masoud out of the Panjshir Valley, unless he chooses to quit. Assuming hypothetically that he loses support among his people, Masoud would have to quit Afghanistan.

Although the Taliban Information Minister Amir Khan Muttaqi, meeting Masoud in Tashkent in July 1999, praised him, calling him a "patriot" and much else, and invited him to join his side, this was essentially a point-scoring exercise. Unwilling to share power, the Taliban realize this and are prepared for a prolonged war of attrition.

The Taliban are fretful that the world community refuses to recognize their government. They would go out of their way to placate individual governments. But they are rigidly stuck on four points. These are: (a) their medieval cultural code; (b) refusal to compromise with their adversaries; (c) refusal to hand over Osama bin Laden; and (d) regulation and control of NGOs in their territory.

They are dogged about their medieval cultural code. They will not relax their Sharia laws, no matter what the world says about their treatment of say, women and children. The men have to grow a beard of minimum prescribed length and eschew alcohol, cinema and music. Enforcement of the code of conduct is ruthless, and the administration of justice macabre and public, in order to give an object less to the wickedly inclined.

They will not compromise with their adversaries. They have so far scorned any move to get them to talk to their adversaries. They have either not agreed or have recanted on what they agreed at meetings with their adversaries. They have steadfastly refused to share power. Efforts in the last three years to get them to accept even a semblance of compromise have failed.

They refuse to hand over Osama bin Laden. The Taliban have so far been firm about not handing over Osama to the Americans. Under great pressure, they have made conciliatory noises and have also resorted to dilatory methods like announcing that they were themselves disciplining him or that they would agree to his trial in a court in a neutral country. They put up an information smoke-screen in spreading the word that he had disappeared from the Afghan soil. Six months after this charade was played out, Osama was found in Afghanistan, and very much active, keeping a low profile. Osama was also involved in the planning of the intrusion of Kargil in India and later in Kabul's abortive northward push in July–August 1999.[1]

They have regulated the working of international agencies and NGOs operating in their territory. Women workers from outside have been intimidated into covering their heads. Afghan women have been prevented from assisting these bodies. International agencies have also been compelled to operate from a single complex in Kabul. In confrontations with foreigners working in Afghanistan, the Taliban have invariably won. They have no compunction about their own countrymen suffering if relief and assistance is stopped.

Defiant, the Taliban say that the world community has viewed them through its preconceived notions and through its western cultural spectacles. Their treatment of men, women and children, they argue, is culture-specific.

[1] See, for instance, Mullah Umar's interview given to Rahimullah Yusufzai, *Outlook* (New Delhi), 29 November 1999, pp. 56–7.

These and other factors have prevented their acceptance as a government, but that has not prevented other governments from keeping contact with them. The Iranians and the Central Asians in particular have been in contact, if for no specific reason other than to size each other up.

An isolated Taliban have meant business opportunities for some of them. There has been a semblance of border trade whenever peace and wherever terrain has permitted. Uzbekistan supplied power to Mazar-i-Sharif and other towns when they were under Masoud's control. After the fall of Mazar and more territory captured by the Taliban, Uzbekistan has been replaced by Turkmenistan, which also has a thriving US$100 million annual trade with the Taliban. The Taliban go shopping to Ashkabad when not making it to Peshawar. Ashkabad offers a peaceful meeting-point for businessmen and investors.

Until mid-1999 Ariana flights landed at Amritsar in the Punjab state of India even though India does not recognize the Taliban and has an embassy of the Rabbani government in New Delhi. Thanks to the Indian stand on Afghan developments and the Taliban's proximity to Islamabad, the Taliban perceive Indians as not "good" friends. But this has not prevented them from trading with Indian parties. India's trade with Afghanistan, that has seen a series of ups and downs, has never really ceased.

The Afghans have perceived India as a potential market for the Turkmen gas that would pass through their territory. The pipeline ending at Multan in Pakistan is economically viable, but if extended to New Delhi, it becomes an even more attractive proposition for all concerned.

Unocal, the US multinational, formally closed its office in Ashkabad after waiting hopefully for peace to return to Afghanistan. This has been seen as a setback for the Afghan economy. The Fauji Foundation of Pakistan and Delta, the Saudi collaborator of the project, have all incurred losses. The Unocal withdrawal has been a setback for US business interests too, while the Europeans have unhindered access to Afghanistan. The Europeans are not averse to doing business with Iran either, whom the Americans are always suspicious about.

Unocal's withdrawal is seen as tactical in influential quarters. "If they have gone, others will come in. We are already being approached and talks are going on. Several companies want to come in place of Unocal", Arazov Redjebai, Turkmenistan's Oil Minister, claimed.[2] He expressed Turkmen "readiness" to launch the project once political problems are resolved and peace returns to the territory through which the pipeline is to be laid. "We hope the obstacles will be removed. God willing, peace will return. The Turkmen gas will eventually reach India", Redjebai said.

"The pipeline project is a matter of time. The question is not *if* it will take off, but *when*", the representative of a British multinational engaged in oil exploration in Turkmenistan said.

According to well-informed quarters in Ashkabad, the Chinese are taking interest and a construction company, Overland, is laying down a gas pipeline through Afghan territory. This part of the project is to be completed by December 1999. There is, however, no confirmation of this "surreptitious" pipeline laying.

All this points to the Taliban's ability to survive, and perhaps thrive, despite being in isolation from the world community. A combination of the survival instinct, religious motivation, political and military support from Pakistan, moral and material help from the UAE and Saudi Arabia and the fact that its opponents at home are in disarray, keeps the Taliban ticking.

But all this is going to change with the UN economic sanctions, which came into force from 14 November 1999. In consequence, Pakistan will not be able to sell natural gas any more freely to Taliban Afghanistan. Similarly, no firm would come forward to invest in gas pipeline. Now everything has to happen clandestinely and the Taliban will start experiencing the pinch of sanctions, say from January 2000. And Taliban Afghanistan is not Iraq to withstand the pressure.

Till economic sanctions were on, the advent and consolidation of Taliban rule in Afghanistan meant gains for Pakistan, which was the single largest beneficiary. It gave Pakistan tremendous clout. The US had been talking to the Taliban through Islamabad. Even the demand for Osama was frequently routed through Pakistan. The entire Afghan war since the 1980s had been a lucrative opportunity for Pakistan in terms of military and financial aid. It had given Pakistan a military and diplomatic role to play

[2]Interview in Ashkhabad, 27 July 1999.

the mediator and a leader in the region. Pakistan's military had fattened itself on western help during the 1980s and had kept itself abreast on the flow of arms and funds, direct and indirect. After all, it is Pakistan's ISI which launders the drug money, purchases arms and other supplies and conducts much of trade on behalf of the Taliban.

•

What is the future going to be like? Given the ground situation, we envisage five scenarios. These are: (a) Taliban rule; (b) Taliban defeat; (c) arms embargo with the objective of imposing a broad-based government; (d) the emergence of an Islamic emirate of Afghanistan; (e) the emergence of a Greater Pashtunistan, accompanied by break-up of Pakistan.

Scenario One—Taliban Rule. The Taliban's view of what type of society they want to build is limited to a vague concept called a "true Islamic State based on Sharia".

Every Afghanistan watcher wonders how in the dynamic international order rule by Sharia will take Afghanistan forward. The imposition of Sharia will automatically impose restrictions on the Afghan polity in its dealings with the international system. According to almost every outside observer, Afghanistan urgently needs peace and massive international aid to bring in the levels of living of pre-1973. The Taliban seem to perceive that this will come about, in their words, "God willing". They seem to pin enormous hopes on Saudi generosity and their strategic location *vis-à-vis* Iran, an important "rogue" state in the western view of the international order. The unceasing UN anxiety to help the people of Afghanistan seems to have convinced the Taliban that they are on right track. The basis for this perception is the way US oil companies courted them during 1996–97. The Taliban and their sponsors are unwilling to accept the changed ground realities in the international oil market and now the pipeline projects in CARs are on hold. Ironically, the focus on Afghanistan in the international community has shifted from pipelines to harbouring terrorists and drug trafficking by the Taliban.

In addition, the Taliban refuse to acknowledge their limitations, such as, that they are a Pashtun-Sunni dominated group; and they will not be able to rule Afghanistan by force alone and suppress the other ethnic and tribal loyalties. They also seem to be unaware of developments within the Islamic world, such as efforts by Iran and Saudi Arabia, the two major players of the Islamic bloc, to synthesize the two main schools of Islam—Shi'ism and Sunnism. Therefore, it is highly unlikely that the Taliban will be allowed to consolidate their position and rule Afghanistan by other ethnic groups; as also by outside powers within the Islamic world and beyond, with the singular exception of Pakistan.

Scenario Two—Taliban Defeat. Will the non-Pashtun groups be allowed to come to power? According to them the only factor holding them back from defeating the Taliban and driving them back south right up to Jalalabad, is the presence of Pakistan's regular army. Masoud is reported to have pleaded with some of the CARs and the US in April 1999 that if he is given better arms and ammunition and Pakistan is forced to exhibit restraint, he would be able to call the shots. There seems to be some truth in this assertion, and Masoud's supporters in the CARs and the US seem to have acted at his behest. The Taliban's 1999 summer offensive against Masoud failed because Pakistan Army withdrew from the Taliban forces midway. There was almost a stalemate on the battlefront, with Masoud's forces gaining a couple of small towns.

But have the Pakistanis indeed been told unambiguously by their allies that they have to dissociate themselves militarily from the Taliban to facilitate a level playing field for an intra-Afghan dialogue? It does not look likely. The non-Pashtun forces, perhaps aware of this, have always been willing to come to the conference table and thrash out the issue of power sharing. In the last three summits of Taliban–anti-Taliban forces— Islamabad April 1998, Ashkabad March 1999 and Tashkent July 1999—it was only the Taliban who refused to yield any ground.

Scenario Three—Arms Embargo for Compelling a Broad-based Government. Towards this objective, the UN initiative in this regard can be put into action. This can be followed by a UN peacekeeping force to disarm both warring factions and convene a Jirga type of assembly to facilitate a dialogue. But then, Afghanistan is not a Kosovo or a Bosnia for the great powers to get involved in, whether through the UN or directly. There is some chance, nevertheless, that some of the great powers will take an interest in the matter on account of the factor of terrorism and violence emanating from Afghanistan. Some of the Taliban men and their allies having openly declared their hostility towards some of the great powers, they have become a hurdle to the great powers' interests in South and South-West Asia. But a Bosnia type of solution is unlikely in a country that is already in shambles; and any extensive aerial bombing would lead to considerable damage to the civilian population. Also, there is no country other than Pakistan which can physically intervene on behalf of the great powers in Afghanistan and bring about some order. Unfortunately, this is at variance with Pakistan's own strategic interests. However, the first shots in this direction have been fired with economic sanctions coming into force from 14 November 1999.

Scenario Four—Emergence of an Islamic Emirates of Afghanistan. The prospective Islamic emirates could be with or without Panjshir Valley. The Pakistani armed forces have played enough havoc with Afghanistan to have sufficiently undermined its staying power. It will take at least five to six decades for Afghanistan to emerge from the present socio-economic wreckage with some semblance of stability. This they will not be able to do it without help from Islamabad. Having completely neutralized the threat from across the Durand Line in the foreseeable future, Pakistan may allow consolidation by the Taliban in the territory under their occupation with a façade of dialogue with Masoud and his men. The way the Taliban responded to the August 1999 round of Islamabad peace initiatives indicates how things could shape up. Whether others will allow this type of *de facto* division of Afghanistan is another matter. Since one of the original sponsors of the Taliban allegedly wanted to build an alternative model to the Islamic Revolution in Iran, the new emirates may be a theocratic state with the Holy Book of Islam as the law of the land. Whether the agenda still holds in the changed situation of a thaw between Riyadh and Tehran remains to be seen—whether the Saudis would still want the 18 million Afghans to live in the medieval age or allow them to get modernized. It is, in any case, difficult to dismantle threadbare the infrastructure built by the theocratic forces of Pakistan in Afghanistan. The groups that support a theocratic State structure have laced their plans with a clever

Islamic ideology; and are exploiting the underdevelopment as a fallout due to deviation from the ordained Islamic path. Over the years they acquired a clout within the overall polity of Pakistan and Afghanistan. Now that they are operating autonomously, if they are not allowed to bring their mission to its logical end, a number of things can happen, including a backlash on Pakistan. That will also keep the Taliban movement engaged.

Scenario Five—Emergence of Greater Pashtunistan. In such a situation, Pakistan may reap a whirlwind from the wind it sowed in the form of the Taliban, with the Taliban movement itself bouncing back on the Pakistan polity. Pakistan's existing political order having proved thoroughly ineffective, any change might be seen as welcome. A section of the leadership is already talking in terms of Pakistan having become a failed State because its leadership has "deviated from the path of Islam". They argue passionately that democracy is not approved by Islam. But will the international system allow the emergence of an Islamic State with nuclear weapons? With the prospects of becoming a gateway to the CARs diminishing, Afghanistan has more or less become Pakistan's exclusive problem. The attitude of the others in the neighbourhood is evolving towards merely guarding themselves against any spillover.

One of the casualties of India's Independence Act, 1947 was a separate state for the Pashtuns. The Greater Pashtunistan movement, active for a while after 1947, has been revived in a big way, according to travellers' reports. It may be noted that the Taliban movement had its origins in the mountains of NWFP and is dominated by Pashtuns. Already there is enough interaction between the Pashtuns on both sides of the Durand Line. A women's university was opened in Peshawar in early 1999, and more than 2000 Afghan women have enrolled themselves already. The chancellor of the university is a former President of Afghanistan and an Islamic scholar, Sibghatullah Mujaddidi. According to a spokesman of Mujaddidi, the Taliban have supported the university with letters of congratulations from Mullah Muhammad Umar and its minister for higher vocational and education, Mullah Hamdulla Nomani.[3]

---

[3] AFP report from Peshawar, 5 April 1999. We were told in October

Similarly, in November 1998, after a meeting between the NWFP Food Minister, Ghafoor Jadoon and Afghan Counsellor Maulvi Najibullah, the NWFP government asked the Taliban administration to establish flour mills in Nangarhar province for grinding wheat imported from abroad to solve the food problem.[4] The Afghan counsellor was further advised that he should approach the private sector, though the same could be arranged by the NWFP government. He was also informed that certain private parties were interested in setting up grinding mills in Jalalabad, if they were ensured the provision of electricity, water and security.[5] The NWFP government also offered to provide wheat to Afghanistan, as was done during 1998, when 10,000 tons of grains were sent across the Durand Line. The meeting ended with an understanding that the two countries sign an agreement enabling the NWFP government to import wheat from Central Asia through Afghanistan via Turghundi Post. In an executive order, the NWFP government lifted the ban on Afghan timber imports from December 1998.[6]

It should become obvious from these news snippets that a subtle attempt is on to economically integrate the Pashtun-dominated areas on either side of the Durand Line. A Taliban functionary has, in a private conversation, confirmed this, describing it as a part of their "agenda". If true, then as we enter the next millennium, we may be on the verge of witnessing a redrawing of the map of South-West Asia.

•

The flush of the limited success that they have had, whatever may have been the reasons for the success, is already making the Taliban militants to talk in terms of conquering the CARs, India, and so on and so forth. In India itself, they are talking in terms of cutting out not only Jammu and Kashmir, but also Assam from

---

1999 that the university is almost bankrupt and may close down any time. Neither the new regime in Islamabad nor the Taliban are in a position to extend any financial help.

[4]*The News*, 1 December 1998.
[5]Ibid.
[6]*The News*, 4 December 1998.

the Indian Union. Though temporary truce has been achieved, Tajikistan seems to top the list of their agenda, as also the Xinjiang in the PRC. Can they be contained now? In Kargil they were; and probably in Xinjiang too. To contain them, the first step would be to localize their depredations, without allowing spillover on the rest of the region. If the regional powers in collaboration with great powers can do that, the next step would be how not to allow a theocratic State structure emerge in Afghanistan–Pakistan.

Would the Taliban remain a localized phenomenon or will it get extended beyond Afghan boundaries? A similar question was raised at the time of Islamic revolution in Iran 1979. The Taliban *per se* may not like to extend it. But the Taliban have become a role model of governance to many peoples living at the subsistence level in the immediate neighbourhood. There is already talk of Chitral, a town on the Pak–Afghan border having been Talibanized. Similarly, there are stories about the mosque becoming a focal point in some CARs. One can say with reasonable certainty that these developments are quite unlikely to make a serious impact on countries like Iran, India or even Russia. All these countries have evolved a viable State structure where people's lives are secure and there is an endeavour to provide the people with the basic necessities for survival. At the same time, the fact cannot be discounted that Islamist rebels have made inroads in the autonomous republic of Dagestan and in Chechnya. From Yeltsin down, Russian leaders have repeatedly asserted that the rebels were trained in Pakistan or Afghanistan, with Osama's blessings.

Beyond this, there will be some convulsions in other not-so-benevolent authoritarian regimes. With Osama's presence in Afghanistan the Saudi ruling family may well feel threatened, for reasons earlier explained. A similar debate was on among the academics of the great powers after Iran's Islamic revolution, and it resulted in the United States stationing its troops in Saudi Arabia to sustain the status quo. The frequently reported dissident movements' activities have so far not made any significant dent on the survivability of the Saudi regime, which at this point of time in history is a coefficient of that regime's capacity to generate the kind of revenue it does. So long as it does that, Taliban type of movements will remain only perceived threats.

16

Choices Before India
With Kargil a Nasty Reminder

Down the ages, what are today India and Afghanistan were a single, vast geographic entity interspersed with rivers, plains and mountains, and had a common history. Takshashila (Taxila) was a seat of learning in ancient times. Gandhari, wife of King Dhritarashtra of the epic *Mahabharata*, came from Gandhara (Kandahar). Parikshit, the grandson who succeeded the Pandavas, winners of the Mahabharata battle at Kurukshetra, as the king of Indraprastha, was killed by Takshaka. Parikshit's son and successor Janmejaya avenged his father's death by defeating the Takshaka Nagas and performing the *Sarpayajna* at what is today Taxila.

Recorded history has some interesting dates that denote significant events concerning India and Afghanistan. In AD 10 Huemo Kadiphises I, the Kushana chief from Afghanistan, invaded India and established his domain in northwestern India. Kanishka, the great Kushana king, ascended the throne in AD 78.

The millennium that is about to end, began with the invasions of Mahmud of Ghazni. Between AD 1000 and 1026, he raided India fourteen times. After his death in Ghazni in 1030, his son Masud attacked and captured Kashmir in 1034.

Afghanistan as a political entity was separated from India in 1739 by a treaty signed on 26 May that year between Mughal emperor Muhammad Shah and Persian King Nadirshah, who left the Mughal empire bleeding, and deprived of the Peacock Throne and Kohinoor.

The partition of the subcontinent in 1947 took India away from Afghanistan, with a perennially hostile Pakistan emerging as a buffer. Independent India was accused, with a good measure of justification, of ignoring the age-old ties with the Afghan people. This separation particularly hurt the Pashtuns of the North-West Frontier Province, who had decidedly voted against the Muslim League in the 1937 elections, the first to be held in British India under the Government of India Act, 1935, that eventually formed the basis of governance of the subcontinent, till it got divided in 1947. Frontier Gandhi Khan Abdul Ghaffar Khan was to lament this "betrayal" in the years to come, when his people were sought to be subjugated by repressive Pakistani regimes, which did not forgive the Pashtuns for not voting with them.

With a hostile Pakistan trying to dominate the land-locked neighbour, it is Afghanistan which has in the last fifty years sought to reach out to India. And it is India which has been responding in varying degrees. Lack of a common border has deprived a physical contact by which the two people would have interacted better. And yet, Pakistan has time and again accused India of instigating the Afghans. It is accepted on all hands that the territorial division of the subcontinent as made in 1947 is final, and India has not been one to question it.

•

The region northwest of India has been the gateway for invasions and ideas. People of different cultures came down as raiders, traders, conquerors and those in quest of knowledge. Down the ages, they got assimilated with India. Because of this strategic importance, military, politico-economic and cultural, India cannot ignore this neighbourhood. It has been mis-called India's "extended neighbourhood". No neighbourhood can be "extended" or "remote" in the age that the new millennium ushers in. In a world that is fast becoming a global village, for anyone in India, or elsewhere, to think that Indians or their government should not concern themselves with what is happening in Afghanistan would be not only flippant, but also dangerous. First, because India has had age-old ties with Afghanistan that remained uninterrupted even after the British drew the Durand Line.

Second, with drugs and Islamist militancy crossing the Afghan borders in all directions, India, which does indeed have a common border with Afghanistan in what is Pakistan-occupied Kashmir, can hardly ignore the twin phenomenon. Third, what is being preached by the Taliban rulers in Afghanistan, and ready for export through various means, is the debased version of the Wahabi school of Islam which has its roots in Deoband, near Saharanpur in Uttar Pradesh. Funded by Saudi Arabia, hundreds of madrasas that dot the Pak–Afghan border are reputed to have produced over 100,000 students. Taught Islamic theology of the Deoband school, these students have been, in addition, trained in the use of arms. Batches of theology students of different nationalities have been visiting Deoband.

•

In itself, the emergence of a theocratic State in the neighbourhood is not seen as a threat. It could well be an internal affair of that State. But when that State labours and connives at superimposing its concept of State structure on others, the nature of that State ceases to be its internal affair.

When the genie called Taliban was sprung on the world in 1994, unsuspecting India was noncommittal. Its official statements were generalizations, such as that it preferred a peaceful solution to the Afghan crisis. But after the capture of Kabul in September 1996, and Najibullah's hanging, India reacted sharply. There were even unconfirmed reports at the time that Najibullah might seek political asylum in India. When reports appeared of Pakistani soldiers participating in the operation to capture Kabul, the Indian stand changed, demanding a broad-based government.

Ever since the emergence of the Taliban movement, the flow of small-arms and narcotics into India from across the border has increased. Also, over the years the Taliban/mujahideen have become synonymous with drug trade and are responsible for growing small-arms proliferation in the entire region. These two resource-earners are enabling them to whip up emotions and support ethnocentric movements all around.

Leaders of some prominent outfits like Jamiat-Ulema-i-Islam (SH group) argue that jihad is the only means of survival for

Muslims. Muslims, says Samiul Haq of JUI, may join jihad wherever it may be, because the jihadists do not believe in geographic boundaries. As he put it, if jihadi students, after graduating, go to Dagestan to fight, "we will not stop them".

With the Red Army out of Afghanistan the mujahideen/Taliban started talking in terms of reviving the tradition of jihad among Muslims everywhere in order to win back the lost glory of the Muslim world. "Muslims face problems because they have forgotten jihad. Once it is revived we can restore our glory", commented Hafiz Mohammad Saeed, chief of the Dawatul Irshad, the parent organization of Lashkar-i-Toyyaba, Pakistan's largest jihadi organization.

These mujahideen/Taliban have regularly intruded into J&K state and committed terrorist acts. According to the General Officer Commanding, Udhampur, between 1990 and 1998, mujahideen/Taliban from fourteen countries participated in terrorist activities in J&K. In counter-insurgency operations by the Indian armed forces 1,073 of them were killed and 136 were arrested. The mercenaries were from Afghanistan, Bahrain, Burma (Myanmar), Bangladesh, Chechnya, Iraq, Iran, Kazakhstan, Pakistan, Saudi Arabia, Sudan, Turkey and Yemen, and Pakistan-occupied Kashmir.

Their first port of call was Peshawar, and they received basic training in terrorist camps on the Pak–Afghan border. Some of them came initially to fight the Red Army; and others after hearing about the success of the mujahideen against the Red Army felt excited and descended upon Peshawar. Most of them received monetary incentives to fight. As one terrorist confessed during interrogation, generally, the training camp leadership, after seeing their performance during training, decided the remuneration, varying from $1000 to as high as $5000. Normally, 25 per cent was paid in advance, and the remainder after the assigned missions were executed successfully. In case the terrorists were captured or killed, the family received compensation from the employers. "We are told all these actions are to protect Islam; and we have been asked to behave like good Muslims—that is growing a beard, offering prayers five times a day wherever we are, etc." Most of these terrorists also confirmed that their training instructors were people from the Pakistani army.

In this backdrop, the infiltration by these mujahideen/Taliban to the Indian side of the India–Pak border in the Kargil mountains came some time in early 1999. The evidence collected by the Indian Army in terms of identity cards, pass books, letters, personal diaries of Lieut Mohammad Maazullah Khan Sumbal and others killed in Kargil operation, and made available to the public, proves beyond doubt that the men who occupied the Kargil heights were not mujahideen/Taliban but were from the Northern Light Infantry division of the Pakistan Army. NLI battalions 3, 4, and 6 along with sub-units of Special Services Group and elements of supporting arms and services of the Pakistan Army were used. These NLI men used the so-called mujahideen/Taliban as porters and guides in operations. The Pakistani citizens, were able to see the whole evidence marshalled by the Indian Army, courtesy international television channels. The whole myth built around mujahideen/Taliban over the past two decades was thus shattered at the popular level. The assumption of the Pakistan Army that the local population would rise against the Indian Army, also proved incorrect. Initial reports from Kargil in early May 1999 clearly indicated that the intruders were first spotted by a local shepherd who promptly alerted the local army commander.

As the operations in Kargil progressed, the front organizations of the mujahideen like Lashkar-i-Toyyaba talked in terms of readying thousands of volunteers to fight along with the mujahideen in Kargil. Strangely enough, none came forward; and NLI men who occupied the Kargil heights were left to fend for themselves.

Having got over the initial surprise, the Indian armed forces were able to come up with an alternative strategy to evict the intruders from occupied positions, and the NLI men in the mujahideen cover were not able to get fresh reinforcements from across the line of control. How many of them were killed and how many "withdrew" is not known. But the Indian Army says they have buried the NLI soldiers killed in action to the extent they could. According to the Indian Army, estimates of casualties of the Pakistani armed forces would be between 800 and 1000.

For Pakistan the cost of the Kargil campaign has been tremendous. It not only cost them men and materials but also morale. Once again they failed to exercise their clout outside Pakistan–Afghanistan.

When the game was up, the Pakistan government, which was lending "moral, political and diplomatic support" to these mujahideen "appealed" to them to return home. Some brave statements made by the leadership of the Lashkar-i-Toyyaba and Hizbul Mujahideen, on 5–6 July, that they would not heed Pakistan government's appeal was only for public consumption. In fact, they publicly declare even now that their mujahideen are still occupying the Kargil heights. Other organizations like Harkatul Mujahideen said their "withdrawal from Kargil is only a tactical retreat". They all know that if they do not heed the Pakistani authorities their daily bread-and-butter can be made difficult. If they are thrown out of Pakistan they would be hounded by international security agencies. When these "holy warriors" meekly vacated the Kargil heights, the whole aura built around them got shattered. It was clear to the entire world that Pakistan, which soon after its creation in 1947–48 had let loose terror on J&K with its men in the garb of Afridi tribals, was commemorating its golden jubilee by sending its men for an identical mission under the garb of Taliban/mujahideen.

In retrospect, if the fight against the Red Army in Afghanistan by the Pakistan army led to the birth of the mujahideen, Kargil became their nemesis. As one Pakistani commentator observed, the way these mujahideen returned from Kargil heights was far more humiliating than India taking 93,000 PoWs after the 1971 war. These Kargil mujahideen made the whole concept of jihad as enunciated in the Holy Book a travesty. Already many families who sent their children to join the mujahideen ranks as a part of their duty towards their faith have started having doubts about the credentials of their leadership. Therefore one can expect some convulsions both in religious parties like Jamaat-i-Islami and Pakistani armed forces in the coming months.

In the Indian assessment, the Taliban/mujahideen have four groups of people: madrasa students, who are showpieces to justify the Islamic fervour of the movement; Pakistani military personnel, both serving and retired;[1] mercenaries;[2] and misdirected men from various Islamic countries whose life's ambition is to become jihadis. Only the Pakistani military personnel and the mercenaries do the actual fighting. The intending jihadis may be sent to the war zone to get acclimatized and trained in the use of explosives and firearms.

When these mujahideen/Taliban succeed in preparing the ground, the regular armed forces in the garb of mujahideen/Taliban take over the operations and intensify the operations. In fact, this provides a bargaining point to extract concessions from the country where these mercenaries operate. Pakistani citizens, not in ones or twos, but in hundreds cannot cross the border and go into an adjoining country to let loose terror without assurance of some protection by their authorities. They roam around the streets of Pakistan/Afghanistan as "holy warriors" and the respective governments do not crack down on them. In Afghanistan they are Taliban; when they move out of Afghan–Pak territory they become mujahideen. As Taliban they kill fellow Afghan Muslims; and as mujahideen in J&K they kill Indian security personnel in suicide attacks. After one such attack in November 1999, one of the militant leaders declared that they would even attempt an attack on the residence of the Prime Minister of India.

•

The explosion at Kandahar that nearly ripped apart the well-fortified home of Mullah Umar is a clear indication that all is not well with the rulers in Kabul. Portents are not good for a regime that should be celebrating three years of capture of Kabul with winning support from the world community. Conflicting signals are emanating from Afghanistan. In recent weeks, there has been a round of fierce fighting that left over 1200 dead.

[1] An intelligence official told us that some personnel from Pakistani armed forces are asked by the authorities concerned to submit provisional retirement papers to give them the status of ex-servicemen. This would enable the Pakistan Army to claim that no serving personnel are involved in actual fighting.
[2] Mercenaries include veterans from Afghanistan who fought the Red Army, 1980–88.

Conflicting again is the information on this regrouping, particularly on the involvement of the Pakistan Army's regulars and the "volunteers". Images on military satellites indicate that under US pressure, Pakistan has reduced its "presence" in Taliban-ruled Afghanistan to a mere 1400. It was 5000 plus when two Afghan provinces of Kapisa and Parwan and the Bagram airbase were captured from Masoud, and then lost between 27 July and the first week of August.

Like many Indian defence planners, Masood Khalili, who represents the exiled Afghan government in New Delhi, thinks neither the Kargil nor the Kapisa chapter is over. The same combination of Pakistan's forces under ISI control and the Arab mercenaries conducting jihad under the inspiration of Osama are fighting on both fronts. The Kargil–Kabul nexus is complete and this has also been confirmed by noted Pakistani writer Ahmed Rashid.

In establishing this nexus, the die had been cast in October 1998 at a meeting convened by the Taliban, which was attended by officers of the Pashtun-dominated Afghanistan desk of Pakistan's ISI and Osama bin Laden. A major operation was decided for March 1999. But priority was to launch it from Kabul. Kargil was not on immediate agenda, since things seemed fine between India and Pakistan after Prime Minister Atal Behari Vajpayee's bus trip to Lahore. But by mid-April, it became Kargil. Masoud inquired of Khalili from deep inside Afghan territory over his satellite phone: "Is it *Bahisht* (paradise) or *watan?*" "Paradise", alluding to Emperor Jehangir's famous description, was the code word for Kashmir. When told that it was, indeed, Kashmir, he was surprised and relieved. The combined force of the Taliban, the Pakistan Army regulars and "volunteers" and Osama's mercenaries of a myriad nationalities were diverted to Kashmir. The switch-over from Kargil, a failed operation, to Kabul was almost simultaneous. By 22 July, the same force had been moved to break Masoud's formation outside Kabul. It had 2500 Pak regulars, 4000 "volunteers", 2000 Taliban soldiers and 700 Arabs. They were told that they were continuing the same jihad as in Kargil, since Masoud's force had been augmented by arms and ammunition by "Indians, Russians and Uzbeks", Khalili disclosed in an interview.

Two main objectives of the combined operation were: to secure the Bagram airbase for the Pakistan Air Force and to shift Osama close to Bagram, away from his present base at Farmihadda, which is too close to the Pakistan border.

But the Kabul debacle was equally severe, since Masoud had time to prepare. He employed his by now known copy-book method of withdrawing and turning about suddenly to counter-attack. It worked. He regained all territory lost in July end. At a meeting in Jalalabad, Khalili said, the Kargil–Kabul post-mortem was full of angry exchanges among the losers. The next round was decided at another meeting in Kandahar on 5 August, with Mullah Umar presiding. Khalili said this time it could be a 15,000-strong force. Whether it would be Kabul once again, or Kargil first, was something on which like anyone else, he would keep his fingers crossed.

•

Has the military wresting power in Pakistan altered matters notably? The new Chief Executive of Pakistan, General Pervez Musharraf, is known to be a sympathizer of the Taliban. The general is reported to have remarked in an address to a select audience in Karachi in August 1999, that

Pakistan fully supports the Taliban. As the majority Pashtun segment of the Afghan society and State, the Taliban, sharing a historical commonality with our own Pashtun, must be accepted and recognized as such. As for their religious radicalism and zealotry, these could be tempered in due course to bring them round to the Pakistani mind-set.

General Musharraf also called the Taliban's Afghanistan a success story for its spectacular military successes. They brought peace to the war-torn Afghanistan by ending the bitter and protracted intra-mujahideen factional fighting, he said.[3]

This assessment seems not to have changed a whit after 12 October 1999. However, Musharraf is also aware that the tough stand taken by the UN in terms of economic sanctions is limiting his manoeuvrability in the immediate future. Therefore,

---

[3]Cited by Brig (Retd) A.R. Siddiqi, "Pak–US–Taliban: An Uneasy Trio", *The Nation*, 25 August 1999.

his immediate target would be to buy peace with the international community by somehow projecting that the Taliban have learnt their lessons. With the winter on, the Taliban are anyway going to lie low. It would be interesting to watch the moves he will make, if any, to break the impasse between the Taliban and anti-Taliban forces.

Equally important, the new dispensation cannot solve the problems of Pakistan, which are complex and multifaceted. Consequently, they will also not be able to sustain Afghanistan as a surrogate. One country is a shambles after twenty years of civil war. The other appears to be on the way to becoming so, after fifty years of independence from the British, given its economic, political and social mess. Judging by post-Kargil reports emanating from Islamabad, even the men in uniform are disillusioned.

As one observer cynically observed to us, in such a situation mujahideen/Taliban should be allowed to fight among themselves. Otherwise their sponsors will let them loose on the neighbourhood to keep them preoccupied. It may be noted that when the Kargil operations were on, the fighting within the Taliban *per se* became minimal. The Taliban were there; but Pakistani troops were missing to do the fighting. After the Kargil operation was called off, the Pakistani troops moved over, and the supply lines could not be sustained due to exhausting of rations. The new Nissan LCVs might have carried crowds from madrasas to chant right up to Kabul. With no supplies, and protection as in the past from the Pakistani regulars, they became cannon fodder to the anti-Taliban forces.

•

One can argue that Pakistan is taking advantage of the Taliban's facilities as the latter are totally dependent on Islamabad for their very existence. Therefore, if stinger missiles or AK-47 rifles stored with the Taliban are moved around by the Pakistan army stationed with the Taliban, they can do very little about it. One Taliban sympathizer pointed out that the Afghans and Afghan Arabs who were killed in Kashmir valley were mercenaries who could have been hired by Pakistani armed forces. In his perception, the Taliban as such have nothing against India. The point is well taken. But a government which defaults in controlling criminal elements from operating from its soil assumes responsibility for their misdeeds.[4]

For Pakistan, fighting a conventional war with India is no longer feasible or cost-effective, considering that the latter has greater resilience to withstand the trauma of war. A prolonged war would also invite the wrath of the international community. Proxy war then, is the only and most convenient alternative. The organizers of such proxy/low-intensity conflicts employ an ideological framework to make cross-border terrorism look like a freedom struggle. This would generate sympathy among the other followers of the faith. Terrorism is sanctified as jihad and prepares the ground for the regular troops to move in. A mujahideen, flushed with missiles and lethal weapons, can terrorize people, being a holy warrior. He can do no wrong!

•

In the perception of most of the 150 million Indian Muslims, if the people with religious fervour sought to export the Taliban version of Islam through dialogue and persuasion, it might not be objected to. They see use of brute force as anathema. The way Taliban–Pakistan burnt Charar-i-Sharif in J&K is a stigma on them. Many theologians are of the view that India is among the few countries which accepts the contribution of Islam to human civilization. Kabul and Islamabad want to undermine that position. Kashmir, if a problem, they say, is one between the locals and the Government of India. These Taliban/mujahideen claiming to be liberators and holy warriors have not only complicated matters but brutalized the social structure in J&K in general and the Valley in particular. They also point out that these Taliban/mujahideen should first address the problems people in their territory are facing before interfering elsewhere.

[4] It may be noted that when Pakistan sought to publicize the arrest of 200-plus people across the country as a campaign against terrorism, a US State Department official dismissed it as being aimed at local criminals, for domestic cleansing (Reuter report from Washington, 22 December 1999).

The whipped-up emotions in Kashmir in the cause of "Islam in danger" during 1989–90 did mobilize the people, but only to a certain extent. The mujahideen from various outfits that were sent to Kashmir valley (according to one count they were more than 100) and the mayhem they caused discredited these movements, which also became directionless. The traditional ill feeling of a Kashmiri for the Afghan, because of what they underwent under Afghan rulers in the past, brought in yet another dimension. The occupation of Hazratbal mosque, and the hero worship of Mast Gul, responsible for burning down Charar-i-Sharif by Pakistani supporters of these mujahideen, sufficiently alienated the locals from the so-called jihad.

Islamic scholars say that Islam is against the killing of innocent women, children and old people. Kidnapping an unmarried girl and keeping her in custody for a week would invite the death sentence on the kidnapper. Many theologians with whom we have talked, believe that the massacres by these mujahideen/Taliban are not sufficiently publicized by the Government of India. Or even if publicized, the media war from the sponsors is much stronger than that by the government machinery and the media. The result is that some of the faithfuls make liberal donations to the cause propounded by organizers of these forces.

•

In the light of cross-border terror let loose by the mujahideen/Taliban, the training orientation of the Indian armed forces is radically changing to fight this proxy war called jihad. The Indian establishment has also launched a major campaign against cross-border terrorism in close coordination with the entire Pakistan–Afghanistan neighbourhood and in various international forums. India has made it a condition for resumption of any form of dialogue with Pakistan on bilateral issues.

Indian policy aims at making the new rulers of Afghanistan realize that by joining hands with Pakistan they are discrediting themselves in the world community. If they wish to gain acceptance they need to distance themselves from Pakistan, and from being used by it in the name of jihad. Interestingly enough, some maverick in the crowd of mujahideen in Peshawar issued a statement on behalf of Osama bin Laden, the "honoured guest" of the Taliban, that he would extend his jihad into Kashmir valley. This was promptly carried by *Jang* (Karachi). The saner elements in the Taliban/mujahideen realized the damage it can do to them in India; and they issued a prompt denial of their "guest" having issued any such statement. The statement carrying the denial is reported to have caused ripples in the Pakistan Army establishment. Till now this has been the only instance of Osama or his Taliban hosts having denied any involvement in a third country through an official statement.

To break this nexus between the mercenaries in the guise of mujahideen and Pakistani regular armed forces, India has two options. One is to launch a massive awareness campaign in South and South-West Asia about this nexus. Such sensitization of people would put in perspective the Pakistani designs in Afghanistan through the Taliban. That may also help to a certain extent in making the six-plus-two meeting put pressure on Pakistan to withdraw itself from Afghanistan.

A second option could be to break the military muscle of the Taliban by prevailing upon the UN Security Council to pass a resolution restraining Pakistan from extending any form of support to the warring factions in Afghanistan. After the revelations of Kargil, Pakistan can no longer claim innocence and it has to find ways and means to disarm the demystified mujahideen. Once that happens, the so-called Islamic militancy, which is nagging the security scenario of most countries in the region, will change.

•

In this context note may be taken of the many statements made by UN Secretary-General Kofi Annan, expressing concern over the involvement of non-Afghan nationals in the Afghan civil war. In a statement made in September 1997, Annan said:

> ... foreign providers of support to the Afghan warring parties ... continue to fan the conflicts by pouring in arms, money and other supplies to their preferred Afghan factions. These countries unanimously denounce "foreign interference", but are quick to add that arms are delivered only to "the other side".

These external players ... must also be held accountable for building a fire which, they should be aware, is unlikely to remain confined to Afghanistan. Indeed, that fire is already spreading beyond the borders of Afghanistan, posing a serious threat to the region and beyond in the shape of terrorism, banditry, narcotics trafficking, refugee flows, and increasing ethnic and sectarian tension.

If what happened in Kargil in Jammu and Kashmir in May–June 1999 can be considered a prelude to what the Taliban/mujahideen can do in future, some quick thinking needs to be done by India's security managers. So far whatever has been coming out is restricted to saying that the Indian armed forces are being re-equipped to fight a Kargil type of war. That only partially addresses the new threat from these new groups.

What is required immediately is to take cognizance of Kargil type of situations developing in Russia (Chechnya and Dagestan), China (Xinjiang), Uzbekistan and Iran. All these countries are experiencing, in one way or another, the adverse fallout of the turmoil in Afghanistan. All of them at different points of time have pointed an accusing finger at Pakistan; and called it responsible for the deteriorating security environment in the region. A positive US role in the matter may be discounted: US policy so far having revolved round hydro-carbon-specific issues initially and now being Osama-specific. A coordinated policy between India, Iran, Russia and China, call it "IICR networking", to counter the adverse fallout from Afghanistan may yield results. Enjoying greater clout with the Taliban among these four are Iran and China. As has been discussed in the earlier chapters, both Iran and China have opened their lines of communication with the Taliban. Turkmenistan is another country already overtly engaged in a constructive dialogue with the Taliban.

The Durrani Pashtuns in the Taliban, who dealt with India, Iran and China over the decades, understand that unless these three recognize them, their claims to legitimacy will not be established with others. Pakistan even after two decades' involvement has failed to be a legitimizer of the Taliban. It could barely manage Saudi Arabia and the UAE. Even the latter have started cold-shouldering the Taliban since early 1999.

Going by stray reports coming from Kandahar, Kabul and Islamabad, an intense debate is already on within the Taliban and their sponsors. The Mullah Umar faction in the Taliban alone wants to pursue the hard-line radicalism.

Therefore, IICR networking, in which a Sino–Iranian combine can play a significant role in bringing moderation among the Taliban, and disengaging them from interference in the rest of the region should be the focal point. The Kargil operation proved beyond doubt that Taliban/mujahideen can indulge in covert terror operations and nothing more virile. So is the case in Chechnya and in Iran. Therefore, a coordinated line of action through Track II channels with Islamabad/Taliban may give new insights into the Afghan turmoil and enable a way out.

The IICR should at the same time work on strengthening the Northern Alliance. Till now the assistance to it has been in terms of arms and ammunition and human relief, and that too covertly. The Northern Alliance was never able to confront the Taliban, a cohesive unit and better able to manage the area under its governance, with all-out Pakistani support. In the interests of better governance for Afghanistan, the Northern Alliance should be enabled to build a better administrative machinery by its supporters across the border. The problem is being looked through the prism of finding a military solution. This has to change and present a balanced approach.

Lastly, since Pakistan looms large in finding a peaceful solution to the Afghan imbroglio, the IICR should take the stance that any financial assistance to Islamabad should be made conditional to bringing the Taliban to agree to a broad-based government. Simultaneously, countries like the UAE and Saudi Arabia should be persuaded to stop supplying POL to the Taliban. In the same way, the CARs should be dissuaded from having any dealings whatsoever with the Taliban until peace is restored.

All this requires a major diplomatic offensive. In August–September 1999, it seemed very much on the cards. The approaching winter of 1999, however, seems to have cooled the ardour of the initiative.

Epilogue
Taliban and the Hijacking of Indian Airlines Flight IC-814

This study on Talibanized Afghanistan was all ready to go to the press, when the hijacking took place, on 24 December 1999, of the Kathmandu–New Delhi Indian Airlines flight IC-814. For the next eight days, world focus zeroed in on Kandahar, where the weary itinerary finally ended, and on the Taliban's way of doing things.

There is little doubt that the hijack was masterminded by Pakistan's ISI. Available evidence indicates, but does not conclusively establish, that Kabul was very much part of the ISI plans.

The ISI has attained experience of masterminding hijacks of Indian aircraft. Each time, except in 1971, after much acrimony with India, it returned the passengers and the aircraft, gaining propaganda mileage in the bargain. The principal difference this time was that the ISI successfully used Afghanistan as its strategic backyard. Pakistan has thus been able to draw attention not only to the Kashmir issue, but also to the Taliban, whose legitimacy it has been canvassing.

India got back its aircraft, crew and the passengers after eight days of tortuous waiting. In the interim, it has had to change its approach to Afghanistan. External Affairs Minister Jaswant Singh referred to "Afghanistan authorities" for the first three days, shifting to "Taliban authorities" from the fourth day. It is quite apparent that the Taliban insisted that Jaswant Singh visit Kandahar. Following protocol dictated by circumstances, he shook hands with Wakil Ahmed Muttawakil, the Taliban's Foreign Minister, and addressed him, once again following protocol, as "Your Excellency". Just the same, Prime Minister Atal Behari

Vajpayee during the hijack crisis, and Jaswant Singh thereafter, have said that there is no move to recognize the Taliban.

•

The way the Taliban put pressure on India, setting deadlines, it was clear that they did wish to strengthen the hijackers' hands. More than one hostage has said that the hijackers received more arms, including AK-47s, after they reached Kandahar.

Yet, one cannot ignore some nuances in the way the drama unfolded, and the way it ended. After the departure of the flight from Dubai, the hijackers planned to land in Kabul, but the Taliban authorities refused permission. The hijackers were then asked to proceed to Kandahar, the headquarters of the Taliban's spiritual leader, Mullah Muhammad Umar, by their Pakistani bosses. It is reasonable to assume that by the time the aircraft landed in Kandahar, Mullah Umar was contacted; and necessary permission was obtained by the Pakistani bosses of the hijackers.

The Taliban's initial response indicated confusion. Their actions on the first two days were mostly providing humanitarian assistance to the hostages. But by day three–four, they seemed to have sorted out their priorities. In fact after this initial floundering, they publicly announced that the safety and security of the hostages would be their priority number one. If any harm was caused to the hostages, they threatened to storm the plane.

According to one version of the events, a report on a TV news channel from India, that the Vajpayee government was planning to trade the terrorists in Indian prisons in return for the hostages, sent confusing signals. Pakistan Television (PTV) repeated this news throughout days four and five. This appears to have led the Taliban to conclude that the Government of India had not ruled out this option.

Their next logical step, in their perception, was to be honest brokers, and ring down the curtain on the hijack drama as soon as possible. When the Taliban succeeded in narrowing down the hijackers' demand to the release of three terrorists, which incidentally was the first demand made by them, they started exerting pressures on India to clinch matters within a definite time-frame.

A day after the departure of the hijacked plane back to India, the Taliban authorities announced that they had left the hijackers and the three terrorists released from the Indian prisons on the Pakistan–Afghanistan border near Quetta.

•

From the sequence of events, it would appear that the Taliban tried to remain as neutral as they could in the matter. Any other course of action would have had a backlash on them. Many Indian commentators initially felt that the Taliban could have at least tried the hijackers under the judicial system of the Islamic Emirate of Afghanistan. They had done it for Osama bin Laden.

At this point of time, there seem to be three reasons why they did not do so. One, it would have invited considerable wrath from their friends and sympathizers in Pakistan. If, for instance, Pakistan closed down its trade and transit points on the Pak–Afghan border, land-locked Afghanistan would have been hard put to manage. Two, by keeping the hijackers in their prison they would have retained world attention for the wrong reasons. Three, it would have subjected the Taliban to avoidable pressures from outside, particularly from India.

In this hijack drama, some other deft moves made by the Taliban may be noted. First, they made it abundantly clear that they would not use the hostage crisis as a pressure point on India to gain diplomatic recognition. On more than one occasion, they made this publicly known. This in itself placed them on a higher pedestal. In fact, Jaswant Singh publicly acknowledged the help and cooperation from the Taliban authorities during the entire crisis. They were seen as a responsible and reasonable group.

The Taliban also made it known that in resolving the crisis they received much counselling from the US. This surprise announcement by the Taliban spokesman in New York was not denied by the US official spokesperson. One may safely infer from this, despite all the anti-Taliban posturing by the US, that the latter is engaging the Taliban in a constructive dialogue without any known preconditions by either side. This independent posturing by the Taliban on their foreign policy front seems to indicate that they made the first tentative moves to distance themselves from their difficult neighbour Pakistan.

By officially announcing that they had released the hijackers and terrorists on the Pak–Afghan border, the Taliban have made it known to the rest of the world that they endorse the Indian assessment of Pakistan's role in the hijacking episode. They apparently wanted to clear themselves of any type of involvement in this "un-Islamic" action in the holy month of Ramadan. It also shows that the Taliban, in their own unorthodox fashion, conveyed to their creator and benefactor, Pakistan, that they were not happy with what it had done by bringing the hijacked plane on Afghan soil.

•

How the Indian mindset will accept these subtle moves remains to be seen. India's External Affairs Minister showed extraordinary swiftness in the matter, uncommon in Indian diplomacy, by positively responding to the Taliban's moves. His willingness to go to Kandahar to oversee the deal, though unconventional diplomacy, demonstrated to the Taliban authorities that India can take decisive steps to improve its strained relations with them.

The next Indian step will need watching. India has publicly advocated for a long time that in the ongoing civil war in Afghanistan, the territorial integrity of that country cannot be compromised; and that Kabul should have a broad-based government. While conceptually, the Taliban seem to be in no disagreement with the Indian formulation on civil war, they are loath to accommodate anti-Taliban forces in governance. At the same time, they are not in a position to ignore people like Ahmed Shah Masoud, who is a leader in his own right in today's Afghanistan. Whether Indian diplomacy can at all play a role in bringing these warring factions to the conference table and help douse the flames of the civil strife in Afghanistan is a matter to ponder.

Index

Abdel-Rahman, Sheikh Omar 31, 78, 79
Abdul Malik Pehalwan, General 168
Abdulayev, Irfan 244
Abdullah, Sheikh Taseer 78–9, 81
Afghanistan
  "original seven sinners" of 18–20
  psyche of 14
  Soviet invasion of 13, 16, 42, 50, 81, 154, 155, 163, 164, 174, 190, 201, 207, 221, 265
  US cruise missile attack on (1988) 83, 144, 181
Afghan National Liberation Front 161
Aga Khan, Karim, Prince 137
Ahmed, Hussain, Qazi 231
Akayev, Askar 212, 232, 243
al-Faisal, Turki, Prince 34, 64, 72, 75, 148, 168
Alaptagin, Erkin 216
al-Bashir, Omar 59
Albright, Madeleine 245
Aligarh Muslim University 39
Almaty Declaration (October 1996) 244
al-Oteibi, Junayman bin Mohammad bin Seif 61, 195–200, 203
al-Qahtani, Mohammad bin Abdullah 196, 197
al-Quaide 193

al-Zawahiri, Ayman 79, 81
Amanullah 15
Amin, Rasool 47, 49, 50
Annan, Kofi 264
Arafat, Yasser 60, 77
arms running 233, 256, 265
Asian Muslims Human Rights Bureau 217
Atef, Mohammed 78
Ayub, Gohar 247
Aziz, Abdul, Lt Gen 151
Aziz, Sartaj 238
Azzan, Sheikh Abdullah 78

Babar, Naseerullah, Maj-Gen 26, 27, 106, 156, 157, 190
Beg, Mirza Asmal, Gen 187
Bevins, Anthony 230
Bhutto, Benazir 26, 156, 231
Bhutto, Z.A. 153
bin Abdul Aziz, Nayef, Prince 76
bin Laden, Osama 16–17, 59–77, 151, 164, 181, 182, 194, 195, 199, 201, 204, 217, 245, 252, 253, 261, 269, 270, 274
Border Management Scheme 138
Bosnia 257, 258
Brahimi, Lakhdar 239, 244
Bridas (Argentina) 148
Burke, Jason 60, 61
buzkashi, nature of 13, 14

Cambodia 108, 211
Castro, Fidel 77

Central Asia, stakes in 13
Central Asian Republics 16, 33, 131–40, 231–51, 221–34, 254, 257, 260, 275
  bomb blasts in 229
  border management 233
Charar-i-Sharif, burning of 272, 273
Chechnya 68, 74, 77, 84, 134, 261, 265, 275
China 16, 112, 142, 184, 207–20, 237, 243, 275
  nuclear tests of 212
CIA 72, 91, 94, 99, 107, 153, 163, 163, 177, 230
"conflict of civilizations" 23, 38

Dagestan 84, 218, 261, 265, 275
Dalai Lama 217
Dars Nizamya 40
Davies, Anthony 34
Dawatul Irshad 265
Delta Oil Company 148, 254
Deoband, Dar al of 39, 156, 264
Dewa, Yashwant, Maj Gen 157
Dostum, Abdul Rashid, Gen 21, 31, 34, 35, 37, 42, 47, 92, 95–9, 101, 192, 241, 244
Durand Line 156, 170, 190, 258, 259, 260

Eastern Turkestan Movement (ETM) 216, 217
ethnic divisions 15, 25, 32, 37, 42, 48–9, 52, 97, 100, 106–7, 161, 163, 171, 191, 192, 194, 222–3, 231, 256–7, 259–60, 275
Exxon 148

Fauji Foundation (Pakistan) 148, 254
Ferghana Valley 232, 233
  and narcotics production 139, 140, 228

Gandhi, M.K. 189, 193

Germany 243
Gilani, Syed Ahmed 19, 89
Gilman, Benjamin 73–4
Gorbachev, Mikhail 98, 230
"Great Game" 13
Gujral, I.K. 86

Habibullah, Amir 15
Habibya School 15
Hamas 21
Haq, Samiul 265
Harkat-i-Inqilab-i-Islami party 27
Harkatul Mujahideen 267
Harkat-ul-Ansar 97
Hashem, Mohammad 136
Hazara-i-Wahdat 36
Hazratbal mosque, occupation of 273
Hikmatyar, Gulbuddin 19, 20, 21, 31, 35n, 36, 47, 87, 89, 91, 92, 95, 178, 232, 244
Hizbi-at-Tahry 233
Hizb-i-Islami 31, 35, 95
Hizb-i-Wahdat 34, 49, 95, 96, 97, 176, 180
Hizbul Mujahideen 267
Hizbullah 193, 217
Ho Chi Minh 189
Human Rights Watch 28
Huntington, Samuel 38
Hussein, Saddam 60, 72, 77, 202

ICRC (International Committee of the Red Cross) 17, 91, 249
Islamic Front for Deliverance of Afghanistan (IFDA) 22, 96, 73, 132, 252
IMF 230
Inderfurth, Karl 69–70, 73, 237, 241, 242
India 38, 39, 243, 254, 260–1, 263–76
  ethnic conflicts in 108
  narcotics menace in 134–5
India/Iran/Russia/China policy coordination (proposed) 275–6

Indian Ocean 13
Institute of Regional Studies, Bishkek 139
Iran 33, 36, 38, 74, 140, 148, 156, 162, 165, 174–86, 187–94, 201, 204, 228, 237, 261, 275
  Islamic Revolution in 153, 154, 187–94, 195, 196, 216, 258, 261
  killing of diplomats of 74–5, 162, 180–2
Iraq 68, 72, 201, 255
Iraq-Iran War 174, 191, 202
ISI (Inter-Services Intelligence) 26, 63, 73, 84, 94, 99, 105, 106, 107, 134, 151, 154, 169, 218, 256, 262, 269
Islam
  export of 20–1, 38, 74, 81, 84, 154, 155, 164, 191, 204, 207, 219, 222, 225, 228, 229, 230–1, 234, 236, 241, 256, 260, 264, 265, 273–4, 272, 273
  sectarianism in 175, 191, 201, 256–7
Islamic Bomb 152, 162
Ittehad-ul-Islami 97

Jamaat-i-Islami 97, 231, 268
Jamiat-i-Islam 20, 49, 94
Jamiat-i-Ulema-Islami 156, 157, 162, 265
Japan 243, 246
jihad 36, 42, 43, 64; see also Islam, export of
Jombesh-i-Milli Islami 36, 49

Ka'bah, seizure of 195–200
Kanju, Mohmmad Sadiq Khan 244
Kansi, Mir Aimal 73
Kapisa 86, 269
Kargil, Pakistani incursion in 86, 146, 218, 236, 253, 266–70, 271, 274–5
Karimov, Islam 98, 99, 133, 222, 228, 229, 230, 241

Karzai, Hamid 37
Kashmir 74, 81, 85, 134, 215–16, 260, 267, 268, 272–3
KGB 244
Khalili, Karim 244
Khalili, Masood 93, 171, 236, 269–70
Khalsi, Yunus 19, 20
Khamenei, Ali, Ayatollah 182
Khan, Chaudhry Nisar Ali 146
Khan, Gohar Ayub 171
Khan, Khan Abdul Ghaffar 263
Khan, Sayyed Ahmad 39
Khatak, Afrasiab 50
Khattami 179, 180, 205
Khomeini, Ayatollah 83, 153, 187–9, 191, 192, 193, 195, 199, 201, 202
Kosovo 134, 257

landmines 18
Lashkar-i-Toyyaba 23, 265, 266, 267
Libya 162

Mamunovich, Ibrahimov Israeil 213, 215, 216, 219
Mao Zedong 38
Masoud, Ahmed Shah 20, 21, 22, 25, 35–7, 42, 46, 47, 51, 52, 73, 87–100, 105, 107, 132, 152, 165, 171, 176, 178, 182, 192, 235, 236, 238, 239, 241, 244, 249, 252, 254, 257, 258, 269–70
Mast Gul 273
Mazar-i-Sharif, changing fortunes in 33, 34, 59, 70, 105, 133, 157, 160, 162, 175, 176, 179, 180, 183, 185, 187, 192, 202, 244, 249, 254
McGirek, Tim 34
Medina, University of 196, 197
military equipment 101–29
military structure 101–29
Miraboutalebi, S. Mehdi 185

Mohammadi, Mohammad Nabi 27
Moldaliyev, Orozbek 137, 138, 233
Muhammadi, Mohammad Nibe 217
Muhammadi, Nabi 19, 20
Mujaddidi, Sibgatullah 18, 19, 20, 161
Mukti Bahini 155
Musharraf, Pervez 83, 151–2, 270–1
Muslim Brotherhood 21
Muttaqi, Amir Khan 70, 105, 238–9, 241, 252
Muttawakil, Wakil Ahmed 68, 181, 246, 247, 250
Myanmar 211

Najibullah 94, 98, 99, 133, 192, 227
  hanging of 264
narcotics 21, 73, 82, 108, 110, 112, 131–40, 149, 164, 194, 232, 233, 246, 256, 265
  Taliban stand on 27
  and arms connection 138
Nasser, G.A. 60, 201
necessity, doctrine of 21
Niyazov, Supermurat 133, 147
Nizamud-din, Mullah 40
NLI 86, 236, 266–7
Northern Alliance 47, 48, 96, 107, 110, 132, 144, 157, 165, 170, 176, 180, 185, 187, 248, 249, 275–6; see also IFDA
NWFP 39

Oakley, Robert 71
Obaidulah, Mullah 105
OIC 179, 246, 247
Osh Deadlock Convention 138
Overland company 142

Pakistan 16, 21, 107, 110, 111, 151–73, 190, 228, 237, 247n, 255, 257, 258, 259, 265, 268, 276
  and export of Islam 231
  army coup in 86, 242, 250
  as a collapsing state 146, 173, 242, 256, 271
  as narcotics route 134
  nuclear explosions of 146, 162
  religious sectarianism in 84, 163–4
Palestine conflict 38
Parcham 49
Pashtunistan, prospective 172–3, 259–60
peace initiatives 235–51
People's Democratic Party of Afghanistan 49, 50
pipelines 14, 16, 141–9, 156, 163, 254, 256, 275
PLO 21, 197
POK 39, 154, 264, 265
Pol Pot 211
POL 251, 276
Putin, Vladimir 232

Qaddafi 60, 77
Qanouni, Mohammad Younis 249
Qian Qichen 212

Rabbani, Burhanuddin 19, 20, 26, 28, 31, 32, 33, 36, 46, 46, 76, 88, 89, 91, 94, 95, 96, 136, 164, 170, 171, 192, 203, 236, 241, 242, 243, 244, 254
Rabbani, Mullah 106
Rakhmanov, Imomali 133
Rashid, Ahmed 31, 32, 71, 111, 169, 229, 230, 246, 269
Rasul, Abdul 217
refugees 18
Rehman, Fazlur, Maulana 157, 162, 191
religion in politics 188–94
religion, export of 229
Richardson, William 48, 245–7
Russia 13, 33, 36, 38, 45, 60, 110, 131, 165, 176, 237, 243, 245, 261

Saeed, Hafiz Mohammad 265
Saudi Arabia 16, 21, 51, 59, 60, 68, 74, 75–6, 82, 110, 111, 153, 162, 164, 165, 189, 190, 195–205, 212, 219, 228, 254, 255, 257, 264, 265, 275, 276
  bomb explosions in 203–4
  dissident movements in 261
  see also bin Laden, Osama
Saudi National Guard 196, 203
Saur Revolution 14, 49
Save the Children Fund 18
Sayyaf, Abdul Rab Rasool 19, 20
Shah, Amir 136
Sharif, Nawaz 52, 83, 84, 85, 86, 151, 161, 168, 169, 231, 242
Sharif, Shahbaz 84
Shatt al-Arab 174
Sheehan, Michael 84
Shen Guofeng 207
Shola-i-Javed 49
Shoora-i-Nazar 20
Sikhmuradov, Boris 138, 146, 226, 239
Sitam-i-Milli party 49
Six-plus-Two meeting 69, 94, 147, 208, 235–51, 274
SLOC 211
Somalia 68
Soviet Union 13
Sri Lanka 108

Tabyshalieva, Anara 139, 221, 228–9
Tajikistan 74, 81, 132
Taliban 25–57, 60, 193, 207, 210, 217, 219, 220, 225, 235, 238, 245, 248, 249, 250, 254, 256–7, 260–1, 264–5, 270, 276
  cohesiveness of 25
  composition of 40–1
  divisions in 47–8
  hierarchical structure of 42, 44–5
  military structure of 51
  moral code of 43, 45, 252–3
  origin of 26, 39, 174
  positive qualities of 256
  prospects of 38, 46
  world-view of 46
  and anti-Taliban disarray 26, 37
Taliban-Pakistan connection 16, 21, 23, 32–3, 34, 36, 50–2, 65, 71, 74, 82, 86, 174–5, 190–1, 194, 202, 208, 235, 261, 272
Taraki, Noor Muhammed 15
terrorism, export of 20, 23, 256, 258, 272; see also Islam, export of
Tibet 216

UAE 21, 51, 164, 255, 275, 276
Ukraine as arms supplier 110
Umar, Muhammad, Mullah 17, 20, 23, 26–7, 41, 42, 47, 61, 75, 105, 164, 169, 190, 192, 193, 205, 238, 245, 246, 248, 259, 269, 270, 275
UN 33, 40, 45, 46, 47, 112–13, 159, 207, 243, 245, 246, 247, 257, 264, 274
  sanctions by 22, 72, 83, 140, 250, 255, 258, 271
UN Drug Control Agency 132, 164
UNHCR 226, 227
Unocal 141, 148, 254
US 16, 46, 51, 64, 70–2, 82–4, 165, 190, 237, 243, 245, 257, 275
  bombing of embassies 16, 59, 64–5, 70, 71, 73, 76
  sanctions by 68
Uygurs 211–20
Uzbekistan 111

Vajpayee, Atal Behari 269

Wali, Abdul 94
women, Taliban's treatment of 43, 47, 51, 54–7, 70, 82, 45–6, 193, 207, 225, 229, 245, 246, 253

World Bank 230

Xinjiang Autonomous Region 74, 81, 209, 211–20, 261, 275

Yang Wenchang 208
Yeltsin, Boris 99, 232, 261

Yusufzai, Rahimullah 78, 170

Zahir Shah, King 17, 20, 22, 48, 93, 251
Ziaul Haq, Gen 153, 154, 190, 191
Zulsov, Igor 74

About the Authors

SREEDHAR is a Senior Fellow at the Institute for Defence Studies and Analyses, New Delhi. A graduate from the National Defence College, New Delhi (1983), he was visiting Fellow at the Woodrow Wilson School of Public and International Affairs, Princeton University (1978-79) and the Strategic and Defence Studies Centre, Australian National University, Canberra (1981-82). He has done pioneering work on the Taliban phenomenon with *Taliban and the Afghan Turmoil* (edited, 1997), and *Afghan Turmoil: Changing Equations* (1998, co-authored). His works on South Asia include *Pakistan: A Withering State?* (co-authored, 1999); *Pakistan Bomb* and *Pakistan after Zia*; and on the Persian Gulf, *Gulf: Scramble for Security*, *Tanker War*, and *Iraq-Iran War*. He is among the leading strategic analysts in the developing world.

MAHENDRA VED, Deputy Chief of Bureau at the *Times of India*, New Delhi, has combined writing on government and political matters with work on national security affairs. He covered the 1971 Indo–Pak war. Posted to Dhaka by the United News of India, he reported crucial developments in Bangladesh during 1974–76. He has written on South Asian affairs as Chief of Bureau of *The Daily* (1981-83) and for the *Hindustan Times* (1984–95), besides writing for the Institute for Defence Studies and Analyses, New Delhi. Publications include *Taliban and the Afghan Turmoil* (ed. Sreedhar, 1997), and *Afghan Turmoil: Changing Equations* (co-authored with Sreedhar, 1998).

Of Related Interest

PAKISTAN: A WITHERING STATE?
by Sreedhar and Nilesh Bhagat

Will the community of nations in the present millennium witness the disappearance of Pakistan as a member? With authenticated facts and thorough-going analysis, this book foretells that it is a distinct probability.

Some notable features of the quicksands called Pakistan are: inability, even after half a century of its existence, to come to a clear conclusion about its own identity; open contempt for institutions of governance by the armed forces; intimidation of the judiciary; economic collapse; survival of the state on drug money; export of terrorism across the borders; grim ethnic divide; public disdain for state authority; lack of leadership, vision and strategy.

Evidence is emerging of the close links of the ruling elite of Pakistan, including its Prime Minister, with the drug runners. Pakistanis in the know themselves assert that the country's nuclear programme is financed with the drug money. As the country goes under, overwhelmed by its economic, sectarian, ethnic and moral crisis, the resort to drug money will increase still further.

When US cruise missiles overflew more than 1,000 kilometres of Pakistan airspace to attack terrorist camps in Afghanistan, Pakistan had to accept it with just a whimper of protest. Most explosive, perhaps, is the detailed exposure of Pakistan's terrorist activity in the Jammu and Kashmir state of the Indian Union, identifying locations, Pakistani officials involved, and the nature of their subversive enterprise..

The malaise of such a state may, finally, end up in a second break-up of Pakistan, resulting in the formation of a separate Pakhtunkhwa, merged with the Pashtun region of Afghanistan. More worrisome for India, perhaps, are the hordes of directionless youth, being trained in the mushrooming *madrasa*s in Pakistan, to carry their antiquated mission of converting the rest of the world to their version of Islam.

208 pages; demy 8vo; hard cover   Price Rs 450/-; US$35

Published by: WORDSMITHS